The Novels of George Meredith: A Study

BY

ELMER JAMES BAILEY

HASKELL HOUSE PUBLISHERS Lᴛᴅ.
Publishers of Scarce Scholarly Books
NEW YORK, N. Y. 10012
1971

First Published 1908

HASKELL HOUSE PUBLISHERS Ltd.
Publishers of Scarce Scholarly Books
280 LAFAYETTE STREET
NEW YORK, N. Y. 10012

Library of Congress Catalog Card Number: 75-163892

Standard Book Number 8383-1312-4

Printed in the United States of America

TO

ALGERNON SIDNEY CRAPSEY

" Our spoken in protest remains.
A young generation reaps."
MEREDITH : *The Empty Purse.*

CONTENTS

I

INTRODUCTION

PAGE

Compensation in Literary Renown — The Probable
Permanence of Meredith's Fame — The Periods of
His Career 1

II

THE APPRENTICE

Meredith's Early Life — Literary Conditions in Nineteenth Century England before 1860 —The "Poems"
of 1851 — "The Shaving of Shagpat" — "Farina" . 13

III

THE JOURNEYMAN

Assimilated Influences — "The Ordeal of Richard
Feverel" — "Evan Harrington" — "Sandra
Belloni" — "Vittoria" — "Rhoda Fleming" . . 45

IV

THE MASTER-WORKMAN

The Period of Free Invention — "The Adventures of
Harry Richmond" — "Beauchamp's Career" —
"Short Stories" — "The Egoist" — "The Tragic
Comedians" 100

V

THE MASTER-WORKMAN

The Period of Concentrated Interest — "Diana of the
Crossways" — "One of Our Conquerors" — "Lord
Ormont and His Aminta" — "The Amazing Mar-
riage" — The Meredith School 148

VI

A List of the Characters in Meredith's Novels, with an
Enumeration of the Chapters in which they appear 193

THE NOVELS OF GEORGE
MEREDITH: A STUDY

I

INTRODUCTION

COMPENSATION IN LITERARY RENOWN—THE PROB-
ABLE PERMANENCE OF MEREDITH'S FAME—THE
PERIODS OF HIS CAREER.

THE fame which comes to an author is no less a
result of the action of moral law than is the glory
of a general, the renown of a statesman, or the beati-
fication of a martyr. Long ago the clear-eyed
Greeks perceived that although Fortune dealt out
her gifts with sovereign disregard of merit or desert,
she was sooner or later followed by Nemesis, the god-
dess of due proportion, who ruthlessly shattered
such prosperity as seemed even moderately beyond
the mean. In the long run, the alternating movement set up by repeated visitations of the two deities,
satisfied the mind of Justice; and the balance in
her steady hand fell to rest. As forces, however,
Fortune, Nemesis, and Justice did not become powerless with the passing of Athens and Rome. On the
contrary, still existing, they were renamed by later

generations; and the law of their harmonious interplay was restated for the benefit of those who had
ears to hear. Because of this evolution of expression, therefore, we no longer talk with the Greek
philosophers of Nemesis, but we find no difficulty
whatever in speaking with Emerson and Browning
of Compensation.

Nor is this law or principle, in so far as it has to
do with literary fame, difficult of statement. Baldly
expressed, it is this: The duration of attention attracted is in direct ratio to the time consumed in
awakening adequate appreciation. In other words,
if renown is the growth of a night, its continuance will
be hardly more than for a day; but if it is slow in
coming to maturity, it is likely to be persistent,
and in some cases permanent. A man, for example,
writes a story which is immediately looked upon as
the greatest novel of the year; soon it is advertised
as being in its tenth, its twelfth, or possibly its sixteenth edition. For a time it heads the list of best-
selling books; then it runs the gauntlet of women's
clubs; and finally it rushes comet-like on its par-
abolic course from our sight. On the other hand,
should a serious-minded, high-purposed author produce a book which must needs be read with the mind
as well as the eye, his readers, at first, are almost
certain to be few, barely "the remnant," perhaps.
Nevertheless, if the work is deserving, the audience
steadily widens; and the author's writing gradually
ceases to be confused with his wife's, if she happens
to be a blue-stocking, or with the weaker pro-
ductions of some man whose pseudonymous name

misleads those who read as they run. Such a writer, furthermore, is occasionally forced to pass through the purgatory of having a club formed for the purpose of studying his work. But even this agony enters as a factor into the problem of due compensation, for if an author withstands that test of his power, the ellipticity of his orbit is in all probability computable; and although he may disappear from sight or even from memory for a time, he is likely, none the less, to return at intervals with an ever increasing splendor of renown.

What Homer was to those who heard him recite his poems, no one now can ever know; but critics were not wanting even among the Greeks, who proved beyond a shadow of doubt, that the blind poet of the seven cities was altogether lighter than vanity. Even in recent time, it has been shown to the satisfaction of not a few, that no such man as Homer ever lived; yet the Iliad and the Odyssey remain, and by the many iconoclastic critics are remembered chiefly because they raised their unshamed hands against a master. Dante, indeed, had literary recognition in his life-time; for as he moved through the streets of Ravenna, not only did the nobility pay him a certain forced respect, but simpleminded mothers gathered their children about them, and whispered in trembling awe that the stern-faced, silent man had looked upon the sufferings of those who writhed in the torments of Hell. Yet when Fortune tardily sought out one of the greatest of the children of men, she found that, over-weary with the climbing of others' stairs, he could draw no comfort from the high regard which she was then willing to bestow. Shakespeare, too, was no very great man in the sight of his friends at the Mermaid Tavern; and the best reply which Dryden and Pope could give to Milton's inquiry, "What needs my Shakspear for his honoured bones?" was to emasculate the most virile work which the literary world has known. There is little question about these great men now, however, for Fame has crowned their work; and in compensation for her delay, she has made the wreath immortal.

In the narrower field of English fiction the working of the law is no less evident and sure. We are in the habit of assuming that Scott, and Thackeray, and Dickens, and possibly George Eliot, are our greatest novelists; and consequently few of us stop to realize, even if we know, that G. P. R. James, and Lever, and Bulwer were, at one time, very much more eagerly read, and their enduring fame much more earnestly prophesied. It cannot, of course, be held with truth that our greater novelists received no recognition in their day. Indeed, Scott's contemporary popularity and present renown would seem to be an exception to the rule, if it could be proved that more than a very small number of those who now feel compelled to buy his books and to speak glibly of his characters, ever sit down even to cut the leaves of their purchase. Thackeray and Dickens, it should be admitted, both expressed their satisfaction in the recognition with which their books were met: but neither of them at any time received a modicum of that extravagant praise, or a tithe of that large return in money, which is the present lot of nearly every man who discovers the cheapness of paper and ink, and thinks it his duty to bring them together. But this evenness of renown in the case of Thackeray and of Dickens does not confute the principle of compensation as laid down. It rather shows the action of the law when recognition has been neither too long delayed, nor too excessive; for the appreciation which Thackeray and Dickens and George Eliot received from their contemporary readers was no greater than was due; and, therefore, creating no disturbance in the balance of justice, it has ever since continued with only that occasional fluctuation of interest, which is the systole and diastole of living, pulsating renown.

With the thought of compensation in mind, therefore, one feels assurance in predicting the permanent fame of George Meredith, the last of those great creative artists whose novels bear nearly the same relation to the reign of Victoria as the dramas of the sixteenth century bear to that of Elizabeth. Beginning to strive for the ear of the public as early as 1849, the year in which Dickens was bringing out "David Copperfield," and Thackeray was writing "Pendennis," Meredith during the next half century placed before the public a dozen novels, several volumes of poetry, a few short stories, and occasionally an essay or a review. In no possible sense of the word, however, did he become popular. Editors of certain magazines, it is true, had the courage to print some of Meredith's work in their pages; but such publication seems not to have awakened any distinct appreciation of the contributor, nor to have increased the length of the subscription lists; indeed, it is said that, now and then, it shortened them.   The first editions of the novels and of the poems supplied the public for years; there was no marked demand for them at circulating libraries; and until recently a uniform issue of Meredith's works was the last thing which a publisher would have considered with the expectation of adequate financial return.

Meredith, however, did not cease to keep the road which he had chosen for himself.   Publishers and editors found that there was no use in tempting, friends that there was as little in advising, until, finally, nearly all of even those who wished him well began to shake their heads and mourn over the inevitable shipwreck which they prophesied must be the lot of perverse genius.   This stubborn following of his own bent by Meredith may have been the chief cause of the general indifference with which he was regarded; but nevertheless, little as he was known, he was not without an audience, and this audience endeavored, almost vicariously, it might be said, to proselytize readers.   Yet, laudatory advertisements, enthusiastic review-writing, and affected admiration accomplished next to nothing.   Despite the apparent indifference, however, George Meredith and his works would not down.   Many who reviled him openly read him privately, while others, who found themselves unable to understand him at all, looked superior and "knowing" when his work was mentioned.   Meredith was happy, certainly, in escaping the lot of Browning who was called upon to endure

the formation of societies named in his honor, but
doing him the dishonor of explaining the obvious
and muddling the clear. Still, small groups here
and there did talk about the novelist to good purpose, and three or four presumably serious studies of
his work also appeared. These, it is true, were somewhat thin in character; but they served to force the
conclusion that there must be something worth while
in George Meredith, since, like Christianity, he was
able to endure in spite of defenders.

Such was the condition of things toward the close
of the nineteenth century, when a wide-spread appreciation of Meredith was seen to be in existence.
Those who admired him were surprised to learn that
he had long been the favorite writer of their next-
door neighbors. Buyers of books ceased to think
that "The Ordeal of Richard Feverel" was a ballad
bound up in complete editions of Owen Meredith's
poems; and although some of them never got beyond that knowledge, others, who were readers as
well as buyers, began to feel that George Meredith
possessed the qualities which abide. To his admirers this long delay in the general recognition of his
genius has been a source of regret; but, on the whole,
perhaps it is best. The tardy appreciation of Meredith means, if the law of compensation holds, that his
present repute must persist. There has been no
rocket-like flight, accompanied with pyrotechnic
whizzings; but there has been, it is now evident, a
steady forward movement, which has resulted in the
capture and possibly the permanent occupation of
one of the higher citadels of renown. In other

words, the probable compensation of George Meredith's long wait for adequate recognition is enduring fame.

Meredith's insistence upon ordering his methods and plans to suit himself has often been the subject of comment on the part of the critic; but while such insistence must be admitted, it should not be construed into meaning that his work, as a whole, is not subject to differentiation. The close reader soon discovers a larger unity in the consistent purpose and the well-ordered system of philosophy which runs throughout Meredith's work. He furthermore perceives, if he makes a study of the novels, that they readily fall into four groups, each of which was produced in a period of about ten years. The seeming artificiality of such a division becomes still more striking when it is added that to each of these groups, except the first, just four works belong. But, however arbitrary a classification based upon time and number may appear, especially when it permits such mathematical exactness of statement, it becomes convincing, if, upon being observed from another point of view, it is still found to be accurate and adequate.

The decade beginning in 1849 seems to have been for Meredith a period of experiment or preparation. Not quite sure of the kind of literature which he should cultivate, he began his career with the publication of a poem called "Chillianwallah" in the issue of *Chambers's Edinburgh Journal* for July 7. Two years later a volume of poems appeared, and then in 1856 and 1857 respectively, "The Shaving of

Shagpat" and "Farina." The composition of the
poems, of the extravaganza, and of the medieval
tale showed no fixity of purpose; and these works
may be said, without undue disparagement, to exhibit a hesitancy which characterizes the apprentice
rather than the experienced workman.

The last years of this first period were no doubt
spent in writing "The Ordeal of Richard Feverel,"
for its publication in 1859 opened the second
decade of Meredith's literary activity. This book
showed a decided advance in power; and, viewed in
the light of his subsequent work, it marked an awakening to a realization of the form of literature in
which the writer could best express himself. The
several novels beginning with "The Ordeal of Richard Feverel" and ending with "The Amazing Marriage," therefore, exhibit a homogeneity which does
not exist in the works of the first period. They
are, none the less, easily separated into three
groups, each including four stories. The three
decades, in each of which one of these groups was
published, may receive a designation determined
by the vantage ground from which the novels are
studied. Such possible points of view are of course
many; but the most important are those from which
one may come to conclusions with regard either to
Meredith's emancipation from the influence of other
writers, or to the development in his philosophy of
life.

If the possibility of such a classification be admitted, the decade beginning in 1859 may be called
the period of influenced production, since "The Or-

deal of Richard Feverel," published in that year,
"Evan Harrington" in 1861, "Emilia in England,"
as "Sandra Belloni" was originally called, in 1864,
"Rhoda Fleming" in 1865, and "Vittoria," which
should be regarded not as a separate novel, but only
as the completion of Sandra's story, in 1867,—all
show striking lines of connection with the writings
of Meredith's predecessors and contemporaries.
Moreover, since these same novels make a systematic onslaught upon sham and conventionality, the
time in which they were produced may be called
the period of attack upon sentimentalism.

The third decade, separated from the second by
two years of silence, began in 1871 with "The
Adventures of Harry Richmond," and was still
further marked by the publication of "Beauchamp's
Career" in 1876, "The Egoist" in 1879, and "The
Tragic Comedians" in 1880. These novels show almost no traces of any other writer's influence, and
may therefore be regarded as belonging to a period
of free invention; but if emphasis is laid upon their
philosophical content, since they present studies of
selfishness or, to use Emerson's term—"selfism,"
they may be looked upon as having been produced
during the period of attack upon egoism.

After the publication of "The Tragic Comedians,"
Meredith permitted a lustrum to pass before he entered upon the final period of his activity as novelist.
Like the novels of the preceding decade, those of this
time, "Diana of the Crossways," published in 1885,
"One of Our Conquerors" in 1891, "Lord Ormont
and His Aminta" in 1894, and "The Amazing Mar-

riage" in 1895, present no striking instances of outside influence; but since they centre themselves
around a single problem, the unhappy marriage, they
may be said to belong to the period of concentrated
interest. Furthermore, since each of the novels in
this group is a study of the separation of a husband
and a wife through troubles arising from incompat-
ibility of temper, disparity of age, or inequality of
rank, and since Meredith apparently approves of the
parting of man and wife under such circumstances,
the works of the last decade belong to the period of
attack upon conventional ideas of marriage.

Not a few objections may be urged against the
classification just outlined; and at least two merit
reply. The classification, it may be said, ignores
the several volumes of poetry which Meredith has
written. This is true undoubtedly, but save in so
far as certain poems throw light upon the novels in
matters of method, purpose, or expression, they may
be ignored in a study of the prose writings. Again,
many threads of connection between the different
groups are disregarded, and this might lead to the
hasty conclusion that there is a lack of unity in
Meredith's work. Now a classification is of greatest
help when it is reduced to its lowest terms; and at
this point it must be remembered that such a reduction involves the casting out of all common factors
and the retention of those alone which are unlike.
Such a classification, however, still remains helpful
even when elements eliminated earlier for the sake
of clearness are reintroduced.

The novels of Meredith, then, may be studied, if

it is permissible to borrow terms from the artisan rather than from the artist, as works produced during years of activity in which he showed himself successively an apprentice, a journeyman, and a master-workman.   In the first stage, he wrote those books already mentioned as belonging to a period of experiment and preparation; in the second, he published the works of the ten years designated as the period of influenced production or of attack upon sentimentalism; and in the third, he spent the greater part of his time upon the novels of two separated decades, of which the earlier may be characterized as the period of free invention or of attack upon egoism; and the later as the period of concentrated interest or of attack upon conventional ideas of marriage.

II

THE APPRENTICE

MEREDITH'S EARLY LIFE—LITERARY CONDITIONS IN
NINETEENTH CENTURY ENGLAND BEFORE 1860—
THE "POEMS" OF 1851—"THE SHAVING OF SHAG-
PAT"—"FARINA."

THE first decade of Meredith's literary career was
the third of his life-time. Born in Hampshire,
February 12, 1828, he lost during his childhood
his Welsh father and Irish mother, and thereupon
becoming a ward in chancery was sent to Germany
for his education. Critics are probably not far
wrong when they say that the man in whom was
thus mingled blood drawn from two branches of the
fancy-loving, quick-witted Celtic race, and whose
training was received among a people posssssed of
searching analytic intelligence, showed by his sparkling wit and his almost mystical treatment of nature
the influence of his ancestry on one hand, and by
his penetrating insight into motives of conduct and
his philosophical criticism of life the no less potent
influence of his education on the other. But however interesting and valuable it may be to point out
the possible connections of earlier conditions and surroundings with later thought and methods, the fact

13

that Meredith was placed at a school upon the continent would imply, in so far as the mere events of his life are concerned, that his parents had left the boy provided with at least some little property. Such a conclusion, however, is hardly trustworthy, for we are often told that when Meredith in the first years of his manhood returned to England, he found himself compelled to enter immediately into a struggle with poverty. In all probability allowance should be made for exaggeration when one reads that the young man lived for several months upon oatmeal; yet there is no reason to doubt that he labored for years with pecuniary difficulties which to many would have been wholly disheartening. Under conditions, then, which must have been far from easy, Meredith, at the age of twenty-one, turned his attention to the study of law; but his interest, never more than lukewarm, soon cooled, and in a short time he abandoned all thought of the bar as a satisfactory profession.

Journalism, as a means of livelihood, perhaps, rather than as a calling, next claimed him, and proved sufficiently attractive to make him willing in later life to serve at intervals upon various newspapers and magazines. But a greater interest than either law or journalism was stirring within him. Indeed as early as 1849, the year in which he was articled, Meredith, roused by the heroism of the English soldiery in the bloody battle of Chillianwallah, made his first appearance as author with a poem commemorative of the victory. The stanzas were not included in the definitive and so called complete edition of Meredith's works published in 1898; but whatever crudeness they may show, their author need not have been ashamed to reprint them.

CHILLIANWALLAH

Chillianwallah! Chillianwallah!
  Where our brothers fought and bled!
Oh! thy name is natural music,
  And a dirge above the dead!
Though we have not been defeated,
  Though we can't be overcome,
Still, whene'er thou art repeated,
  I would fain that grief were dumb.

Chillianwallah! Chillianwallah!
  'Tis a name so sad and strange,
Like a breeze through midnight harp-strings
  Ringing many a mournful change;
But the wildness and the sorrow
  Have a meaning of their own—
Oh! whereof no glad to-morrow
  Can relieve the dismal tone!

Chillianwallah! Chillianwallah!
  'Tis a village dark and low,
By the bloody Jhelum River,
  Bridged by the foreboding foe;
And across the wintry water
  He is ready to retreat,
When the carnage and the slaughter
  Shall have paid for his defeat.

Chillianwallah! Chillianwallah!
  'Tis a wild and dreary plain,
Strewn with plots of thickest jungle,
  Matted with the gory stain.

There the murder-mouthed artillery
    In the deadly ambuscade,
Wrok the thunder of his treachery
    On the skeleton brigade.

Chillianwallah! Chillianwallah!
    When the night set in with rain,
Came the savage plundering devils
    To their work among the slain;
And the wounded and the dying
    In cold blood did share the doom
Of their comrades round them lying,
    Stiff in the dread skyless gloom.

Chillianwallah! Chillianwallah!
    Thou wilt be a doleful chord,
And a mystic note of mourning
    That will need no chiming word;
And that heart will leap with anguish
    Who may understand the best;
But the hopes of all will languish
    Till thy memory is at rest.

The publication of "Chillianwallah" has, of
course, a certain interest as the starting point in
Meredith's literary career. A mere date in itself,
however, is usually of very little value in the life of
an author. Far more important is the place which
he holds relatively to other writers, especially if he
makes his appearance at a time favorable to his best
development. Such was the case with Meredith.
Even going back to the beginning, one learns that
Meredith's birth preceded Ibsen's by but one month,
and Dante Gabriel Rossetti's by only three. The
year of 1828 also saw the establishment of *The
Athenæum* and *The Spectator*, two reviews which

for many years disagreed whenever a work by Meredith appeared, since the first was nearly always favorable, despite any restrictions which it saw fit to suggest; while the second was seldom other than depreciatory, whatever merit it was grudgingly forced to allow.

In 1828, of the poets favorably known during the early part of the nineteenth century, Byron, Shelley, and Keats were dead; and Moore, Coleridge, Southey, and Wordsworth had all done their best work, although Southey was still Poet-Laureate, and Wordsworth was to succeed to that office in 1843. Tennyson and Elizabeth Barrett were but just known, and Browning had not printed "Pauline." Among the essayists and reviewers, Hazlitt and Lamb were near the end of their lives; Hunt, DeQuincey, and Landor were in mid-career; Macaulay had contributed his first vigorous articles to *The Edinburgh Review;* Carlyle was at the close of his period of extreme admiration for things German; and Ruskin was a boy of ten. Scott, of course, was the acknowledged leading novelist; but the roll of the "*Waverly*" series was nearly complete. Thomas Love Peacock, who was to become Meredith's father-in-law, was very popular as the author of several satirical tales of English life, Susan Ferrier was between "Inheritance" and "Destiny," and Maria Edgeworth between "Ormund" and "Helen." Disraeli had just published "Vivian Gray;" Bulwer, not yet raised to the peerage, was in the period of his wild and wicked heroes; and G. P. R. James, foolishly encouraged by Scott, was at work upon "Richelieu."

Between 1828 and 1859, that is during the thirty years which lay between Meredith's birth and the appearance of his first novel, important changes took place in literary England. Tennyson steadily forged ahead until he succeeded Wordsworth as Poet-Laureate in 1850, and by publishing "In Memoriam" in the same year, so effectually silenced the sneers which "The Princess" had awakened in 1847, that he was felt to have placed his fame upon no doubtful foundation, a belief greatly strengthened by the appearance of the first four "Idylls of the King" in 1858. Browning was making his way more slowly, but he completed the series called "Bells and Pomegranates"; and somewhat later, "Men and Women," despite the cheap flings of critics, gained him no mean following. His wife, however, was regarded by nearly everybody as the greater poet of the two, though that very mild poem, "Aurora Leigh," was looked upon as a rather shocking piece of work for a lady. Arnold was severely criticised again and again for his attempt to write English poetry in accordance with Greek methods; Rossetti's verses awaited their resurrection from the grave of his wife; and Swinburne was probably no more than beginning to think about those naughty "Poems and Ballads" which eventually troubled the sentimental propriety of England.

During the same period Peacock amused his readers with his satire of "Crotchet Castle"; and Disraeli dabbled in various themes. Bulwer managed to escape from his melodramatic heroes and colorless virgins, and after trying to balance himself in writing historical novels, subsided into his complex period of the highly moral mingled with the supernatural; while G. P. R. James placed an almost endless succession of wooden horsemen, one by one, upon nearly every plain which the world afforded. The Brontë galaxy all ran their brilliant courses, although many considered the sisters inferior to Samuel Lover, Charles Lever, and Frederick Marryat; Trollope began his systematic writing of a fixed number of pages each day, and produced, on the average, three novels every two years; Kingsley gained the reputation of being ready to speak in sincere defense of every just cause; but, after exhibiting himself in "Alton Locke" as a champion of the workingman, he turned his attention to historical tales. Before doing this, however, he let his mantle fall upon Charles Reade, who had already gained favorable recognition as a playwright, but who thereupon began the composition of novels which inveighed against social wrongs and abuses. At the very close of the period George Eliot astonished herself no less than the world by the success with which she met in writing, at the suggestion of George Henry Lewes, the three stories now collected under the title, "Scenes of Clerical Life"; and Wilkie Collins set about the composition of "The Woman in White," that attractive example of a story told for the story's sake. But the two men who alone were mentioned in the same breath with Scott were Dickens and Thackeray. Born within a twelve-month of each other, they both began their literary work soon after the year of Meredith's birth, and publishing their writings with marked regularity, had completed nearly all their important novels when "The Ordeal of Richard Feverel" appeared in 1859.

Among prose writers other than novelists, Carlyle and Ruskin were preaching the nobility of labor, and fulminating against cant and sham; while Macaulay continued to write his brilliant essays and began his no less brilliant history. The Tractarian movement ran its course with its remarkable display of fine rhetoric, enthusiastic zeal, and deep religious feeling. The opposing leaders, Pusey and Newman, both equally sincere, shook the English Church to its foundations; while Gladstone, though not in the midst of the conflict, hovered with much apprehension upon the outskirts of the battlefield. George Eliot hardly helped to simplify matters by translating German inquiries into the authenticity of Christianity; and the works of Darwin and of Spencer in natural science and in philosophy not only added to the confusion, but forced thinking men to give up long accepted doctrines, and to reformulate many sacred beliefs.

Such then were the literary conditions in England while Meredith was getting his schooling upon the continent, and was later serving his apprenticeship at home. In wealth of genius these years have often been compared with justice to the Elizabethan Age. Poetry flourished as freely in one period as in the other; the novel in the later took the place of the drama in the earlier; and discoveries in science were hardly less important in opening new vistas to men's imagination than were the explorations of Raleigh and Drake. In other words, the later period, like the former, did not so much try men's souls, as it permitted their full development. Under such conditions, therefore, an intellect like Meredith's must beyond a doubt have found sustenance on every side and incentives at every turn.

But however much it may be evident in after years that a writer's work has been influenced by his ancestry, his education, his early struggles with poverty, and the literary conditions which have surrounded his first sallies into the fields of authorship, it is not always found that in the beginning he exhibited a knowledge of the form in which he could best express himself. Such at all events, is the case with Meredith. His first poem of "Chillianwallah" was perhaps but an accidental utterance of patriotic admiration for those who snatched victory out of defeat while fighting for their country's honor. Be that as it may, the young law student spent the next two years in preparing a small volume of verse to which he gave no more ambitious title than "Poems by George Meredith." Five years later, in 1856, he published in prose, an Arabian story called "The Shaving of Shagpat"; and this was received with sufficient favor to encourage his further testing the temper of the public in the following year with a German tale named "Farina, A Legend of Cologne." These two stories, wholly dissimilar in diction, character drawing, and plot, force the reader to feel that Meredith was at the stage of experiment, rather than at that of conscious power.

Certainly all this earlier work betrayed a lack of finality, thus standing in direct contrast to the convincing firmness of tone which characterized "The Ordeal of Richard Feverel." With this book, published in 1859, Meredith's period of apprenticeship came to an end; his ten years of experiment had taught him that his work must be done in the field of novel-writing. The classification of the earlier writings of Meredith as experimental, however, does not permit their immediate dismissal from our attention. At the time of their publication, it is true, he had not determined his style, nor formulated his philosophy; but he was writing under influences which remained powerful with him for several years; he was trying methods of expression, not a few of which became characteristic of his style; and he was giving voice to ideas which in their later development caused many to regard him as almost an oracle.

The "Poems" of 1851 made no very distinct impression upon the public, though William Michael Rossetti praised the book in *The Critic*, and Charles Kingsley reviewed it appreciatively in *Fraser's Magazine*. The critics in general, however, seemed to feel that they were tempering justice with mercy when they dealt Meredith the rather dubious and disheartening compliment of saying that the poems showed promise. As a matter of fact, they really deserved greater commendation. Crudities appeared on almost every page, it is true, but there was none the less a spontaneous, limpid flow in many of the stanzas, which may be favorably compared with the smoothness of Tennyson's first volume; and further-more, there also appeared abundant evidences of a vigor of thought and a boldness of diction which more than offset an occasionally obvious strain after originality. Without any endeavor to be nice in making selections, one may turn immediately to the simple stanzas which open the poem called "The Sleeping City."

> "A princess in the eastern tale,
> Paced thro' a marble city pale,
> And saw on ghastly shapes of stone,
> The sculptured life she breathed alone;
>
> "Saw, where'er her eye might range,
> Herself the only child of change;
> And heard her echoed footfall chime
> Between Oblivion and Time;
>
> "And in the squares where fountains played,
> And up the spiral balustrade,
> Along the drowsy corridors
> Even to the inmost sleeping floors,
>
> "Surveyed in wonder chilled with dread,
> The seemingness of Death, not dead;
> Life's semblance but without its storm
> And silence frosting every form."

Here certainly is an atmosphere reminding the reader of the success with which Tennyson drew the loneliness of Mariana in the moated grange, or with which Shelley pictured the lovely lady of "The Sensitive Plant." But if one is in quest of the quality of atmosphere, one finds it beyond a doubt in "Will

o' the Wisp," where the lightsome eeriness of lilt and
rhythm seems to echo the mocking laughter of
the crazy hobgoblin flying over the oozy marshes
of the woods.

> "Follow me, follow me,
> Over brake and under tree,
> Thro' the bosky tanglery,
>> Brushwood and bramble!
>> Follow me, follow me,
>>> Laugh and leap and scramble!
>> Follow, follow,
>> Hill and hollow,
>> Fosse and burrow,
>> Fen and furrow,
> Down into the bulrush beds,
> 'Midst the reeds and osier heads,
> In the rushy soaking damps,
> Where the vapours pitch their camps,
>> Follow me, follow me,
>>> For a midnight ramble!
> "O! what a mighty fog,
> What a merry night O ho!
> Follow, follow, nigher, nigher—
> Over bank, and pond, and briar,
> Down into the croaking ditches,
>> Rotten log,
>> Spotted frog,
>> Beetle bright
>> With crawling light,
>> What a joy O ho!
> Deep into the purple bog—
>> What a joy O ho!
>
>   .   .   .   .
>
> "Down we go, down we go,
>> What a joy O ho!
> Soon shall I be down below,
> Plunging with a gray fat friar,

Hither, thither, to and fro,
Breathing mists and whisking lamps,
Plashing in the shiny swamps;
While my cousin Lantern Jack,
With cock ears and cunning eyes,
Turns him round upon his back,
Daubs him oozy green and black,
Sits upon his rolling size,
Where he lies, where he lies,
Groaning full of sack—
Staring with his great round eyes!
    What a joy O ho!
Sits upon him in the swamps
Breathing mists and whisking lamps!
    What a joy O ho!
"Such a lad is Lantern Jack,
When he rides the black nightmare
Through the fens and puts a glare
Iu the friar's track.
Snch a frolic lad, good lack!
To turn a friar on his back,
Trip him, clip him, whip him, nip him,
Lay him sprawling smack!
Such a lad is Lantern Jack!
Such a tricksy lad, good lack!
    What a joy O ho!
    Follow me, follow me,
Where he sits, and you shall see!"

These lines recall the goblin passage in Milton's "L'Allegro," and suggest, though more remotely, the meeting of Shakspeare's weird sisters in the cauldron scene of "Macbeth." Their best analogy is found, however, not in literature, but in the kindred art of music, where the "Humoresken" of Grieg and the "Marche Grotesque" of Arensky express the same odd effervescence of spirit.

Of an entirely different nature were nine quatrains each dealing with the work of one of the greater writers who preserved the true traditions of English poetry from Chaucer to Keats. Unrhymed, and to a certain extent careless of the laws of metre, they show a strength of thought and a fullness of tone somewhat suggestive of Whitman.

THE POETRY OF MILTON

Like to some deep-chested organ whose grand inspiration
Screnely majestic in utterance, lofty and calm,
Interprets to mortals with melody great as its burthen,
The mystical harmonies chiming forever throughout the
bright spheres.

THE POETRY OF WORDSWORTH

A breath of the mountains, fresh born in the regions majestic,
That look with their eye-daring summits deep into the sky.
The voice of great Nature; sublime with her lofty conceptions,
Yet earnest and simple as any sweet child of the green lowly vale.

Submitted recently to an enthusiastic admirer of Wordsworth in America, these lines called forth strong approval; but that Meredith at the age of twenty-one showed sufficient insight to write them, cannot be looked upon as a mere accident. A large number of these early poems have to do with nature themes; and that not a few of them might have emanated from Dove Cottage is well instanced, for an example, by the concluding verses of "The Southwest Wind in the Woodland."

> "The voice of Nature is abroad
> This night; she fills the air with balm;
> Her mystery is o'er the land;
> And who that hears her now and yields

His being to her yearning tones,
And seats his soul upon her wings,
And broadens o'er the wind-swept world
With her, will gather in the flight
More knowledge of her secret, more
Delight in her beneficence
Than hours of musing, or the love
That lives with man, could ever give!
Nor will it pass away when morn
Shall look upon the lulling leaves
And woodland sunshine, Eden-sweet,
Dreams o'er the paths of peaceful shade;—
For every elemental power
Is kindred to our hearts, and once
Acknowledged, wedded, once embraced,
Once taken to the unfettered sense,
Once claspt into the naked life,
The union is eternal."

But Wordsworth was not Meredith's only teacher;
he learned also from Shakespeare. Certainly no
unprejudiced reader can fail to hear in the lyrics
called "Spring" and "Autumn" the haunting lilt
of such songs as "When Daisies Pied and Violets
Blue" in "Love's Labour's Lost" or "It was a
Lover and His Lass" in "As You Like It."

SPRING

When buds of palm do burst and spread
    Their downy feathers in the lane,
And orchard blossoms, white and red,
    Breathe Spring delight for Autumn gain;
    And the skylark shakes his wings in the rain;

Oh then is the season to look for a bride!
    Choose her warily, woo her unseen;
For the choicest maids are those that hide
    Like dewy violets under the green.

AUTUMN

When nuts behind the hazel-leaf
  Are brown as the squirrel that haunts them free,
And the fields are rich with the sun-burnt sheaf,
  'Mid the blue corn-flower and the yellowing tree;
  And the farmer glows and beams in his glee;

Oh then is the season to wed thee a bride!
  Ere the garners are filled and the ale-cups foam;
For a smiling hostess is the pride
  And flower of every harvest home.

Despite the weakness of the ending of each of the poems just quoted, the verse, if not Shakesperean, is at least Elizabethan in simplicity and sincerity. Now it happened that both these terms were watchwords, though hardly in a Shakesperean sense, with the pre-Raphaelite Brotherhood, who, about the middle of the nineteenth century, were astonishing both the English nation and themselves with their new ideas in art and literature. Just what the acquaintance between George Meredith and Dante Gabriel Rossetti may have been when both in 1851 reached the age of twenty-three, is not very well-known; yet a connection between Rossetti and other writers has been asserted on much more dubious ground than need be assumed for the relation between the chief pre-Raphaelite poet and Meredith. The Brotherhood, in their commendable effort after sincerity, made the unfortunate double mistake of most reformers, that of going too far, and that of ignoring the corrective influence of common sense. Meredith unfortunately exhibited both the presumable

merit and the actual fault, when in urging his lady
to a ramble over the fields, he wrote the lines:

"Thou art no nun, veiled and vowed; doomed to nourish a
        withering pallor!
    City exotics beside thee would show like bleached linen at
        midday
    Hung upon hedges of eglantine!—"

Such a quotation, of course, cannot by itself prove
that Meredith wrote under the influence of Rossetti;
but the eighth stanza of "Love in the Valley," as it
appeared in the "Poems" of 1851, is pretty convincing.   It is Rossetti through and through, not indeed
the Rossetti of "The Blessed Damozel," but rather
the poet of "The Ballads" and the painter of
"The Annunciation."

"When at dawn she wakens, and her face gazes
    Out on the weather thro' the window panes,
Beauteous she looks! like a white water-lily
    Bursting out of bud on the rippled river-plains.
When from her bed she rises clothed from neck to ankle
    In her long nightgown sweet as boughs of May
Beauteous she looks! Like a tall garden lily
    Pure from the night and perfect for the day."

It is easy to say that the lines just escape being
ridiculous; but for the matter of that the pre-Ra-
phaelites spent most of the earlier days of their
movement in trying to make such escape both in
their poems and in their paintings.   On the other
hand, there are some people who think the stanza
beautiful, a pretty conclusive proof that there is no
profit in disputes concerning taste.   Nevertheless, it

would be unfair to leave the impression that the best poem in the volume is not better than its weakest part. Tennyson and Rossetti looked upon the lyric with favor; and Meredith himself cared sufficiently for it to subject it to careful revision in 1878, when it appeared in *Macmillan's Magazine* for October, and to include it in "Poems and Lyrics of the Joy of Earth" published in 1883. Even before its revision, it contained among others such wellnigh perfect stanzas as these:

"Shy as a squirrel, and wayward as a swallow;
    Swift as the swallow when athwart the western flood
Circleting the surface he meets his mirrored winglets,—
    Is that dear one in her maiden bud.
Shy as the squirrel whose nest is in the pine-tops;
    Gentle—ah! that she were jealous as the dove!
Full of all the wildness of the woodland creatures,
    Happy in herself is the maiden that I love!

    .   .   .   .

"Happy, happy time, when the gray star twinkles
    Over the fields all fresh with bloomy dew;
When the cold-checked dawn grows ruddy up the twilight,
    And the gold sun wakes, and weds her in the blue.
Then when my darling tempts the early breezes,
    She the only star that dies not with the dark!
Powerless to speak all the ardor of my passion
    I catch her little hand as we listen to the lark."

Here indeed is the lyric cry; and its sweetness is all Meredith's own.

The fact that on the whole these early poems show the influence of Wordsworth, Shakespeare, and Rossetti may not at first thought seem to have much bearing upon Meredith's prose work.

But as Nature is often a determining force in the novels, as Meredith professedly uses dramatic methods in presenting his characters, and as truth in self-expression is one of his principal teachings, it is not without interest to know that in his very earliest work he shows the influence, however slight and remote, of our chief nature-poet, of our foremost dramatist, and of a young enthusiast not unjustly called by his contemporaries, the apostle of sincerity.

Meredith's practice in poetic diction undoubtedly played an important part in forming the style of his first prose work; but the influence which appears to have been felt most strongly in the writing of "The Shaving of Shagpat" was foreign, rather than native. There are, it is true, striking resemblances between Meredith's eastern tale and Beckford's "Vathek"; but the similarity is due to their common origin in "The Arabian Nights" rather than to any study which Meredith might have made of Beckford's romance. No doubt Meredith knew the elder writer's book, for its popularity hardly waned from the time of its publication in 1786 until well on towards the middle of the nineteenth century; and its influence, moreover, was as openly admitted by writers, as it was freely discussed by readers. Byron, for instance, did not hesitate to say that he owed certain parts of "Lara," of "The Corsair" and even of "Childe Harold" to Beckford; and if Moore and Southey flattered themselves with being more discreet, they did not succeed in misleading anybody by their silence. Under these circumstances, it may be concluded that probably Beckford's stories suggested possibilities to Meredith. However that may be, it still remains true that "The Shaving of Shagpat" is more nearly like "The Arabian Nights" than like "Vathek," and that it is also much better sustained throughout than is Beckford's work. In execution, like its eastern predecessor, Meredith's extravaganza shuts up one story inside another, much as do those magic boxes sometimes brought from the Orient; while its exuberance of detail, its brilliancy of color, and its quickness of movement present the alternating chaos and order of the kaleidoscope. Successful, however, as the book is on the whole, it must be admitted that there is discernible here and there an artificiality, a suggestion of the author playing the showman, which prevents the reader's mistaking "The Shaving of Shagpat" for the thousand-and-second tale of Scheherazade.

The character of Meredith's Arabian entertainment, as he called it, permitted or perhaps even demanded the use of an ornate and florid style; yet the luxuriant profusion of figures, indicative of an unusually fertile imagination, the gorgeous display of sparkling diction due to a glowing appreciation of color and form, and the smooth flowing cadences traceable only to accuracy in the author's understanding of tone, were so well managed as to save Meredith from falling into the production of that mongrel kind of shilly-shally writing called "poetic prose." The frequent use of metaphor and simile in the book, no doubt, had something to do with awakening in Meredith that predilection for figurative language which often laid his later books open to the charge of obscurity; but in "The Shaving of Shagpat, at least, the motive for each figure is obvious; and when one is introduced, it is sufficiently developed to prevent any misconception of the author's meaning. In the later works, on the contrary, Meredith often involves one trope in another, until the reader in his confusion drops the thread which is his only means of escape from the beautiful but tangled maze.

Hardly less frequent than the figures of speech which wind through these stories are the flashes of direct and ironic wit which illuminate nearly every page. The book is bright with sharp epigrams and strong aphorisms which pale only beside the scintillating brilliancy of "The Pilgrim's Scrip," in "The Ordeal of Richard Feverel." Hardly separable from this wit is a humor which forces the reader near to immoderate laughter. The history of the doleful thwackings which befel Shibli Bagarag in the city of Shagpat the clothier, the shameful punishments which Shahpesh the Persian visited upon Khipil the builder, and the frightful agonies which were suffered by Baba Mustapha through the persecutions of the Genie Karaz in the form of a flea, are perhaps as ludicrous as anything English literature can show in the field of sheer fun. The story, of course, is written in mock-heroic vein, and is full of whims and absurdities, which are often expressed in language purposely grandiose and inflated; but there are, none the less, passages of true pathos and unusual beauty. Certainly to one who is moved by the charm of an exquisite mingling of melodious

words informed by noble thoughts and poetic feeling, "The Lily of the Enchanted Sea" is altogether
lovely, and "The Story of Bhanavar the Beautiful"
is well-nigh perfect from beginning to end.

Of the many phases of beauty appearing in "The
Shaving of Shagpat," the treatment which Meredith
accorded to nature is not least important   The
book has numerous bits of landscape description,
although, rather surprisingly, sustained passages of
this sort are few.   After the amount of attention
given to nature in the early book of poems, Meredith
might have been expected to show growth in a power
already possessed in a high degree; and, furthermore, taking into consideration the attention paid
to nature in "The Ordeal of Richard Feverel," a
reader wonders why Meredith allowed this field of
his art to lie so nearly fallow even for a time.   But
despite the apparent neglect on his part, he did exhibit a tendency towards what became an important
element in his later work.   This was his recognition
of a sympathetic connection between Nature and
Man, that is of a dynamic relationship between
scene and character which through interaction are
made to gain from each other.   This treatment of
Nature was indeed not new in literature, for Shakespeare used it frequently, and Tennyson cultivated
it carefully.   Scott, too, recognized its value, but it
is safe to say that it has been more fully developed
by Meredith than by any other English novelist.

Still another tendency, although not connected
with the preceding in any way save in time and place
of appearance, was the use of a device which has

come to be looked upon as a characteristic of Meredith's novels. It consists in the formal introduction of a proverb, a stanza of poetry, or even a prose passage of some length, as a kind of general criticism upon the conduct of the characters. By this is meant not the method frequently employed by Thackeray and George Eliot and sometimes by Meredith himself, that of suddenly appearing upon the stage for the purpose of calling attention to the actors or perhaps of pointing a moral; but rather the method of the old Greek drama in which the chorus comments as fate upon the meaning of the impulses, the words, and the deeds of the men and women in the play. Occurring but occasionally in "The Shaving of Shagpat," this device almost ran riot in "The Ordeal of Richard Feverel." Thereafter, Meredith was more restrained in its use, but the tendency reappeared in "Sandra Belloni" and in "The Egoist," and became pronounced in "The Amazing Marriage."

These comments as they occur in "The Shaving of Shagpat" have a second significance probably not dreamed of by Meredith in writing them. Usually in this particular story they take the form of quatrains, which in spite of a difference in the succession of rhymes, are a curious anticipation of Omar Kháyyám as translated by Edward Fitzgerald. A few stanzas taken at hazard are convincing.

> "The curse of sorrow is comparison!
>   As the sun casteth shade, night showeth star,
>   We, measuring what we were by what we are,
>   Behold the depth to which we are undone."
>
> .   .   .   .

> "On different heads misfortunes come:
> One bears them firm, another faints,
> While this one hangs them like a drum
> Whereon to batter loud complaints."

.　　.　　.　　.　　.　　.　　.　　.

> "Thou that dreamest an event,
> While Circumstance is but a waste of sand,
> Arise, take up thy fortunes in thy hand,
> And daily forward pitch thy tent."

Although Fitzgerald's translation of Omar Kháyyám was published in 1859, three years after the appearance of "The Shaving of Shagpat," it is known to have been circulated in manuscript for some time before it was printed. There is no evidence, however, that either of the writers actually borrowed from the other, though the striking similarity of tone between the two works is, to say the least, interesting.

The lot which has befallen Meredith of always being taken too seriously or not seriously enough is evidenced in the two or three attempts that have been made to interpret "The Shaving of Shagpat" allegorically. To the most recent, it is said, Meredith courteously replied that the elaborate exposition recalled some of the thoughts which he had when writing the fantasy, but that as a matter of fact, the book was no more an allegory than Crummles was a Prussian. This commentator might have been spared his work, interesting as he undoubtedly found it, had he been acquainted with the second edition of "The Shaving of Shagpat." This appeared in 1865 and contained a Prefatory Note denying that the story was susceptible of any esoteric interpretation. The note is not reprinted in editions now accessible; characteristic of Meredith, however, it well deserves reproduction.

"It has been suggested to me by one who has no fear of Allegories on the banks of the Nile, that the hairy Shagpat must stand to mean umbrageous Humbug conquering the sons of men; and that Noorna bin Noorka represents the seasons, which help us, if there is health in us, to dispel the affliction of his shadow; while my heroic Shibli Bagarag is actually to be taken for Circumstance, which works under their changeful guidance towards our ultimate release from bondage, but with a disappointing apparent waywardness. The excuse for such behavior as this youth exhibits, is so good that I would willingly let him wear the grand masque hereby offered to him. But, though his backslidings cry loudly for some sheltering plea, or garb of dignity, and though a story-teller should be flattered to have it supposed that anything very distinct was intended by him, the Allegory must be rejected altogether. The subtle Arab who conceived Shagpat, meant either very much more, or he meant less; and my belief is, that, designing in his wisdom simply to amuse, he attempted to give a larger embrace to time than is possible to the profound dispenser of Allegories, which are mortal; which, to be of any value, must be perfectly clear, and when perfectly clear, are as little attractive as Mrs. Malaprop's reptile."

Of more importance than either the meanings

which have been read into "The Shaving of Shagpat," or the beginnings of those peculiarities of expression which became a striking characteristic of the later works, or even those possible sources and influence which are easier to assert than to prove, is the promulgation of principles which Meredith in after years used as more or less important parts of a consistent system of philosophy. Character with him no less than with Shakespeare is the source of destiny. A man's conduct in a crisis is determined by his previous thoughts and acts. Pride and cowardice, avarice and fear as surely bring to nothing, as courage and faithfulness, honor and humility lead to triumph. Egoism, the undue worship of the perishable self; sentimentalism, the elevation, according to Meredith, of the constantly changing conventional above the "eternal verities," are perhaps for a time their own exceeding great reward; but the ironic laughter of truth is heard at last, the illusions are dispelled, and the king is glad to propitiate the people by the voluntary resignation of the crown to Shibli Bagarag, the Master of the Event. The words of the sage are indeed seen to be the words of wisdom when he says:

> "Power, on Illusion based o'ertoppeth all;
> The more disastrous is its certain fall!"

But the mere recognition of a truth does not bring salvation, nor having touched success at one point may the race of mankind be content.

"For the mastery of an event lasteth among men the space of one cycle of years, and after that a fresh

Illusion springeth to befool mankind. . . . As the
poet declareth in his scorn:

> 'Some doubt eternity; from life begun,
> Has folly ceased within them, sire to son?
> So, ever fresh Illusions will arise
> And lord creation, until men are wise.'

And he adds:

> 'That is a distant period; so prepare
> To fight the false, O youths, and never spare!
> For who would live in chronicles renowned
> Must combat folly, or as fool be crowned.' "

Of the many illusions which are constantly ham-
pering mankind in its advance toward full perfection, Meredith, judged by all his writings, from beginning to end, seems to look upon the conventional
attitude towards women as the most stubborn,—
as an Event, indeed, to an assistance in the mastery
of which he himself has heard no uncertain call.
Even in this early work he did not hesitate to take
the stand that without the aid of woman, man must
leave much undone, since from her chidings he
learns many things, and through her encouragement
he becomes strengthened to retrieve his errors and
to save himself from complete overthrow. Indeed,
so strongly does Meredith insist upon these doctrines, that he may himself be regarded as the Sage
who said in speaking of the Laws made in honor of
Noorna by Shibli Bagarag for the protection and
upholding of woman,

> "Were men once clad in them, we should create
> A race not following, but commanding, fate."

Serious as some of these teaching are, however, "The Shaving of Shagpat" is on the whole to be regarded as an extravaganza in both thought and expression; yet even from that point of view, the work has to be taken more seriously than the story which immediately followed it. "Farina" bubbles with laughter from beginning to end; and the reader seems to hear the author calling out from every page "That's the fun of it!" Only once in later life did Meredith give another exhibition of such unrestrained humor; but "The Case of General Ople and Lady Camper" has nothing in common with "Farina" save the jester's spirit which animates both. The story of the retired officer with his "gentlemanly residence" and of the lady who reformed both his speech and his manners, is an episode in recent English social life; but the history of the siege which Farina laid to the heart of Margarita is a German romance of the Middle Ages. It is a rollicking tale of love and adventure, of blood and thunder, of kidnappings and rescues, of maidens and duennas, of knights and robbers, of saints and sinners, of nixies and devils, and, indeed, of pretty nearly everything in heaven above, in the earth beneath, or in the waters under the earth. Its supernatural elements suggest the pseudo-Gothic romances of Horace Walpole and Ann Radcliffe; its ridicule of the chivalry of mediæval Germany recalls the picaresque novel as modified by Cervantes; the Water-Lady is own sister to Fouqué's Undine; and Aunt Lisbeth, judged from her suspicious watch over Margarita, must have learned her lesson in the same

school with the Aunts von Landshort who guarded
the heiress of Katzenellenbogen in Washington Irv-
ing's story of "The Spectre Bridegroom." But suggestive as the story is of other authors' creations,
the probability of its actually owing anything whatever to Meredith's contemporaries or predecessors
is very remote. The most that can be said with cer-
tainty is that "Farina" was Meredith's first book to
show any traceable influence of his school days in
Germany.

The style of "Farina" is much less ornate than
that of "The Shaving of Shagpat," the character
and the setting both demanding a pruning of the
diction which was fully appropriate to the earlier
work. On the other hand the burlesque facetious-
ness, at times approaching audacious nonsense,
finds fitting expression in words and turns of phras-
ing best described as piquant and quaint. Wit and
humor play as freely here as in the story of Shibli
Bagarag's adventures, but there is a noticeable absence of pathos. The sayings of the Minnesingers
serve the purpose of the Greek Chorus, as did the
verses of the sage in "The Shaving of Shagpat;"
and now and then there is a glint of the philosophy
emphasized in the preceding book, such, for instance,
as the corrective power of laughter, the inevitable
fall that waits on pride, and the foolishness of placing the conventional above the absolute. On the
whole, however, a decided increase in power of description is perhaps the most important advance
which Meredith made in this story. Not as yet, it is
true, did he show himself an artist in sustained pas-

sages, but he exhibited an unusual skill in painting
a picture with a few strokes; and, rather strangely,
most of these have the Rembrandt-like characteristic of possessing a single point of light. Two
scenes, the first from "The Lilies of the Valley,"
the second from "The Silver Arrow" adequately
show this new development of Meredith's genius.

"The moon was dipping down, and paler, as if
touched with a warning of dawn. Chill sighs from
the open land passed through the city. On certain
colored gables and wood-crossed fronts, the white
light lingered; but mostly the houses were veiled in
dusk, and Gottlieb's house was confused in the
twilight with those of his neighbors, notwithstanding
its greater stateliness, and the old grandeur of its
timbered bulk."

.   .   .   .

"They wound down numberless intersections of
narrow streets with irregular-built houses standing
or leaning wry-faced in row, here a quaint-beamed
cottage, there almost a mansion with gilt arms,
brackets, and devices. Oil lamps unlit hung at
intervals by the corners near a pale Christ on cruci-
fix. Across the passages they hung alight. The
passages and alleys were too dusky and close for
the moon in her brightest ardor to penetrate;
down the streets a slender lane of white beams could
steal. . . . After incessant doubling here and there,
listening to footfalls, and themselves eluding a chase
which their suspicious movements aroused, they
came upon the Rhine. A full flood of moonlight
burnished the knightly river in glittering scales, and

plates, and rings, as headlong it rolled seaward on from under crag and banner of old chivalry and rapine. Both greeted the scene with a burst of pleasure. The gray mist of flats on the south side glimmered delightful in their sight, coming from that drowsy crowd and press of habitations; but the solemn glory of the river, delaying not, heedless, impassioned—pouring on in some sublime conference between it and heaven to the great marriage of waters—deeply shook Farina's enamoured heart. The youth could not restrain his tears, as if a magic wand had touched him. He trembled with love; and that delicate bliss which maiden hope first showers upon us like a silver rain when she has taken the shape of some young beauty and plighted us her fair fleeting hand, tenderly embraced him."

With "Farina," Meredith ended his work as mere apprentice, and during the next two years gave his attention to the composition of "The Ordeal of Richard Feverel. Still, although the "Poems" of 1851, "The Shaving of Shagpat," and "Farina" are to be regarded as belonging to the period of experiment and preparation, their importance is not slight. Therein are discernible the determining influence of two or three great writers, the beginnings of a powerful and unusual style, the first applications of methods new to English fiction, and certain fundamental ideas in a remarkable philosophy. In studying the growth of an author's genius, such things as these cannot be ignored, although the average reader may look upon them as of little value. But even he, however, though he cares nothing about the genesis of a style, or the institutes of a philosophy can well afford to take down the early stories of Meredith and spend a little time with Shibli Bagarag as he proves himself worthy of the love of Noorna bin Noorka, or with Farina and the Goshawk while they rescue Margarita from the clutches of Baron Werner and his robber band.

III

THE JOURNEYMAN

ASSIMILATED INFLUENCES—"THE ORDEAL OF RICH-
ARD FEVEREL"—"EVAN HARRINGTON"—"SANDRA
BELLONI"—"VITTORIA"—"RHODA FLEMING."

THE journeyman differs from the apprentice
mainly in that he has discovered the bent of his
genius, and is consciously possessed of power and
skill. From observation and practice he has gained
a certain self-confidence, and believes that he ought
to be trusted to do ordinary work well; but if he
has the making of a master-workman in him, this
self-confidence does not let him fall into the trap
of thinking that he has nothing more to learn. On
the contrary, he still studies whatever has met with
general approval, but he is now animated by a desire to become acquainted with methods and means
rather than with results. The old inquiry of his
apprenticeship, what must be imitated that proper
training may be effected, gives way to the deeper
and more important questions, how was this work
done, and to what extent may the same methods be
followed without the sacrifice of originality. He
gets his answer, much as he did in earlier days,
through experiment and imitation; but it is through

experiment of a higher kind, and through imitations of a rarer sort. No longer satisfied with the simple reproduction of what he has seen, he strives to express his own ideas as completely as he may without violating long accepted traditions and well authenticated principles. As a result, what he now places before the world, although it may still be suggestive of the work of others, is far from being a mere resemblance. In other words, the process of absorption is replaced by that of assimilation, and he is thus enabled to turn to his task with ever increasing energy, in the hope that he may yet produce a masterpiece which shall give lasting joy to both maker and user.

The apprenticeship of Meredith seems to have been spent in a pretty close study of English, Arabian, and German models; but there came a time when the young author, after having fully decided to devote himself to novel writing, felt that he might trust somewhat freely to his own originality. Not so self-confident, however, as to consider himself a master-workman, he did not wholly emancipate himself from the influence of other authors, but spent his time upon four or five works which have much in common with the writings of his predecessors, Richardson, Fielding, and Sterne, and with those of his contemporaries, Dickens, Thackeray, and George Eliot. This does not mean that Meredith merely copied these authors, nor that he deliberately borrowed from them. Indeed, whatever charges the most hostile critics have brought against him, none have taken it upon themselves to accuse him very loudly of plagiarism, but have rather gone to the opposite extreme, insisting that in his self-sufficiency he refused to learn from those who could have taught him much. Writers of such criticism would have said far less, had they known a little more. The true student of Meredith, whether admirer or not, plainly sees that the earlier novels, at least, are the resultant of some of the most important forces in the world of English letters. Appropriating whatever he deemed admirable, wherever he could find it, Meredith, either consciously or unconsciously, turned such material to account, first, however, so thoroughly assimilating it, that in its transformation it appeared wholly his own. Indebtedness thus incurred is by no means censurable. Meredith simply used a method which has been characteristic of the greatest authors from Homer to Molière, from Chaucer to Browning. Indeed, it is not impossible that an overscrupulous care to be original from every point of view, is the mark of a second-rate mind rather than of a genius.

For any young novelist writing during the middle years of the nineteenth century to have wholly rejected what his surroundings abundantly offered would have been well-nigh impossible. So far as Meredith is concerned, the corrective power of his genius fortunately saved him from mere imitation, and helped him to the preservation of an original and striking individuality. Nevertheless, his environment was not without its disadvantages. At a time of great intellectual activity, the chorus of those who have gained the attention of the public is often so overpowering, as to drown the voice of any new aspirant to fame; and this was the unfortunate lot which befell Meredith when he published "The Ordeal of Richard Feverel." In 1859, readers asking for the newest books could make choice of Dickens's "Tale of Two Cities," Thackeray's "Virginians," Trollope's "Bertrams," Reade's "Love me Little, Love Me Long," Fitzgerald's translation of the "Rubáiyát," Darwin's "Origin of Species," and Mill's "Essay on Liberty." Moreover, during the same year, occurred the deaths of Leigh Hunt, Macaulay, De Quincey, and Hallam, thus giving the pessimist some excuse for shaking his head and mourning over the irreparable thinning in the ranks of literary men. Certainly the minds of those interested in books and authors were taken up with many things; and it is therefore little surprising that, despite several favorable reviews, the first edition of "The Ordeal of Richard Feverel" supplied all demands for nineteen years. But whatever disappointment Meredith may have felt over the reception accorded his first novel, its publication was an important event in his career. It showed conclusively that he was ready to abandon such cherry-stone carving as "The Shaving of Shagpat," and that he was sufficiently sure of himself to enter into competition with other novelists, and to submit to measurement by their standards.

"The Ordeal of Richard Feverel," was followed as rapidly as careful work would permit by "Evan Harrington," "Sandra Belloni," "Rhoda Fleming," and "Vittoria," all of which, as has been said, pos-

sess in common at least one characteristic, that of
recalling the writings of other authors.   This sugges-
tiveness, however, is much stronger in some cases
than in others.   Sometimes it is a feature of style;
often it is a similarity of incident, or a likeness in
character-drawing; now and then it is almost safe
to say that a certain personage could not have been
created, had it not been for the existence of some
other novelist's work; and occasionally striking par-
allels of considerable length can be pointed out
between Meredith and others.   True as these statements are, however, the influence which predecessors
and contemporaries seem to have exerted upon Meredith is to be felt rather than seen.   Often there is
no more than a whiff or a tang of the borrowed
flavor, and even these are lost as soon as tasted.
Clearly, anything so evanescent will hardly bear
much insistence.   Still if Meredith himself should
rise up in protest, and assert that he was uncon-
scious of any outside influences whatever, the comparison would still remain true and have a certain
interesting value.

When "The Ordeal of Richard Feverel" appeared, some reviews called it a Shandean romance,
and others said that it betrayed the influence of
Bulwer's "Caxtons": nor can it be denied that the
critics had some warrant for their statements.   Richard Feverel's Uncle Algernon had been a gentleman of the Guards, but had unfortunately lost his leg
as the result of an injury received in a cricket match;
Pisistratus Caxton's uncle Roland had lost a leg
at the battle of Waterloo; and Tristram Shandy's

Uncle Toby had been severely wounded in the leg at the siege of Namur. Now, of course, the presence of one-legged uncles in novels hardly constitutes a similarity which is to be taken as other than accidental; but in addition, all the uncles and, even more, all the fathers in these three stories had various hobbies, not the least important of which were their remarkable ideas of how the several young heirs should be brought up. Sterne refers more than once with some humor to what he calls the Shandean system of Tristram's father; and Meredith is constantly pointing the finger of scorn at Sir Austin's theories and their application. In the first book, too, there are passages descriptive of the elder Shandy, which might almost have been written of Sir Austin, "It is the nature of an hypothesis," says Sterne in the character of his hero, "that it assimilates everything to itself, as proper nourishment," a sentence certainly applicable to the Baronet's suspicious and condemnatory train of thought, when he was nursing his wrath against Richard for marrying Lucy. "There are a thousand unnoticed openings which let a penetrating eye into a man's soul," says Sterne, thereby expressing an aphorism worthy of a place in "The Pilgrim's Scrip," and at the same time furnishing a terse anticipatory comment upon Sir Austin's unsuccessful endeavor to entrench himself in studied and unnatural reserve.

The elder Caxton, whose name, by the way, was shortened from Augustine to the more familiar Austin, like the fathers of Tristram and of Richard, also used a system in bringing up his son. He had a method, however, which stood in direct contrast with that of the lord of Raynham Abbey. Pisistratus was sent to school that by mingling with his fellows he might become a man, Richard was kept at home that he might escape the corruption which Sir Austin thought to be rife in educational institutions; the former was allowed the greatest freedom, the latter was under constant surveillance, for it was a fundamental theory with Sir Austin that "young lads might by parental vigilance be kept secure from the Serpent until Eve sided with him—a period that might be deferred, he said." Both parents hoped to retain the confidence of their sons by inviting it at every opportunity, and by assisting, though not dictating, in the choice between good and evil. In carrying out the plan, Austin Caxton never for a moment forgot that he was dealing with a human being, and through this sanity of attitude he was able to keep his child as a companion until the end; but, in the words of Adrian Harley, "Sir Austin wished to be Providence to his son," and only at fleeting intervals entertaining "a thought that he was fighting with fate in his beloved boy," he failed at the crucial moment, and there was an end to true confidence between father and son.

Yet Sir Austin deserves our sympathy. His love for Richard was really deep and strong, and he did nothing but what in his blindness he thought was for the best. Demon-ridden by the Great Shaddock doctrine, and marked by the "total absence of the humorous in himself (the want that most shut him out from his fellows)," he was unhappily without the faculty of laughter. "For a good wind of laughter," says Meredith, "had relieved him of much of the blight of self-deception, and oddness, and extravagance; had given him a heathier view of our atmosphere of life; but he had it not." It is not surprising that under such conditions a tragedy took place. The System must prevail, although the boy for whose good it was formulated should be sacrificed to its exactions. Had Sir Austin but possessed the clearer vision, clouded though it was, of Lady Blandish; or better still had the penetrating eye of the far-seeing Bessie Berry been his, he might have preserved his son alive. But he would not see. Ever declaring to himself that, so far as his son was concerned, all love and all wisdom were his own, he merited in the hour of his grief over his son's waywardness and agony, exactly the same criticism which had been spoken of him many years before:

"If immeasurable love were perfect wisdom, one human being might almost impersonate Providence to another. Alas! love, divine as it is, can do no more than lighten the house it inhabits—must take its shape, sometimes intensify its narrowness—can spiritualize, but not expel the old life-long lodgers above-stairs and below."

Pity the Baronet deserves, no doubt, but his nature was seldom other than cold and hard. In the very crises of his son's life, he could steel himself to utter an aphorism; and by the irony of fate he characterized himself most fully when he wrote, "A maker of Proverbs—what is he but a narrow mind, the mouthpiece of narrower?" These sayings of his from that first startling statement, "I expect that woman will be the last thing civilized by man," to that final penetrating observation, "Which is the coward among us? He who sneers at the failings of Humanity!" are never less than brilliant, and frequently strike at the roots of the folly and the mistakes of mankind. Recalling them, the reader is again carried back to "The Caxtons," for the father of the hero in that book was engaged upon the composition of "A History of Human Error." The absent-minded scholar and the analytic nobleman thus both turned their eyes upon the world about them, and put down the lessons they drew therefrom, but one looked from within and was moved by sympathy and pity, while the other stood aloof and felt little but contempt and scorn.

At one other point, certainly, there is a faint resemblance to be found between Meredith and Bulwer, although it might not suggest itself, if the presence of larger and more striking similarities did not lead the reader to find analogies where perhaps none really exist. Nevertheless, the extreme deference paid by Mrs. Caxton to her husband, her ready acceptance of every word of his as the utterance of incarnate wisdom, remind one of the earlier attitude of Lady Blandish toward Sir Austin. Fortunately for Mrs. Caxton, no rude shock ever disturbed her admiration. Her husband, inferior as he was to the nobleman, was always simple and sincere, as simple and sincere, in fact, as the Vicar of Wakefield. Lady Blandish, on the other hand, was destined to a harsh awakening. The Autumn Primrose, as

Meredith called her love for Sir Austin, bloomed for
the Baronet's pleasure, and more than once he
seemed on the point of plucking it for his wearing,
but the blighting frost of his egoism wrought in
time its destructive work.   During the first weeks of
her stay at Raynham Abbey, Lady Blandish was
awed into approval by the stupendous claims made
for the System, nor would she permit herself to doubt,
either when her heart went out to the modest loveli-
ness of Lucy, or when in pity she gazed upon Richard
lying pale and motionless, with fever on his cheeks
and strange unseeing eyes.   But when the nobleman
hearing of Richard's deceit and disobedience, as he
called it, endeavored still to be the Sage, still to
maintain his pose as one who could be surprised by
nothing in nature, then was the veil lifted somewhat.
Daily, thereafter, she saw him more and more as he
was, and at the end she could write with sane indig-
nation to Austin Wentworth:

"Oh! how sick I am of theories, and Systems, and
the pretensions of men!   There was his son lying
all but dead, and the man was still unconvinced of
the folly he had been guilty of.   I could hardly bear
the sight of his composure.   I shall hate the name
of Science till the day I die.   Give me nothing but
commonplace, unpretending people!"

But the chief victim of Sir Austin's strange perversion, the object of Lady Blandish's pity, and the
butt of Adrian Harley's wit, Richard himself, is a
study in character, not unlike that made by one of
the founders of the English novel.   Almost without
question, "The Ordeal of Richard Feverel" may be

looked upon as a purified "Tom Jones." Fielding
in his chief work presented a hero as fully and as
truthfully as Rousseau in his "Confessions" endeavored to picture himself. That Fielding succeeded, no reader denies; and attempts have been
made, now and then, to gain renown in a similar
way. But of the several authors who seem to owe
a part of their inspiration to Fielding's frankness in
portrayal, Meredith comes nearest to a reproduction
of his spirit. Meredith freely admits the natural
impulses of his hero, and shows whither, under certain conditions they would inevitably lead him.
That is, Meredith dared to do, what Thackeray almost feared to undertake. In the preface of "Pendennis," its writer remarked that since the death of
Fielding, no writer of fiction had been permitted to
depict a man as he really was. Instead, the hero
had to be carefully draped and be given a conventional simper, since readers were determined not to
hear what moved in the real world; what passed in
society, in the clubs, college mess-rooms; what was
the life, the talk of young men. Thus hampered,
Thackeray felt that he had need to apologize for his
frankness in drawing the character of Arthur Pendennis, and that he must ask the charitable favor
of his readers for presenting the truth. This timidity on Thackeray's part—one hardly likes to call it
cowardice—this deference to conventional ideas not
yet wholly abandoned, is a state of mind which
Meredith stigmatizes by the name of sentimentalism; but Thackeray possibly had been made a trifle
fearful by the cry of disapprobation which in 1847

had greeted the publication of "Jane Eyre."   Charlotte Brontё living quietly in the rectory at Haworth
had been too far removed from the stiff propriety
of the cities to be trained in the elegant accomplish-
ment of squeamishness, and had portrayed the natural passions as they are, rather than as London
then said that they must be assumed to be.   Nevertheless, limited as her opportunities for observation
were, what Charlotte Brontё could do, she did; on
the other hand what Thackeray felt he ought to do,
he went nigh to shirking; and it is therefore not a
little to the credit of Meredith that in the very beginning of his career as novelist he did not hesitate
to follow the path of the woman rather than of the
man.

Readers are not now so daintily fastidious as they
used to be, and they accept without adverse comment the baldest portrayal of the animal passions;
but Charlotte Brontё and George Meredith were
leaders in the renascence of the realistic presentation of the natural instincts, subjects which no healthy
mind now considers it beyond the right of the novelist
to present.   That they were for a time taboo to
writers of fiction was perhaps partly due to the rise
of a false modesty, but probably more to the fact
that their calm and well-balanced treatment by
Fielding and Richardson was brought into disre-
pute by the salacious suggestions of Smollett and
the "knowing" leers of Sterne.   Under circumstances
like these, certain chapters in "Jane Eyre" and in
"The Ordeal of Richard Feverel" might have been
expected to make readers uneasy, a condition of

mind which was by no means greatly soothed when
Charles Reade's "Griffith Gaunt" appeared in
1866. No wonder that shocked propriety of that
time exclaimed, "What are we coming to!" nor can
we doubt that the destruction of Sodom and Gomor-
rah would have been prophesied for the present day
and generation, had anyone foreseen the unblush-
ing immorality of many of our plays, and the shame-
less coarseness of not a few of our popular novels.
For the inexcusable length to which recent writers
have gone, however, Charlotte Bronté and George
Meredith and Charles Reade are not to blame. In
that cyclic movement which the world exhibits as
it makes its onward progress, this age is repeating to
a certain extent the degraded artificiality of the Restoration drama as compared with the frank natural-
ness of the Elizabethan play, the evil mental conditions which permitted the reading of Smollett and
Sterne as compared with the healthier attitude which
found Richardson and Fielding acceptable.

If the readers of Meredith's first novel really
were over-shocked by the narration of Richard's
adventures with the Enchantress, they could hardly
deny that it had brought them face to face with an
everyday truth. Depressing this experience may
have been to some, and doubt as to the wisdom of
the author's daring may have affected others; but no
just person could have been blind to the fact that
the colors had been laid upon the canvas by no uncertain hand. Nor even in the drawing of minor
characters could any tendency toward carelessness
or indifference be found. The strokes might be few,

but they were sufficiently bold and telling to give the figures life and animation. Ripton Thompson, for instance, though sometimes regarded as an unsuccessful portraiture of vulgarity, is more than a mere foil to his high-born friend. A reading of his fight with Richard, and of the part which he played in the Bakewell comedy will carry any man back to his own boyhood days. His conduct in his father's office was natural to the last degree, and his following of Miss Random was, to a youth of his temperament, inevitable. Nor is the subtile distinction which he made as to the propriety of his conduct in comparison with Richard's, anything unusual. The specious argument by which he explained away his logical inconsistency, is known and repeated and acted upon still by nearly every young man whom one meets. Ripton's desire to watch over and preserve the purity of his headstrong companion, therefore, is not to be ridiculed: rather one is touched by the pathos in his reply to Richard's scorn at his words of warning, "It would be different with me, because Richard, I'm worse than you." Such guardianship, such affectionate desire to protect, recalls William Dobbin's faithful following of George Osborne in "Vanity Fair." Even more,—as the crude, ungainly son of the grocer in Thames Street dared to worship Amelia Sedley at a distance, so Ripton Thompson found his mission in striving for Lucy Feverel's welfare. Indeed, the very words in which Meredith describes Ripton's awakening might have been written by Thackeray himself— even to the little moral with which they conclude:

"He spoke differently; he looked differently. He had the Old Dog's eyes in his head. They watched the door she had passed through; they listened for her, as dogs' eyes do. When she came in, bonneted for a walk, his agitation was dog-like. When she hung on her lover timidly and went forth, he followed without an idea of envy, or anything save the secret raptures the sight of her gave him, which are the Old Dog's own. For beneficent Nature requites him. His sensations cannot be heroic, but they have a fullness and a wagging delight as good in their way. And this capacity for humble, unaspiring worship has its peculiar guerdon. When Ripton comes to think of Miss Random now, what will he think of himself? Let no one despise the Old Dog. Through him doth Beauty vindicate her sex."

Far more important than Ripton Thompson is the garrulous, large - hearted, simple - minded Bessie Berry. In that mad world where the inmates of Raynham Abbey played their many parts, she is almost the only well-balanced human being. The mention of her name, however, and the recollection of her doings immediately suggest a number of other characters in English fiction. In portraying her, Meredith used a method characteristic of Dickens, that of summing up a person in one grand, all-containing trait. As Tommy Traddles in "David Copperfield" possesses a sort of "hearth-broomy kind of expression," as Mrs. Fezziwig in "A Christmas Carol" is "one vast substantial smile," as Benson, Sir Austin's butler, is "the saurian eye,"—although that designation also brings to mind De

Quincey's dubbing the coachman in "The Glory of Motion" "a crocodile"—so is Mrs. Berry made to live and breathe before us as "the bunch of black satin." Coarse she is at times, as coarse as Sairey Gamp, as racy in her speech as Dame Quickly, and as slyly insinuative, but withal as sympathetic, as the nurse in "Romeo and Juliet." She is marked, too, by a pronounced interest in cooking which places her besides Mrs. Todgers in "Martin Chuzzlewit," while her common-sense ideas upon morality, and her shrewd observations upon life in general make her an own sister to Mrs. Poyser in "Adam Bede."

We trust her, yes, we love her, the moment we meet her at the door of her lodging house in Kensington. Nor are we betrayed. She is the *Dea ex machina* of Richard's life. Married she has been, and at the hands of her husband she has suffered much; but despite her sad experience, her ideas upon men and matrimony are safe and sane. One sight of Mrs. Mount enables her to analyze and label the woman a Bella Donna, a use of terms which, as Meredith remarks, would have startled that lady by its accuracy. Incisively penetrative in her understanding of Sir Austin, she adequately sums up his character when she says to Lady Blandish, "A man that's like a woman, he's the puzzle o' life!" Greater wisdom than is usually admitted, underlies her bridal gift to Richard's young wife; and a full knowledge of the world causes her to make no delay in hastening to the Isle of Wight, when she hears that Lucy lies unprotected at the mercy of Brayder and Mountfalcon. Mrs. Berry's keenness of vision also shows

her that beyond a doubt all would be well if she could
but bring Richard and Lucy together. In her attempt to assist in the consummation of her hope she
makes her famous speech on the separation of husband and wife:

"Three months dwellin' apart! That's not matrimony, it's divorcin'! what can it be to her but
widowhood? Widowhood with no cap to show
for it! And what can it be to you, my dear? Think!
you have been a bachelor three months! and a bachelor man, he ain't a widow woman. . . . We all
know what checked prespiration is. Laugh away,
I don't mind ye, I say again, we all do know what
checked prespiration is. It fly to the lungs, it gives
ye mortal inflammation and it carries ye off. Then
I say checked matrimony is as bad. It fly to the
heart, and it carries off the virtue that's in ye, and
you might as well be dead!"

After that how can one say, as has been said more
than once, that Mrs. Berry simply wandered into
"The Ordeal of Richard Feverel" from the show-
box of Gadshill! Meredith did far more than imi-
tate the creator of "David Copperfield." He borrowed a part of that writer's panoply, perhaps, but
in the tilt he beat Dickens on his own ground.

And what is to be said of Clare and Lucy? They
also are not unsuggestive of Dickens; yet the quiet
grief with which Clare obeyed her mother's com-
mands, and the tragic struggle which Lucy made
against her fate, can never become a mere matter of
laughter or contempt, a misfortune which has over-
taken many a passage in Dickens, once looked upon

as the perfection of pathetic writing. Critics say far too much, when they assert that the point of bathos is reached in the description of the death of little Nell, for after more than half a century that chapter in "The Old Curiosity Shop" still rings true. Nevertheless, there is a dignity, a reserve in Meredith's treatment of Richard's watch beside his dead cousin, which protects the younger writer from serious adverse criticism. A similar self-restraint appears also in his description of Lucy's death, for she, too, must die, not because she is misunderstood, but because she must be broken on the wheel of Sir Austin's magnificent system. Hers was a stronger character than Clare's; too strong, indeed, to meet death in the same way. The deepest pathos of her life, therefore, is not in the agony of her last hours, but rather in that meeting with her husband when, rising to her noble forgiveness of his unfaithfulness, she is rent and torn in the very moment of triumph, by his blind and wilful persistence in a mistaken conception of honor. In that hour, the souls of Richard and Lucy lie bare before us; we are at the very springs of spiritual life; and we learn anew that the still small voice sometimes speaks to the heart of man as plainly from the words of the novelist as from the pages of Holy Writ.

"The Ordeal of Richard Feverel" is a tragedy— a tragedy, indeed, in the Shakspearean manner. This means not simply that the reader is led into the presence of death, but that the heart-racking catastrophe of the end is foreshadowed at the very beginning. The tragic note sounds with no uncertain

tone in the earliest pages, and from then on it is per-
sistently repeated with increasing intensity until it
becomes the knell tolling the few years of Lucy's
troubled life. Not for a moment in reading the book,
not even in its humorous scenes, is one allowed to
deceive oneself with the hope that in some miraculous
way the outcome may be happy. Instead, there
seizes upon the reader that kind of frenzy which lays
its grasp upon him as he watches the unrelenting
advancement of the plot against Cordelia, or the
ravening progress of the feud which deflowered the
houses of Capulet and Montague. Convinced for
the time that the woes of Richard and Lucy are real,
one feels that one must turn back the wheels of fate,
that the inevitable must not be.

Powerful as Meredith must have seen that his first
novel was, however, he did not again permit himself to make an equally extensive incursion into the
same field of writing. "The Tale of Chloe" is
tragic, it is true, but nearly perfect as it is, still no
more than a short story; "Rhoda Fleming" with its
lesson that the consequences of sin are eternal, is
pretty serious reading, but it is not tragedy, not at
least in the technical sense of that term; the death
neither of Roy Richmond nor of Nevil Beauchamp
takes the novel in which each of those men appears,
out of the realm of comedy; and although "Vittoria,"
"The Tragic Comedians" and "One of Our Conquerors" may seem to hover upon the borders of
lands presided over by the tragic rather than the
comic muse, it is clear that in comparison with
"The Ordeal of Richard Feverel," all the succeed-

ing novels form a group of which the homogeneity is much disturbed by any attempt to class the earlier work with them.

Meredith's second novel, therefore, "Evan Harrington," stands in almost as great contrast with the book immediately preceding it as that with the writings of its author's apprenticeship. The tragic element is practically eliminated, for although Juliana Bonner's death brings about the union of the man whom she loves with the woman of his choi?e, her story awakens no more than a quickly passing impulse of pity. The woes of the unfortunate Susan Wheedle are but faintly outlined, and are included probably for no other reason than to show the kindliness of Evan's heart; and finally the unhappy lot of the beautiful and attractive Caroline Strike is perhaps purposely but little more than mentioned, that the story of her temptation and escape may not seriously interfere with the gradual unfolding of Evan's rise to true manhood, or with the mirth-provoking treatment of the complications surrounding the Countess de Saldar. The book, indeed, is pervaded by humor of every sort, the extravagant, the grotesque, the refined, the delicate, the subtle, and the funny, until it would seem that Meredith is on the point of breaking through the bounds of what in the drama would be called legitimate comedy, and of permitting himself to revel for a time in the fields of hilarious farce. But as a matter of fact, he is ever mindful of the demands of true proportion; and consequently, never degenerating into the harlequin, he can force home, despite his fun,

the serious lesson of the hollow foolishness which lies
in attempting to appear what one is not.

Different as Meredith's first two novels are in
most respects, however, the second is like the first
to the extent of presenting three or four characters
somewhat suggestive of those found in the writings
of other authors. John Raikes, for instance, it has
been said by some critic, might easily have been created by Thackeray; but such a statement shows a
strange forgetfulness of the words and ways of Dick
Swiveller in "The Old Curiosity Shop;" and certainly the solicitous care and the deferential respect
which Evan's old school-friend has for his much
worn hat vividly recalls the outward appearance
though not the swindling nature of Mr. Tigg, the
shabby-genteel gentleman in " Martin Chuzzlewit."
The Cogglesby brothers, too, unlike the Cheeryble
twins as they are in many respects, must still suggest Nicholas Nickleby's benefactors, in their kindness of heart, their delight in dry jokes, and their
sly plans for helping the deserving and circumvent-
ing the insincere. The chapters in which these two
men carry out a conspiracy to reduce the pride of
old Harrington's daughters—a conspiracy only too
successful since Andrew found himself caught in his
own trap—is like Dickens almost at his best in the
humorous; and the first chapter, also, in which the
inn-keeper, the butcher, and the confectioner discuss
the death of the tailor is reminiscent of Dickens, but
of Dickens, rarified, sublimated, and refined. While
the Lymport shopkeepers talk, the reader learns
that the Great Mel, as the sartorial Melchisedec

Harrington was called, had a soul much above but-
tons and would gladly have moved in aristocratic
circles. Realizing that he could best attain this end
by not making too many pretensions, he assumed a
modesty which really irked his heart, a humility
which was ever on the watch for opportunity, a kind
of Uriah Heepism, so to speak, raised to the n'th
power. Nevertheless there was nothing cringing in
Mr. Melchisedec Harrington, Tailor of 183, Main
Street, Lymport-on-the-Sea, for it must be remembered that Melchisedec had a Presence; and according to Meredith:

"A Presence would seem to be a thing that directs
the most affable appeal to our human weakness. . . .
Beau Brummel, for instance, had a Presence. Many
it is true, take a Presence to mean no more than a
shirt-frill. . . . But that is to look upon language
too narrowly."

The wife of the Great Mel, has a far fainter Dickens flavor than he. The way in which she bullied
Dandy is not without a suggestion of Quilp's treatment of Tom Scott, nor is her servant's devotion to
her beyond a comparison with Tom's affection and
admiration for the master by whom he was habitually
beaten and abused. But Henrietta Maria Harrington, a woman endowed with a Port as her husband
with a Presence, does not permit herself to be dismissed with the mere statement that she faintly
recalls a character in "The Old Curiosity Shop."
She was a strong-minded, common-sense woman,
perhaps best summed up in Dandy's epithet of
"iron," a word which he frequently muttered when

he found himself reduced to subjection by the mere glance of her eye. Like Mrs. Berry in "The Ordeal of Richard Feverel," she is, with the possible exception of Lady Jocelyn, the one sane person in the story of Evan Harrington from the time she stands unawed before the patronizing Lady Roseley until she comes to think it fully in keeping with a Port to look after the management of Tom Cogglesby's house. She might have been a little more gentle with Evan the night after his return from his father's grave, a greater display of affection at that time would have been no weakness on her part; but true to her nature she "gave her cheek for his kiss, for she never performed the operation, but kept her mouth, as she remarked, for food and speech, and not for slobbering mummeries."

Mrs. Harrington knew her children, even as with penetrating insight she knew all men and women whom she met. In her daughters she expected to find neither sense of mind nor greatness of soul, for they were true descendants of their father; but in Evan her hope was centred, although she was far from being blind to the knowledge that he could not win his battles unaided. Determining, therefore, that her son should not be ruined by what she termed a "parcel of fools," she appeared more rigid and less kind than perhaps her heart prompted. Such reserve, however, might be expected to go with the commanding strength of character which showed itself in the calm scorn irresistibly quelling Tom Ogglesby's irascibility, and in the self-respecting motherhood reaching out to save her son from hypocrisy and deceit.   There was more than dignity, there was grandeur in her bearing and in her soul when she appeared at the picnic in the grounds of Beckley Court.   Evan, she felt, must be saved at any cost to his pride.

"There was in her bosom a terrible determination to cast a devil out of the one she best loved.   For this purpose, heedless of all pain to be given, or of impropriety, she had come to speak publicly, and disgrace and humiliate, that she might save him from the devils that had ruined his father.   'My lady,' said the terrible woman, thanking her in reply to an invitation that she might be seated, 'I have come for my son.   I hear that he has been playing the lord in your house, my lady.   I humbly thank your ladyship for your kindness to him, but he is nothing more than a tailor's son, and is bound to a tailor himself that his father may be called an honest man.   I am come to take him away.'"

If the reader of these words has any adequate conception of the circumstances under which they were uttered, if, indeed, he has even a remote understanding of the woman who said them, he has convincingly borne in upon him the fundamental truth in Meredith's philosophy of life.   So, indeed, Mrs. Mel is more than a mere character in a novel, she is more than what critics call a type, she is rather an embodiment of that perfect sincerity before which, in the long run, artificiality and sham must always go down.

In strong contrast with their mother stand the three daughters, Caroline Strike, Harriet Cogglesby, and Louisa, Countess de Saldar. Inheriting their father's social ambition to rise in society, they emancipated themselves as far as possible from what they called the Demigorgon of Tailordom and strove with courage and pertinacity to make their footing firm in aristocratic circles. Much as the reader may laugh at them, however, he feels at times that Caroline Strike is not undeserving of pity. The beautiful wife of a brutal husband, she is saved from disgrace through the one sincere trait in her character, her love for her brother. Faintly sketched as she is, she plays her part with a stately sweetness which makes the story of her life pathetic in spite of all her failings. Her next younger sister, Harriet, the wife of the wealthy brewer, Andrew Cogglesby, is even more lightly drawn. Unendowed with the beauty of her elder sister, and lacking in the strategical power of the Countess, she was content to remain in the background, to sacrifice herself for the good of the cause, and to furnish funds for the campaign in which the daughters Harrington hoped to vindicate their right to forget their humble birth.

In the siege thus laid to the citadel of society, the Countess de Saldar was the general. Attractive, vivacious, far-seeing, and cautious, she knew where to marshal her forces, how to place her artillery, and when to fly the flag of truce. Her very success wins our approval; and the reader feels almost guilty of treason as he breaks into irresistible laughter, when the father, whom she had denied, was pitilessly served up to her at the dinner in Beckley Court, or when the awful catastrophe of her mother's unex-

pected appearance at Lady Jocelyn's picnic, sub-
verted her plans and spiked her guns. The Countess
de Saldar has been called "the most consummate
liar in literature," but this, as Meredith said in another connection, is to look upon language too narrowly. Her perversion of the truth was too artistic to
be regarded as mere lying; rather let it be called a
poetic idealization of unattractive fact. But if
the generalship of the Countess awakens admiration
in the hours of siege and of attack, it wins even
greater applause, when in unbending dignity she with-
drew from a well-fought, if unsuccessful battlefield.
It was not in her nature to admit defeat. Repulsed
from one position, she marched away, with colors
flying, to recruit her forces at another vantage ground.
Her letter from Rome showed her occupying a new
eminence, ambitious, unconquered, and courageous
still.

The Countess has only one peer in English literature; Becky Sharp in "Vanity Fair." As Thackeray's interesting heroine, forgetting that her mother
was an opera girl, used to say that her maternal
ancestors, the Entrechats, were a noble family of
Gascony, so the Countess sunk the identity of the
Great Mel in Abraham Harrington of Torquay; as
Becky took advantage of a certain lack of gallantry
in Jos Sedley to make him her lover, so Louisa de
Saldar boldly drew Harry Jocelyn from a group of
scoffing critics, and taught him to fetch and carry at
her will. Again as the governess in Queen's Crawley
determined to make friends with everyone around
her, who could at all interfere with her comfort, so

the tailor's daughter at Beckley Court undertook to make capture of all who could in anyway assist or prevent her making her position sure. As Miss Sharp overreached herself in marrying Rawdon Crawley, so the Countess now and then, taking advantage of what seemed to offer firm footing, found herself upon treacherous ground. And thus the comparison of character and plot might be continued even to those last scenes in which Mrs. Rawdon Crawley, born Sharp, betook herself to deeds of charity, went to church regularly and placed her name upon subscription lists for the Destitute Orangeman, the Neglected Washer-woman, and the Distressed Muffin-man, while the Countess de Saldar found a haven and a refuge in a religion which, according to her own words, gathers all in its arms, not even excepting tailors.

Despite the likeness between the two women, the Countess is far less repellent than Becky. Either of them, it is true, might unsheath her claws and mark one with a cat-like scratch; but their ways were different. Becky was careless whom she hurt, if the injured person could not retaliate; the Countess with a certain lady-like magnanimity exhibited her weapons only to keep some envious woman in well-disciplined subjection. Still further Becky was an egoist who sacrificed everything and everybody to her own ambition, while the Countess, gathering up her two sisters, her brother, and the memory of her dead father, endeavored to carry them all with her to a secure and lasting niche in high society. In the attainment of their ambition both of the women

failed, yet while the reader feels that Thackeray
meted out to Becky her proper deserts, he wonders if
Meredith did not suffer an occasional qualm for not
permitting the Countess to remain master of the situation at Beckley Court.   Such a triumph would have
been hardly more than poetic justice due that lady's
adroit and consummate genius.

As studies in character, Mrs. Mell and her titled
daughter are of such importance as to make it a
matter of some surprise that neither Evan Harrington himself nor the two women who regarded him
with romantic affection approach anywhere near
being unique.   Nevertheless, the reason for the existence of the novel rests first of all in its presentation
of the struggle which a young man undergoes, when
for good and almost sufficient reasons he would like
to appear other than he is; and also in its setting
the not unimportant problem of what a young
woman shall do, when her heart has been given to
the keeping of a man socially her inferior.   Evan's
nature even in its undeveloped state partook sufficiently of his mother's sturdy sincerity to earn for
him from the angry Countess the frequent accusa-
tion of being but a Dawley—an epithet by which the
lady meant that her brother was willing to remain on
a level with the commonplace family from which the
Great Mel had presumably raised his wife when he
made her Mrs. Harrington.   Partly moved by his
sister's prodding, but influenced still more by the
fact that he had fallen in love with the daughter of
Sir Franks Jocelyn, Evan wavered between the desire to call himself a gentleman, and the wish to be

loyal to truth and write himself a tailor. Nor does
Meredith permit his readers to feel that Evan was
called upon to make any insignificant choice. It involved a question of moral strength; on the young
man's decision his future rise or fall is so plainly made
to depend, that one breathes a sigh of relief when
one learns that Evan has determined to make his
way to Mr. Goren's unattractive London shop. If
by so doing he in any way ceased to be a gentleman,
he at least showed himself a man.

The struggle through which Rose Jocelyn passed
in becoming reconciled to her lover's calling was
hardly less significant than Evan's own. But her
native good sense and strength of character did not
fail her in the crucial moment; despite an occasional feeling of repugnance to becoming a tailor's
wife, she showed herself worthy of the man who
loved her. Unfortunately, circumstances for a time
forced Evan to appear a dastard even to her, and
their engagement, as a result, seemed irrevocably
broken. For artistic reasons the bond had to be
reknit, but it is disappointing to find that Meredith's hand suddenly lost its cunning, and that the
first four thoroughly satisfying acts of the comedy,
as its author calls it, are followed by a group of scenes
which it is scarcely too harsh to speak of as cheap
and commonplace. Meredith's solution of his
concluding problem is as little satisfactory as the
closing chapters of "The Vicar of Wakefield" where
Goldsmith, suddenly seeming to realize that he had
before him a Gordian knot of his own weaving,
abruptly and unexpectedly struck it through, be-

cause he lacked the patience and, possibly, the ingenuity necessary to its untying.

In the same way Juliana Bonner's death and the influences which it set in motion seem hardly more than a sorry makeshift to unite the parted lovers. Just why Meredith introduced the young woman in the first place is hardly clear. Evidently he did not care for her and apologized more than once for her existence. It is true that she is faintly suggestive of Richard Feverel's cousin Clare, probably for no other reason than because she was an invalid, but on the whole she was a despicable little creature and the way in which she gloated over Evan's bodily strength and physical attractiveness makes her at times positively repulsive. Meredith's chivalry now and then forced him to present her in such a light as to awaken a glimmer of pity; but in general it must be admitted that a reader feels little better than shocked to have the likeness of Juliana Bonner hang in the same gallery with portraits of Lucy Desborough, Clara Middletown, and Diana Warwick. Yet, the ending, despite its weakness, does not lessen to any great extent the satisfaction and delight, with which one recalls those early scenes made memorable by the presence of the tall and stately Henrietta Maria Harrington, the versatile and vivacious Countess de Saldar, the eccentric Tom Cogglesby, and the beautiful Caroline Strike.

"Evan Harrington" first appeared in the popular magazine called *Once A Week,* and ran from February 11 to October 13, 1860. It was reprinted the following year; and the story proved enough more

successful than "The Ordeal of Richard Feverel"
to create a demand for a second edition in 1866.
Meanwhile, of course, Meredith did not cease writing;
but he did turn aside for a time from prose to poetry,
and in 1862 published a volume entilted "Modern
Love and Poems of the English Roadside." Of
the twenty-three pieces of varying length in that
book but four are now included in sets of Meredith's
presumably complete works—"Juggling Jerry" and
"The Old Chartist," both in method reminding one
of Browning, "Marian," a lyric recalling Tennyson's
early studies in portraiture, and, most important of
all, the cycle of fifty sixteen-line stanzas collectively
given the title which stood as the leading name of
the whole volume. Upon its appearance the book
was so severely handled by *The Spectator* as to pro-
voke a sharp letter of protest from Swinburne, who
did not hesitate to say that no man then living had
ever turned out a more perfect piece of writing than
the forty-seventh poem of the series entitled "Modern Love." This rather sweeping statement, it
should be remembered, was made at a time when
Tennyson was felt by most readers to be the greatest
writer since Milton; and Browning, by at least a few,
to be the greatest since Shakespeare.

That Swinburne's challenge was made not without
reason, is best proved, perhaps, by letting the poem
mentioned speak for itself.

> "We saw the swallows gathering in the sky,
> And in the osier-isle we heard them noise.
> We had not to look back on summer joys
> Or forward to a summer of bright dye;

But in the largeness of the evening earth
Our spirits grew as we went side by side.
The hour became her husband and my bride.
Love that had robbed us so, thus blessed our dearth!
The pilgrims of the year waxed very loud
In multitudinous chatterings, as the flood
Full brown came from the West, and like pale blood
Expanded to the upper crimson cloud.
Love that had robbed us of immortal things
This little moment mercifully gave,
Where I have seen across the twilight wave
The swan sail with her young beneath her wings.

In accordance with just what theory of selection
the remaining score of poems in the volume was
afterwards suppressed is not at all clear. Some,
it is true, show but little improvement over the
"Poems" of 1851, and for that reason were perhaps
rightly rejected; but on the other hand two or
three are not unworthy of a place beside the best
lyrics produced during the latter half of the nineteenth century. "Margaret's Bridal Eve," for instance, led Swinburne to say in his "Essays and
Studies" that it stands not very far below Rossetti's
"Sister Helen," a poem which the same critic ranked
as being "out of all sight or thought of expression
the greatest ballad in modern English." In spite
of such praise Meredith ruthlessly omitted the
piece from all later collections of his poetry, and
with as little hesitation pruned away the nearly
flawless verses called "The Meeting." It is interesting to learn that this particular poem received
the distinction of being praised by Thackeray at a
time when he was almost a dictator in the world of

English letters. The great novelist and editor said
to Peacock who showed him the lines in manuscript,
"They have the true ring about them. Were it not
my fate to make enemies of so many of my contribu-
tors by not always being able exactly to meet their
views, I should ask you to let your friend fill many
pages of the *Cornhill*." These were no insignificant words, but, flattering as they were, they seem,
when one takes the subject of "The Meeting" into
consideration, to exhibit Thackeray in the same
unfortunate light as does the introduction to "Pendennis"—that is, suffering from an obsession of
timidity. At all events the poem appeared for the
first time not in *Cornhill*, but in *Once A Week*, where
in compensation for its rejection by Thackeray, it
was illustrated by Sir John Millais.

THE MEETING

The old coach-road through a common of furze
    With knolls of pine ran white;
Berries of autumn, with thistles and burrs
    And spider-threads, droop'd in the light.

The light in a thin blue veil peered sick;
    The sheep grazed close and still;
The smoke of a farm by a yellow rick
    Curled lazily under a hill.

No fly shook the round of the silver net;
    No insect the swift bird chased;
Only two travellers moved and met
    Across that lazy waste.

One was a girl with a babe that throve,
    Her ruin and her bliss;
One was a youth with a lawless love
    Who clasped it the more for this.

The girl for her babe hummed prayerful speech,
The youth for his love did pray;
Each cast a wistful look on each;
And either went their way.

From these quotations at least two conclusions may
be safely drawn, that Meredith was no mere poetaster,
and that his work in verse showed a considerable
growth in 1862 beyond what it had been ten years
before.   Still, although poems by Meredith appeared
now and then in the magazines, he did not see fit
to collect them into a volume until twenty years
had gone by.   On the other hand, beginning in 1864,
he published three novels in three successive years,
"Sandra Belloni," "Rhoda Fleming," and "Vittoria."   Of these the third is connected with the first
in much the same way as Thackeray's "Virginians"
is related to "Henry Esmond." The heroine,
Emilia Alessandra Belloni, however, is the same in
both stories; and the steady growth of her character
is continuously kept before the reader instead of its
being presented at two contrasting periods of her
life, as was Thackeray's method with Beatrix Esmond.   Nevertheless, Meredith's two novels present several points of difference.   "Sandra Belloni"
was originally called "Emilia in England," a title
which it kept until 1887, and which indeed it should
have retained, since it presents the experience of an
Italian exile's daughter.   "Vittoria," or as it might
better have been called "Emilia in Italy," relates
the events in the life of the same young woman
after her arrival in her father's native land, and the
identification of herself with the unsuccessful at-

tempt which that country made in 1849 to throw off
the Austrian yoke. In the two novels dealing with
the life of Emilia Belloni, therefore, peaceful England is set off against troubled Italy, society small-
talk against political intrigue, enthusiasm for art
against devotion to country, youthful sentiment
against womanly affection, ridiculous scenes pro-
vocative of laughter against grim incidents inspir-
ing horror, and pictures almost wholly lacking in
tragic elements against those which are strongly
colored by sorrow and bloodshed.

But if "Sandra Belloni" stands in noticeably
strong contrast to its sequel, its similarity to "Evan
Harrington" is hardly less remarkable. In fact,
had Meredith's third novel been for any reason
published anonymously, its authorship would have
been immediately suspected. The three daughters
and the son of the Lymport tailor simply reappear
as the children of the City of London merchant, at
least so far as there is concern with their social ambition or with the ascendency which the three sisters
in either novel had over their only brother. Nor
is the truth of this comparison weakened by the
daughters of Samuel Pole being less strongly dif-
ferentiated than those of Melchisedec Harrington,
or by the fact that Evan Harrington in proving
himself a man rose, while Wilfred, never becoming
wholly sincere, steadily declined. That many of
the minor characters in both novels should be much
alike is of course little surprising, for Lady Gosstre,
Lady Chillingworth, the Hon. Mrs. Bayruffle, and
even Edward Buxley and possibly Tracy Running-

book must have moved in the same social circle
with Lady Jocelyn, Mrs. Barrington, and Drummond Forth.   In addition to this likeness in character drawing, there is also a similarity of incident
too striking to be overlooked.   The picnic on Bes-
worth lawn is essentially a repetition of that which
occurred at Beckley Court, even to the placing of the
superior guests upon an eminence apart from the
common crowd.   The supper also in which the delicate feelings of the sisters Pole were scourged by
the vulgar Mrs. Chump inevitably suggests the dinner
at which the Countess de Saldar and Caroline Strike
writhed beneath the lash of hearing their father's
memory bandied about as a thing for sport and
laughter.

Now and then, too, in "Sandra Belloni" Meredith seems to hark even further back than to "Evan
Harrington," since Braintop's admiration for Sandra
is not wholly unsuggestive of Ripton Thompson's
worship of Lucy; and Mrs. Chump occasionally recalls Mrs. Berry.   But in neither case is there any
strong appeal made to our sympathy.   Braintop, in
consequence, never appears other than foolish and
silly, nor Mrs. Chump other than common and of-
fensive.   The latter, however, is of interest from
another point of view, for she is a study in caricature
after Dickens's broadest style.   Early pictured as
"a shock of blue satin to the eye" and afterwards
characterized as "a simmering pot of emerald
broth," she lives before us by virtue of Dickens's
method of concentrating upon a striking trait.   Her
speech as represented by Meredith is hardly realistic

or convincing in itself; but it suddenly takes on versimilitude when the exasperated Adela Pole bursts out with her characterization of the woman's talk. "Her brogue! Do you remember it? It is not simply Irish. It's Irish steeped in brine. It's pickled Irish!" Of course Dickens would not have written in just that way, but his custom of portraying a person by making three or four ridiculous strokes of the pen has been pretty closely imitated. In drawing Mrs. Chump, Meredith, it must be conceded, availed himself of the privilege of being farcical; but in so doing he barely escaped being repulsive. Nevertheless, vulgar, coarse, and repellent as Mrs. Chump is, there is sufficient reason for her existence since she is a righteous retribution—or to use the diction of criticism, an artistic nemesis, visited upon the Pole sisters for their assumption of a pose which shows them to be only less vulgar, coarse, and repellent than she through their possession of a greater subtilty in self-expression.

Arabella, Cornelia, and Adela Pole stand as the embodiment of that attitude of mind which, knowing itself to be wholly commonplace, still undertakes to deceive not only the world but itself also into the belief that it is possessed of innate grace and charm. This mental condition and the conduct to which it gives rise, Meredith looked upon as a phase of what he terms "sentimentalism." As expressed in the three sisters, it shows that they felt themselves to be in exclusive possession of the Nice Feelings and unsurpassed in comprehension of the Fine Shades. This confidence on their part led to a proceeding

which they called "Mounting." That is, conscious
of what they regarded as dross in those surrounding
them and consequently to a certain extent contemptuous, they none the less were not unwilling to make
use of others if by so doing they might advance
themselves. "To be brief," wrote Meredith, "they
were very ambitious damsels aiming at they knew
not exactly what, save that it was something so wide
that it had not a name, and so high in air that no one
could see it." For this reason they endured Mr.
Pericles because of his wealth, they associated with
Lady Gosstre because of her title and assured social
position, and they decided to patronize Emilia hoping
by means of her wonderful voice to become known
as a sort of triple modern Mæcenas, a kind of
earthly agent of the Muses.

Nor did those more closely related to them escape
paying tribute to their ambition. Their father's
success as merchant was the more gratifying, since
it rendered possible their escape from a city circle;
but they had to admit that his unaspirated speech
made them shudder. They thought themselves sincere when they professed to love their father, but
they could not bring themselves to look upon his
grammar as paternal. Their brother, too, an in-
valided Cornet recently returned from India, they
loved tenderly and admired when necessary. But
coming to the conclusion that valor is not an intellectual quality, they soon exhausted their sensations concerning his deeds of arms, and fancied that
he had served their purpose. All of which goes to
show that they were certainly lacking in sincerity,

not to say in truth and honor. Meredith therefore
does not hesitate to subject the Fine Shades and the
Nice Feelings to frequent scourgings which would
awaken pity if the punishment meted out were not
so richly deserved.

Wilfred Pole, the brother, was also a sentimental-
ist, and differed from his sisters only in presenting
another aspect of the same insincerity. Imagining
himself to be in love with Emilia, because he was
desirous of sharing in the renown which her voice
must eventually bring her, he was not perfectly sure
that her birth and personality would permit of her
being introduced to the members of the social circle in which he moved. Again, partly to please
his father, but more to gain the satisfaction which
would redound from a union with a woman of title,
he proposed marriage to Lady Charlotte Chillingworth. When she accepted him as her lover, he
found himself in a dilemma. Equally pledged to
two women, he could not decide to which he should
remain faithful. Seeking release from each, he
learned that neither would give him up, Emilia because she could not believe him insincere, Lady
Charlotte because she was determined to keep him
at all hazards. Thus Wilfred cut a ridiculous figure;
and the reader feels artistic satisfaction, when at
the close of "Sandra Belloni," the sentimental youth
was unexpectedly jilted by both the singer and the
lady.

But his woful experience taught him no lasting
lesson. Reappearing in the novel called "Vittoria,"
he surrounded himself in Italy with conditions

strikingly similar to those which had brought about
his humiliation in England. After becoming engaged to the Austrian Countess Anna von Lenkenstein he again met Emilia whom three years of study
had made a cantatrice of no ordinary ability. No
more truly in love with her than before, he felt his
earlier ambition revive, and attempted to repeat
his trick of paying addresses to one woman while
still bound in honor to another. Less uniformly successful in his second experiment than in his first, he
soon found the tables completely turned upon him.
He received but cold treatment from Emilia and a
colder dismissal from the Countess. Truly, sentimentalism led its possessor through thorny paths;
and Wilfred Pole must have felt it a hard school
in which he learned the lesson, that he who will
not when he may, may not when he will. Surely
if the victim of his own insincerity awakened the
laughter of the gods in his early disappointment,
Olympus must have rung with their shouts when
they gazed upon the boy-like chagrin with which
he received his second breeching.

In strong contrast with the Pole sisters and their
brother stands Emilia Alessandra Belloni, Meredith's first minute and elaborate presentation of
admirable womanhood. Endowed by her creator
with all the graces, all the virtues, and all the powers,
youth and beauty, simplicity and honesty, inspiration and genius, Sandra was a favorite with Meredith at the beginning and, according to those who
claim to know, was never in the author's mind replaced as a study of ideal womanliness by any char-

acter of the later novels. Confident of her charm, yet never in any sense egotistical, she offended only the hypercritical when she offered to sing, assuming without question the desire of her audience to listen. Simple as Nature itself, she failed to comprehend the subtle reasoning which caused Cornelia Pole to conclude that the woods, the night, and the moon gave inspiration not elsewhere found. As sure as the Lady in "Comus" that virtue is its own protection, she saw no cause for concealing her early acquaintance with Captain Gambier, nor for hesitating in later years to visit the offices of the disgusting Pericles.

Practical, too, she was calmly unconscious of the humor in her account of her careful preservation of the potatoes which her angry father used as ammunition against her first lover. Unashamed of those whom she knew, she impulsively introduced Purcell Barrett, the poor organist, nor knew that she had erred, even when the sisters gave him the three shades of distance, called respectively from the coldness of their recognition, Pole, Polar, and North Pole. Simple and sincere herself, she expected to find others no more complex or divided in mind than she, and in consequence, not for a moment did she suspect Wilfred as implying less than he said, when she sat with him beside the white-twisting fall of Wilming Weir. Unsuspicious of his restless shallowness, she saw no reason to bind him by promise. He loved her, she thought, as she loved him, and two souls so loving had no need of spoken oath. Thoroughly convinced, therefore, of the righteousness of her belief in her lover, she could see nothing strange or unwarrantable in her going to Samuel Pole for the purpose of asking his consent to her marriage with his son.   No reader can be much surprised at the effect which her unconventional methods had upon the London merchant; but the ludicrous conduct of the man when the fear comes upon him that Emilia is insane, makes neither her nor her pleadings in any degree ridiculous to us.

Despite her simple, trusting nature, however, Emilia did not lack in depth or in strength of character.   True, she was struck down at the revelation of Wilfred Pole's perfidy, when Lady Chillingworth, intending to work ultimate kindness by means of present cruelty arranged that the girl should hear her lover's disavowal of any affection for her; but upon her recovery, delayed though it was by her other misfortunes, she adjusted herself to circumstances in a way which showed that her almost girlish conduct was the mere surface play of a truly estimable womanliness.   Rendered somewhat less impulsive by her unhappy experiences, she grew more analytical of herself and of others, and finally came to see that she had the right to ask release from a promise which kept her away from Italy, and upon receiving a refusal, to break that promise herself, in accordance with the dictates of duty and honor. This marked a decided development in her character; still, the reader is startled by the consummate deed of retaliation which closed her life in England. Poetic justice, however, was no more than fulfilled in Lady Chillingworth's being forced to hear Wilfred

Pole make as thorough a repudiation of her as he had formerly made of Emilia. Still it must not be overlooked that her ladyship rose to the occasion. With unconquerable aplomb she moved forward to say, "I like a hand that can deal a good stroke. I conceived you to be a mere little romantic person and correct my mistake." The words are wise and fitted the situation. Moreover, the thought which they expressed may stand for that which must exist in many a reader's mind. Had Emilia left England without performing that act of chastisement, she would indeed have appeared but a mere little romantic person. The stroke as delivered, however, gave balance to her character and at the same time formed a fitting climax to the book which tells the story of her early life. Without it, Meredith's third novel would have been far weaker than his second; with it "Sandra Belloni" is distinctly stronger than "Evan Harrington" and certainly not unworthy of the hand which wrote "The Ordeal of Richard Feverel."

The opening chapter of "Vittoria" presented Emilia in new surroundings. She, however, was unchanged save that to the attributes which had made her admirable were now added a breadth of understanding and a perfection of vision which placed her character in full and stable equipoise. In "Sandra Belloni" she was always beautiful and attractive, in "Vittoria" she was stately and commanding. At the close of her three-year study in the Milan Conservatory of Music, not only her voice but her womanhood as well rose from the

chrysalis stage of youth, and hovered brilliantly
above the hearts and souls of Young Italy. Patriot-
ism and heroism led her in spite of counter-edict and
command, to sing the song which was to precipitate
the uprising against Austrian oppression. Had
the minds of those who listened, possessed but a part
of the wisdom which was hers, the unification of
Italy would have been   immediately secured; but
her   hearers   convinced   that   the   conclusions   of
man's laborious intellectual study are superior to
those of woman's quick insight, made the half-
hearted response which ended in nothing but a
reign of terror and useless bloodshed.   Nor did fate
permit Emilia to escape the havoc which the blindness and timidity of men permitted to ensue.   Nevertheless, the picture which Meredith gives of her
at the very close of "Vittoria" shows that strength
of mind, greatness of heart, and nobility of soul
were hers.

"Merthyr delivered the burden of death. Her
soul had crossed the darkness of the river of death
in that quiet agony preceding the revelation of her
Maker's will, and she drew her dead husband to her
bosom, and kissed him on the eyes and forehead,
not as one who had quite gone away from her but
as one who lay upon another shore whither she would
come. The manful friend, ever by her side, saved
her by his absolute trust in her fortitude to bear the
burden of the great sorrow undeceived, and to walk
with it to its last resting place on earth unobstructed.
Clear knowledge of her, the issue of reverent love,
enabled him to read her unequalled strength of

nature, and to rely on her fidelity to her highest
mortal duty in a conflict with extreme despair."

On the whole, "Vittoria," from some points of
view at least, is unique among Meredith's works.
It is that author's only historical novel, the only one
of which the scenes are laid entirely oui of England
and of which the characters are almost exclusively
foreign to Meredith's native land. It seems not to
have been, nor to be, very popular; and the statement
that it was the fruit of a visit to Italy during the Aus-
tro-Italian war has been met more than once by
the semi-sarcastic remark that readers would have
been better pleased had Meredith stayed at home.
This patronizing bit of criticism, was due of course,
not so much to fact as to the brilliancy of the
writer who first uttered it, since the novel appeared
in *The Fortnightly Review* from January 1 to December 1, 1866, at the very time when, acting as Italian
correspondent for *The London Morning Post*, Meredith was assumed to be collecting material for a
book already written.   However that may be, the
failure of "Vittoria" to win ready acceptance from
its author's admirers may be due to its being more
emphatically a novel of incident than any of his
other books; for readers of Meredith are devoted to
him, not because he can tell a story, but because he
gives careful and minute studies of character.

If Meredith intended to write a novel which should
strongly attract lovers of exciting action, he seems
to have failed in his purpose, not perhaps because the book itself is in any way undeserving
of success, but probably because readers desiring

that kind of book had come to the conclusion
that the author of "Evan Harrington" or of "Sandra Belloni" could hardly write to please them.
If such really was the case, they stood in their own
light, for, as a matter of fact, there is an onrush
in the several chapters presenting the events immediately preceding the abortive uprising, and in
those relating the flight of Emilia, which must carry
readers to the end. Moreover, there is a greater
breadth and freedom of drawing than in any of
Meredith's earlier books; and, indeed, it might be
held with some show of truth that he never again
permitted himself equal liberty. Be that as it may,
the chief defect, apparent to every reader, is that
the great number of characters—there are one hundred and nine—crowd the pages to such an extent
that by the hopeless confusion of Austrians, Italians,
and English; men, women, and children; patriots,
traitors, and enemies; poets, composers, and sing-
ers; nobles, commons, and servants, one is both
blinded and deafened, and is sometimes compelled
to pause and wonder what it is all about.

As the last novel written during Meredith's period
of journeyman work, "Vittoria," whatever its defects, has at least the interest of showing that its
writer was practically emancipated from everything
which looks like the dominating influence of other
authors. Now and then Meredith appears to have
borrowed from his own earlier work, much as in
"Sandra Belloni" he drew from "Evan Harrington"
and "The Ordeal of Richard Feverel;" but so far
as other novelists are concerned, the power which

they had once had over him was spent, and he was ready to depend wholly upon himself. True as this is of "Vittoria," "Rhoda Fleming," the novel which in date of publication separated "Sandra Belloni" from its sequel, gave no promise of any such self-deliverance. Instead, the indebtedness of Meredith to Richardson, Dickens, and George Eliot,—or rather the similarity of certain passages of the novel to parts of "Clarissa Harlowe," "David Copperfield," and "Adam Bede"—came nearer to laying its writer open to the charge of plagiarism than anything else which he had done. Meredith's acquaintance with the works of Samuel Richardson had led him at the close of "Evan Harrington," to make mention of Sir Charles Grandison by name; and in "The Ordeal of Richard Feverel," at least in the unpruned exuberance of its earliest form, to include a humorous, scintillating chapter about a certain Mrs. Caroline Grandison, said to be a legitimate descendant of the famous gentleman whose family name she bore.

"In her sweet youth," it seems, "the lady fell violently in love with the great Sir Charles and married him in fancy. The time coming when maiden fancy must give way to woman fact, she compromised her reverent passion for the hero by declaring that she would never change the name he had honored her with, and must, if she espoused any mortal, give her hand to a Grandison. Accordingly, two cousins were proposed to her; but the moral reputation of these Grandisons was so dreadful, and such a disgrace to the noble name they bore, that she rejected

them with horror. Woman's mission, however,
being her perpetual precept, she felt at the age of
twenty-three bound to put it in practice and, as she
was handsome and most handsomely endowed, a
quite unobjectionable gentleman was discovered
who, for the honor of assisting her in her mission,
agreed to disembody himself in her great name, and
be lost in the blaze of Sir Charles. With his con-
currence she rapidly produced eight daughters. A
son was denied her. Thus was the second generation of Grandisons denied a son. Her husband,
the quite unobjectionable gentleman, lost heart after
the arrival of the eighth, and surrendered his mind
to more frivolous pursuits. She also appeared to
lose heart; it was her saintly dream to have a Charles.
So assured she was that he was coming at last that
she prepared male baby-linen with her own hands
for the disappointing eighth. When in that moment of creative suspense, Dr. Bairam's soft voice
with sacred melancholy, pronounced 'A daughter'
madam!' Mrs. Caroline Grandison covered her
face, and wept. She afterwards did penance for
her want of resignation and relapsed upon religion
and little dogs."

These allusions to Richardson's hero might possibly be explained as the result of chance; but it is
far more than a mere chance, it is a strongly
influenced state of mind to which certain parts of
"Rhoda Fleming" are due. The pursuit of Clarissa
Harlowe by Richard Lovelace has little in common
perhaps with the pursuit of Dahlia Fleming by
Edward Blancove; but the sincere repentance of

the eighteenth century libertine and his earnest wish
that his evil work had been left undone are too nearly
like the deep and manly contrition of the London
banker's son and his desire to make amends so far
as in him lay to leave any doubt in a reader's mind
of Meredith's marked indebtedness to Richardson.

The influence of Dickens and George Eliot,
can hardly be so positively declared, although considerable evidence of its probability is adducible.
The plot of "Rhoda Fleming," centring as it does
about the deception practised by a nobleman's son
upon a young and pretty Kentish girl visiting her
uncle in London, is not in any essential unusual: the
situation is one which has been treated over and
over again, ever since the time when story-telling
began. To hold, then, that Dahlia's elopement
with Edward is traceable either to Emily's flight
with Steerforth, or to Hetty's misplaced confidence in
Arthur Donnithorn would be setting up a claim too
easily refuted; but to allege that Robert's search for
Dahlia owes something to Peggotty's journey to find
Emily, and to Adam's quest for Hetty is to make
an assertion less easily disproved. The despairing
hope with which the man in each case sets out, the
inquiries which are so depressingly fruitless for a
time, the endeavors which are wholly discouraging
for many days, and the final discovery of the crushed
and broken-hearted victim are too much alike for
the reader not to feel, even if he cannot prove, that
George Eliot drew somewhat from Dickens, and
that Meredith was not wholly uninfluenced by both
of his older and popular contemporaries.

In certain minor matters, also, other similarities are noticeable: Rhoda's dogged persistence in refusing to believe that Dahlia could have gone wrong must recall Adam's long unshaken confidence in Hetty; Mrs. Lovell's remarks upon Edward's waywardness when she finds that Dahlia is but a farmer's daughter, suggests Rose Dartle's cruel indifference when she learns that Emily is a Yarmouth sailor's child; and Robert's refusal to allow Edward even a moment with Dahlia brings to mind the essential particulars of the scene between Adam and Arthur in the wood.   Again, the effect which Edward's letter has upon Dahlia is not unlike that which Arthur's has upon Hetty; Dahlia's consent to marry Sedgett—a deed by which her family hopes to restore her to respectability—suggests Hetty's first contemplations of her possible marriage with Adam, after she has been cast off by Arthur; and finally, so far as matters of plot are concerned, Adam's marriage to Dinah Morris at least remotely calls to mind the union of Robert and Rhoda.

In character-drawing, too, certain similarities may be pointed out.   Dahlia and Rhoda as sisters make one think of Nancy and Priscilla Lammeter in "Silas Marner," while the group gathered in the Pilot Inn is not unsuggestive of a far more successful piece of drawing, the company which sat around the fireplace in the kitchen of "The Rainbow." Certainly Meredith suffers here in comparison with George Eliot. The woman painted a scene which is natural, convincing and life-like; but the man's picture is without verisimilitude, for it is not too much to say

that his characters are stiff and unnatural. William
Fleming's housekeeper, Mrs. Sumfit, and his super-
annuated overseer, Master Gammon, are beyond all
doubt in Dickens's style; and his brother-in-law,
Anthony Hackbut, has been felt by many critics to
belong in the same catagory. Nor has Nicodemus
Sedgett escaped being placed there also, though it
seems nearer the truth to say, that he reflects the
manner of Charles Reade. Indeed, however strong
a case may be made in the attempt to show that
"Rhoda Fleming" was produced under the direct
influence of works by Richardson, Dickens, and
George Eliot, it may be remarked in passing that
the whole novel has a flavor distinctly like that
found in "Griffith Gaunt" and in "Foul Play."
These works, however, did not appear until after the
publication of "Rhoda Fleming," a fact which shows
that if it is worth while to assert the existence of a
connection between Meredith and Reade, the latter,
rather than the former, must have been the disciple.

But this treatment of "Rhoda Fleming" as if it
were little more than a mere patch-work of pieces,
artfully chosen and skilfully fitted together, is hardly
just either to the book or to the author. That it is
inferior to the other works of Meredith's journeyman period, few readers will deny despite Stevenson's readiness to give it almost unstinted praise.
Certainly, excuses are frequently made for an apparent carelessness of workmanship not easily par-
donable in an author who expects to be taken seriously. The chief of these, namely, that Meredith,
much to his own regret was forced to place his

book upon the market before he could give it the careful revision which was his custom, appears with a regularity almost computable; yet the excuse can hardly reconcile one to defects which are characteristic of the tyro rather than of the experienced novelist. It would seem far better not to blink the fact, but to admit fairly and squarely, that Meredith was out of his element when he attempted to present the yeoman character. At all events, he certainly learned his lesson, since he never again saw fit to centre the plot of a novel around any but those whose social instincts were actually fine or presumably so. The field in which he could do his best was wide enough without the need of an attempt on his part to enlarge its boundaries and to trespass upon George Eliot's ground.

Fortunately the result of Meredith's mistaken ambition was not an absolute failure. Indeed, whatever lack of finish the story may show, however crude it may seem here and there, "Rhoda Fleming" is neither to be ignored nor to be regarded lightly. If the frequent allusion to their mother's Bible fails to surround the two sisters with the religious atmosphere which envelops Dinah Morris and Adam Bede, the repentance of Edward Blancove is more real and convincing than Arthur Donnithorne's remorse. If Robert Eccles is an inconsistent character through his appearing now a yokel, now a brute, now a blackguard, and now a gentleman, Major Waring's unwavering refinement makes him always attractive, noble, and admirable. If Mrs. Lovell's life in India and the incident of the blood-spotted handkerchief are so briefly touched upon as to leave the reader in a quandary, the careful study and minute delineation of Rhoda are sufficiently satisfying to awaken sympathy, although her convictions may not themselves gain approval.

Nor is it too much to apply the over-worn epithet of "Shakespearean" to a work in which the idea of nemesis is so consistently worked out. Farmer Fleming visited a severe punishment upon his daughter Rhoda, because of her sympathy for a girl who had wandered from the path of virtue, and the time came when the disgrace of his beloved Dahlia was a burden almost too great for him to bear. Rhoda pitilessly insisted that Dahlia against her will should marry Sedgett, and in so doing she produced conditions which all but forced her into an unwilling union with Algernon Blancove. Edward abandoned Dahlia, when he mistakenly supposed that he had grown wholly tired of her, and was afterwards forced to learn that repentance, although it may gain forgiveness, cannot revive a love which cruelty and neglect have crushed. In other words, the book teaches with no uncertain tone that character is its own punishment, its own reward, its own destiny. As clearly from the lips of Meredith as from the mouth of the Apostle issues the message "Be not deceived; God is not mocked; for whatsoever a man soweth that shall he also reap."

"Rhoda Fleming" and "Vittoria" were the last sustained works produced by Meredith in the first period of his career as novelist. During the next few years, a review or a poem signed by his name might be occasionally chanced upon in the magazines of the time; but on the whole, Meredith for some reason preferred to keep silence. Had he persisted in such preference, it may be almost safely asserted that his name would not now be remembered or, if remembered, as that of an author of one book, namely, "The Ordeal of Richard Feverel." At best, indeed, he had done little more by 1870 than furnish an example in proof of Oliver Wendell Holmes's comment at his "Breakfast Table":

"Every articulately-speaking human being has in him stuff for one novel in three volumes duodecimo. . . . There is great danger that a man's first lifestory shall clean him out, so to speak, of his best thoughts. Most lives, though their stream is loaded with sand and turbid with alluvial waste, drop a few golden grains of wisdom as they flow along. Oftentimes a single cradling gets them all, and after that the poor man's labor is only rewarded by mud and worn pebbles."

To regard "Evan Harrington" and the three novels succeeding it as no better than the silt washed down by the gold-bearing river would be to do them manifest injustice; yet it is little doubtful, that in many respects, each of the stories, when viewed in its entirety, is inferior to "The Ordeal of Richard Feverel." That book, far from successful as it was in attracting readers at the time of its appearance, now stands out even among the great novels of Meredith's famous contemporaries as a piece of rare workmanship. Still, the later books, when taken in contrast with the first, exhibit in matters of detail a greater firmness of touch, a more confident breadth of sweep, a surer consciousness of power, indicative of growth in both strength and wisdom. Furthermore, however much or little the influence of other novelists may be truly assumed to have dyed the earlier textures woven in the looms of Meredith's thought, the last fabric which he drew out as a journeyman was beyond all question or suspicion wholly his own. The five years of silence which followed have been mistakenly regarded by some as a period of dissatisfaction and contempt with a world which would not read his books. Rather should it be looked upon as a time of rest preceding great achievement. At all events, when "The Adventures of Harry Richmond" appeared in 1871, a change had occurred in its author: the journeyman had become a master-workman.

IV

THE MASTER-WORKMAN

THE PERIOD OF FREE INVENTION—"THE ADVENT-
URES OF HARRY RICHMOND"—"BEAUCHAMP'S
CAREER"—"SHORT STORIES"—"THE EGOIST"—
"THE TRAGIC COMEDIANS."

THE career of the artisan is largely determined
by the continuous co-operation of two forces—
power and ambition. Either without the other
scarcely ever produces a resultant of any appreciable value, but when the two forces are properly
balanced, they are mutually corrective, since the
possession of power tends to prevent idle dreaming,
and a clearly perceived goal is an incentive to per-
severance. Now, not all of those whose fortune it is
to become journeymen preserve the balance of
inner forces, which leads eventually to master-
workmanship. Either there is a lack of true proportion between their ambition and their power, or
their vision for some reason becoming dull, they are
content to sit down by the highway rather than to
follow it to the end. Others, however, press on to
complete success. Now and then, a man reconciles
himself in the days of his apprenticeship to the hard
labor, the disciplinary task, and the irksome com-

mand, because he is wise enough to see that endurance of these things is necessary to his training. In the succeeding years when as journeyman he is to a large extent his own master, but still has to listen to the orders of an employer, he does not fall into discouragement because of harsh and perhaps unjust criticism, nor does he permit himself to rest satisfied with his past accomplishments because they have called out approving or flattering commendations. On the contrary, too self-confident to be over depressed, and too sane to be unduly elated, he gathers strength from within and from without to strive still for the full realization of his purpose; until at last having reached the goal, he has the right to say, with that mingled humility and pride which is true greatness,

"I stand on my attainment."

The criteria of a master-workman are various. Some, of course, are far more important than others. Most striking of all perhaps is that self-trust which caused Horace to say, that he had builded in his "Odes" a monument more lasting than bronze, and which led Shakespeare to prophesy eternal life for his "Sonnets." This confidence, indeed, does not always express itself in words, for mere persistence in following out theories in spite of adverse criticism is evidence that a man considers his work good. Every piece of art so placed before the world, whether it be a painting, a symphony, or a book is a challenge. Its maker is really saying; "I hear your criticism, I admit that I do not seem to follow the ac-

cepted canons of art; but look at my work, judge for
yourselves, and let it stand or fall by its own worth."
Had it not been for this fearless self-confidence, grow-
ing out of the knowledge that art is for man and not
man for art, the world would have been poorer by the
lack of the best works of such painters and sculptors
as Raphael and Angelo, of such musicians as Bee-
thoven and Wagner, and of such poets as Wordsworth and Tennyson and Browning.   Usually, however, if a man will but continue to force his work
upon the world long enough, he will at last extort
consideration, since contempt for destructive criticism has a charm which eventually attracts attention
and wins admiration.   Popularity, therefore, partic-
ularly if it comes after a period of indifference and
if it shows any tendency to remain permanent, may
be regarded as a second indication that one is a
master-workman.   But a far more conclusive test of
such attainment, for popularity indeed may appear
at almost any time in one's career, is the publication
of studies and commentaries by others, and the
appearance of imitations more or less faithful.   The
former will range all the way from those which insist that there is nothing whatever of good in the
works under discussion, to those which claim that
an acquaintance with them is the final shibboleth
of culture; the latter will include, as extremes, the
exact copy which is too nearly perfect to be called a
plagiarism, and the work which shows its maker to
have been a student of his master's methods rather
than of his mannerisms.

If these four marks are admitted to be true signs

that a man has left the days of journeyman work behind him, certainly the years of Meredith's life after
1870 may be looked upon as his period of master-
workmanship. His confidence that his judgment
and his theories of novel-writing could not be seriously at fault, became more pronounced than ever;
his popularity steadily increased; three extended
commentaries upon his work appeared; a host of
briefer studies presented him at varying angles of elevation; and, in addition, a number of young novelists, flattering themselves that by snatching a shred
from Meredith here and a patch there they might
re-enact the fable of the daw with the peacock's feath-
ers, but escape that foolish bird's unfortunate end,
sought to charm the ear of the reading public with
imitations of the products of Meredith's genius.

Certain minor facts may also be mentioned as
furnishing further proof that Meredith had entered
upon the culminating period of his career. In 1873
"The Ordeal of Richard Feverel" was translated
into Italian; from time to time American publishers issued several of Meredith's novels; the more
important reviews of Germany and France began to
take account of the man and his work; and the
London *Punch* saw fit to print burlesques both of
his prose and his verse, and to present his portrait
in caricature. Still further, two volumes of "elegant
extracts" were prepared for those who were compelled to take their Meredith in homœopathic
doses; and in 1898 there appeared as a final proof
of true greatness—a "George Meredith Birthday
Book!" Among contemporary authors, Thomson,

the poet of despair, Swinburne, the poet of contemptuous discontent; and Tennyson, the poet of faith and hope, each spoke of him in no uncertain words of praise; critics like Symons and Saintsbury and Dowden delighted to do him honor; and novelists varied all the way in their expressions of approval from the extreme worship of Stevenson to Mrs. Humphry Ward's restrained, but true-hearted exclamation, "The Master of us all, George Meredith!" Finally, it is of no little importance in this connection to learn that a Scotch university, never very prodigal of such honors, conferred upon him the degree of LL.D.; and also that when the death of Tennyson in 1892 left the British Society of Authors without a President, no word of dissent marred the prompt election of Meredith as the Poet Laureate's fittest successor.

But although the second half of Meredith's life may be looked upon as a period of realized ambition, the work of the two-score years following 1870, homogeneous as it appears from some points of view, still permits the classification already spoken of, into the novels produced in the decade when his invention allowed itself free play, and those written during the ten years when his interest concentrated itself upon a study of problems presented by ill-sorted marriage. The eight novels of the whole period are alike in that they show their author to be completely emancipated from any obvious outside influence; but, none the less, the grouped works of these two decades of later composition are so strongly distinguished from each other in many respects, that either may be made the subject of separate observation.

The third period of Meredith's literary production, then, may be characterized as "free" in two senses of the word: free, in that the writer was no longer hampered by the study of models; free, also, from the much higher and more important point of view that he showed himself possessed of a range of vision, a power of analysis, and an originality of style, which gave him a unique place among English novelists. "The Adventures of Harry Richmond," it may be urged in partial proof of this claim, is Meredith's only example of autobiographical fiction—that is, in the sense of its being written in the first person; "Beauchamp's Career" is his strongest political novel; "The Egoist" is the most striking study in literature of character dominated by a single trait; and "The Tragic Comedians," since Meredith himself disclaimed the charge that "Diana of the Crossways" was founded upon an episode in the life of the Honorable Mrs. Norton, is the author's only essay in the presentation of a plot dealing with persons who actually lived, and with events which really took place.   In matter of form, Meredith, with even more conspicuous success than in his earlier work, managed to weld the theory of the comedy to that of the novel. And, finally, a return with increased power to the use of the epigrammatic style which was characteristic of "The Shaving of Shagpat" and of "The Ordeal of Richard Feverel," made him widely quotable for his wit, but unfortunately also laid him bare to the charge of being wilfully obscure.

"The Adventures of Harry Richmond," which opened this third decade of Meredith's literary life, made its first appearance in the *Cornhill*, where, embellished with full-page illustrations by George du Maurier, it ran from September, 1870, until November, 1871. Immediately upon its completion here, it was published in book form, and its popularity was so great that a second edition was called for within two months. For the benefit of the curious in such matters, it may be said that this novel is Meredith's longest story, for in the limited uniform edition of the works it consists of fifty-six chapters printed upon seven hundred and sixty demi-octavo pages. The number of characters, too, is remarkably large, there being one hundred and sixty-nine,—that is, more than appear in "The Ordeal of Richard Feverel" and "Sandra Belloni" taken together, and as many more than are found in "Vittoria" as there are personages in "Rhoda Fleming." Unimportant as these details are in themselves, we are forced to regard them as giving some foundation to the frequently repeated charge that the story is a rambling one. Certainly, it is far less compact than any which preceded it; and the events, it cannot be denied, are often episodic and sometimes digressive rather than obviously integral parts of a unified plot. The scene of the action, moreover, touches all the continents of the Eastern Hemisphere; and characters appear from every important European district except Russia and the Scandinavian peninsula. On the other hand, no such confusion arises in the mind of the reader who follows the vicissitudes of that magnificent charlatan, Augustus Fitz-George Frederick William Richmond Guelph Roy, as results from an attempt to thread the intricate maze surrounding Emilia Alessandra Belloni Vittoria Campa. Despite its looseness of construction, therefore, "The Adventures of Harry Richmond," as a story, is indisputably superior to the novel immediately preceding it; and some critics have even gone as far as to hold that it is an improvement upon "The Ordeal of Richard Feverel."

As in "Evan Harrington" the reputed hero is far less important and interesting than his sister, the Countess de Saldar, so in "The Adventures of Harry Richmond," the youth whose name appears in the title of the book, does not at any time make himself so attractive to the reader as does his father, Roy Richmond. The latter is a favorite from the midnight hour when, with his infant son in his arms, he makes his way across the Hampshire heath country, until the night when he perishes at the burning of Riversley Grange, in the only imaginable manner really befitting the end of his strange and eventful career. What if he be a cheat, an impostor, a mountebank? His every action is on a scale so magnificent as to awaken not only interest, but sympathy. He has the generic characteristics of the Great Mel and of the Countess, his daughter, but his ambition is greater than theirs; for while the Lymport tailor and his youngest child would have been satisfied to be written among the nobility, the spur pricking the sides of Roy Richmond's intent was nothing less than a desire to be counted of the blood-

royal.   His preposterous claims, which he himself almost believed authentic, his extravagant conduct,
which by its originality held ridicule and laughter
very nearly in check; his astute planning, which came
close to uniting his son with the Princess of a German
State, go far indeed toward winning the reader to
his side.   Nevertheless, Meredith by causing Roy
Richmond to fail again and again at the moment
when success is almost within reach, awakens suppressed ironic laughter.   Roy Richmond, therefore,
is no mere caricature in Dickens's style, nor, whatever the author of "Sentimental Tommy" has to say
to the contrary, is he to be compared with Thackeray's Barry Lyndon: rather he is the consummate
production of that side of Meredith's genius which
created Mrs. Berry, Tom Cogglesby, Mr. Pericles,
and Anthony Hackbut.

The charge is sometimes made that a man like
Roy Richmond could not in real life be crushed by
the discovery that the source of his mysterious in-
come is Dorothy Beltham instead of a frightened
government eager to buy his silence.   His repentance, too, after his unexpected and overwhelming
defeat, it is said, is hardly convincing, and is certainly the weakest part of the story.   Perhaps; still,
even if these charges be admitted without question,
the earlier chapters describing his life with his boy
are well nigh perfect; so nearly perfect in fact that
they would save any novel from oblivion.   Nor does
Roy Richmond, in spite of all his defects, ever wholly
lose the splendor which there irradiates him.   He
must have been a wonderful father—yet Meredith

never makes him so wonderful as to appear impossible. Whether he was a caravan of wild beasts or the interpreter of Punch and Judy, whether he talked to Harry of Nelson or of Pitt, he must have been a rare delight;—and, beyond a doubt, supreme joy was the lot of a child whose father could make all the mighty characters of Shakespeare's plays live in one grand fantasy!

"The scene where Great Will killed the deer, dragging Falstaff all over the park after it by the light of Bardolph's nose, upon which they put an extinguisher, if they heard any of the keepers, and so left everybody groping about catching the wrong person, was the most wonderful mixture of fun and tears. Great Will was extremely youthful but everybody in the park called him "Father William"; and when he wanted to know which way the deer had gone, King Lear punned and Lady Macbeth waved a handkerchief for it to be steeped in the blood of the deer; Shylock ordered one pound of the carcass; Hamlet offered him a three-legged stool; and a number of kings and knights and ladies lit their torches from Bardolph's nose; and away they flew, distracting the keepers and leaving Will and his troop to follow the deer. That poor thing died from a different weapon at each recital, though always with a flow of blood and a successful dash of his antlers into Falstaff; and to hear Falstaff bellow! But it was mournful to hear how sorry Great Will was over the animal he had slain. He spoke like music. I found it pathetic in spite of my knowing that the whole scene was lighted up by Bardolph's nose.

When I was just bursting out crying—for the deer's tongue was lolling out and quick pantings were at his side; he had little ones at home—Great Will remembered his engagement to sell Shylock a pound of the carcass; determined that no Jew could eat of it, he bethought him that Falstaff could well spare a pound, and he said the Jew would not see the difference; Falstaff only got off by hard running and roaring out that he knew his unclean life would make him taste like pork, and thus let the Jew into the trick."

The boy among whose earliest recollections was the memory of such a story as this, exhibits throughout his life a likeness to his father which is not usual in literature. Novelists frequently present parents and their children in the same book, but seldom would the relationship be suspected if there were not some assurance or some hint that it existed; but here the character of Harry Richmond is so colored as to make the reader exclaim now and again: "That boy is his father's own child!" In his development, it is true, he shows a certain tendency to weakness, which as much interferes with his being unfailingly attractive as it makes him different from his father. This, however, cannot be looked upon as a refutation of the similarity suggested, for no son is exactly like his father, but inherits only certain traits from him. Nor can it be held that the alleged similarity rests upon insufficient foundation because the younger man never acts in precisely the same way as the older. Family traits are most generally seen in some turn of the head, some movement of the hand, or some use of words rather than in any extended line of thought or conduct; but, as is the case with Roy Richmond and his son, the likeness is not the less clear because it is not susceptible of direct proof.

The desultory education which the boy received from his father was first supplemented by attendance at a Mr. Rippenger's school. In a very faint way the life there makes one think of David Copperfield's experience at Salem House, probably because, in a very much fainter way, Temple is something like Traddles, and Heriot like Steerforth. However that may be, throughout the treatment of Harry Richmond's childhood and youth, Meredith again struck those perfect chords which he sounded when he dealt with the boyhood of Richard Feverel, but which he badly jangled when he included Alec Jocelyn and Dorothy Loring in "Evan Harrington." His skill returned, it is true, with the children of Laura Piaveni in "Vittoria" and reached its climax perhaps with Crossjay in "The Egoist." Still, the dozen chapters dealing with Harry's boyhood are infinitely better than all the innumerable stories of abnormal and precocious children parading up and down the pages of recent magazines.

One stops, now and then, perhaps, to wonder if a boy could by any possibility have so many strange experiences as fell to Harry Richmond's lot; but whether he is being fondled by his father, or attaching himself to Julia Rippenger and to Heriot, or wandering with the gypsies, or suffering abduction at the hands of Captain Welsh, or making his way through a German forest, he is

one of the most natural boys in English fiction.
Shortly after his arrival in the court of Prince Ernest,
however, he unexpectedly develops into a youth
capable of making most violent love. This sudden
leap forward startles the reader somewhat; and by
the time things are readjusted, Harry Richmond has
ceased to be of any special interest save in so far as he
is a tool of his father's colossal ambition. The em-
bers of his youth, it is true, do occasionally send
up a fitful glow or aspiring flash, but Harry Richmond unfortunately never fulfills the promise of his
childhood.

For a time, at least, around this young man as a
centre there move, in addition to his father, four
characters of no mean importance, his grandfather,
Squire Beltham of Riversley Grange; his aunt, Dorothy Beltham; and the two women who regard him
with romantic attachment, Janet Ilchester and the
Princess Ottilia of Eppenwelzen-Sarkeld. The Squire
is a straight-forward sturdy character not unlike
Jonathan Eccles in "Rhoda Fleming," though he
is thrown into much higher relief than the Hampshire
farmer. He least of all is befooled by Roy Richmond; and not only in this respect, but in others as
well, stands out as one of the few wholly sane characters in the book. He belongs, therefore, in the
class which includes Mrs. Mel from "Evan Harrington," Agostino Balderini from "Vittoria," and
possibly Major Waring from "Rhoda Fleming."
Coarse and blunt he may be, but he sees clearly and
he speaks with sincerity. In that last scene which
takes place at London not many days before his

death, he rises almost to grandeur. Desirous of sparing his daughter as much as possible, yet disgusted with her foolish infatuation for her dead sister's husband; filled with righteous contempt for his son-in-law, but not unmindful that the man is Harry's father; yearning with love for his grandson, but embittered by the knowledge of his wilful blindness; he bursts out in a masterly invective against Roy Richmond, which at last compels that arch-charlatan to restrain his insolence, and to cower before the storm of well-deserved abuse. Nevertheless, there is that in him which makes it not impossible that Dorothy Beltham should be his daughter. If he is sturdy, she is persistent; when he is nursing his wrath, she is cherishing her affections; when he stands ready to crush, she is eager merely to restrain. Unfortunately, she is never at any time thrown into very great prominence, but, none the less, she permeates the book and adds a sweetness to what without her would sometimes be acid or bitter, and sometimes flavorless or insipid.

The two younger women, the Princess Ottilia and Janet Ilchester, present an interesting contrast. The former idealized Harry Richmond, the latter saw him as he was; the former was romantic, sentimental; the latter far-seeing, sensible; the former was governed by the heart, the latter by the head: yet the former was not unlike Sandra Belloni in many respects, and the latter was not without some likeness to Clare Forey. Each of them to some extent disappoints the reader who is hardly reconciled to Ottilia's contenting herself with Prince Hermann; and the strange

aberration of mind which permitted Janet to engage
herself to the Marquis of Edbury is almost incredible. Surely the well-balanced intellect of the Eng-
lishwoman would have prevented her from taking
such a step out of mere pique at Harry Richmond's
apparent indifference; and it would equally have
stifled in the very beginning any such quixotic whim
as marrying a man to reform him. Her escape at
the stroke of the hour, however, must seem something like a straining of the novelist's art; but of
course the eternal fitness of things demanded that
she should be saved from the Marquis.   Still, her
later marriage to young Richmond suggests that
she was not over-successful in steering her course
between Scylla and Charybdis, since it is a serious
question whether her life could be happier in losing
a rake, only to take up with a stick.

"The Adventures of Harry Richmond" is thought
by some to have been inspired by Marryat's "Japhet
in Search of a Father"; but no very careful reader of
the two books will feel that any real connection exists. The statement in all probability was first made
by some hasty critic who was perhaps analogy-mad
and therefore saw what he was most eager to see.
As a matter of fact, two novels could hardly be more
widely separated or be more unlike. Nor can the
claim that Stevenson's "Prince Otto" had its sources
in Meredith's novel be given much more credence.
It is true that the younger novelist's book received
almost unstinted praise from Meredith; it is likewise
true that Stevenson worshipped the elder writer
nearly to the verge of sentimentality, and took much

delight in referring to him as his master. It is still further true, that the names Otto and Ottilia occur in both books, and that Doctor Gotthold in Stevenson's romance is something like Julius von Karsteg in Meredith's novel; but after all the only extended passage in "Prince Otto" which seems to suggest a comparison with anything in Meredith is that beautiful chapter descriptive of the Princess Seraphina's flight through the forest. That, indeed, has the Meredith flavor and never more than when, after the night of fear and sorrow, she lifted her eyes, and, catching sight of that hue which is never seen but as the herald of the morning, she cried with joy catching at her voice, "O! it is—it is the dawn!"

The hunt for resemblance between authors, whether they live at the same time or are separated by long intervals of years, whether they are of the same nationality or belong to races having little in common, is one of the many interesting studies which literature allows. The pleasure, however, is fraught with danger, since one often runs near to falling into the trap of finding a connection where none exists, of jumping to a conclusion as ill-founded as that of the man who derived "Moses" from "Methuselah," by omitting—ethuselah, and adding—oses. There can be little doubt that any attempt to connect Marryat and Meredith rests upon ground as untenable as this philologist's. Probably, too, the suggestion that there might be some connection between "The Parliamentary Novels" of Trollope and "Beauchamp's Career" by Meredith would be properly rated as hasty rather than well considered.

But it is not too much to say that those who took delight in "Phineas Phinn" and "Phineas Redux," both preceding the publication of Meredith's political novel by only a few years, and who likewise found pleasure in "The Duke's Children," a book which followed it by three or four, must have felt that the atmosphere of Meredith's work was not unlike that of Trollope's splendid series. Further than this, however, the comparison cannot be carried, for Phineas Phinn has little in common with Nevil Beauchamp, and Glencora Palisser reminds one not at all of Reneé de Croisnel or of Cecilia Halkett.

Of greater interest and of more importance than this faintly possible connection with Marryat and Trollope is the fact that "Beauchamp's Career," flanked on either hand by six remarkable pieces of fiction, shows itself almost inextricably bound to both groups. That is, the novel seems to have been the product of much that went before as it was the anticipation of not a little that followed. In the first place, politics had been introduced as a minor element in "The Adventures of Harry Richmond," the book immediately preceding it, and the criticism directed by Dr. Shrapnel against those who accented the Ego was a foretaste of "The Egoist." Again, Meredith here kept up his attacks upon sentimentalism whenever it appeared, whether as idealism or as insincerity; and, furthermore, strongly hinted at the inadequacy of commonly accepted ideas of marriage. Thus there can be found in the book the informing ideas which permit the threefold grouping of Meredith's novels into those making war upon sentimentalism, those ridiculing egotism, and those proving the insufficiency of the conventional attitude towards the marriage question.

Even more striking still is the strong family relationship which the characters of "Beauchamp's Career" bear to those of Meredith's earlier novels. Rosamond Culling, both because of her position in Everard Romfrey's house and because of her regard for Nevil Beauchamp, is near to being a reproduction of the Lady Blandish who suffered from the tongue of gossip and cared for Richard Feverel with a mother's love. Mr. Romfrey himself is, of course, not at all like the lord of Raynham Abbey, but he must suggest in more ways than one Squire Beltham of Riversley Grange. Great-aunt Beauchamp, a sort of half-hidden force in the background, recalls those elderly women, Mrs. Grantley in Meredith's first novel and Mrs. Bonner in his second. Seymore Austin has far more in common with Austin Wentworth than the mere accident of name; and the attitude of Beauchamp towards the former permits comparison with that of Richard towards his older cousin. Dr. Shrapnel, too, is Professor Von Karsteg written large; and Reneé de Croisnel is almost undoubtedly a replica of Ottilia of Eppenwelzen, as Cecilia Halkett is of Janet Ilchester; but it must be immediately added, on one hand, that the French woman is less attractive than the German princess, and, on the other, that the Colonel's daughter is much superior to Squire Beltham's distant relative. Great as is the contrast between the appearances of Reneé and of Ottilia in England, and between the attitudes which their re-

spective lovers take towards them, the two events
and the attendant circumstances have sufficient in
common to show that they must have sprung from
the same creative mind.   At this point therefore,
Nevil Beauchamp and Harry Richmond become at
least tangent to each other; and the later engagement of Janet Ilchester to Lord Edbury may almost
permit itself to be called an intersection with the
marriage of Cecilia Halkett to Blackburn Tuckham.

Yet "Beauchamp's Career," as might be hastily
concluded, is no mere presentation of old puppets in
new relationships.   Nevil Beauchamp and Cecilia
Halkett, at least, stand out in bold relief; and can
hardly be looked upon as inferior to the greatest of
Meredith's creations.   Certainly with the possible exception of Carlo Ammiani in "Vittoria," Beauchamp
is the most interesting study in male portraiture between Richard Feverel and Willoughby Patterne.
It is true that he wavered between two loves, as
did Wilfred Pole and Harry Richmond, and thus
betrayed a weakness which Meredith expects his
readers to condemn, but he possessed much greater
force of character than either of these men, and a
more attractive personality than either Evan Harrington or Edward Blancove.   Chivalrous, impulsive,
ready to draw upon the slightest provocation, he
often carried those who did not sympathize with his
political ideas to ground whither they least wanted
to go.   Over-mastered by his heart when he first
knew Reneé de Croisnel, he was disappointed to
find her less influenced by passion than by fear, although later, when reason had asserted itself, he

was able so to act that the lady was saved from herself. On the other hand, swayed by his intellect, he would not listen to the promptings of his feelings at a time when he might have won Cecilia Halkett; and yet he could find little but blame for her, when he learned that, stiffling her affection for him, she had consented to a union with the prosaic Blackburn Tuckham. It is doubtful if he ever saw that the real trouble lay in his own vacillation of character, in his inability to balance heart and mind with that nice adjustment which means perfection of soul. Poetically considered, he should have been united in the end with Cecilia Halkett; but his loveless marriage of gratitude with Jenny Denham was just what he deserved and just what he would have reached, had he been a character in real life. Still, whether one is able to approve wholly of Beauchamp's extreme Radical idea in politics, or believes that they rose out of a vitiating fallacy; whether one is patient or overtried with him as he struggles for firm footing between passion and reason, one finds that he is a close rival for that sympathy and affection which nearly every reader has for Richard Feverel.

Cecilia Halkett, whom Beauchamp should have married, as compared with Reneé de Croisnel, whom he would have married, and with Jenny Denham, whom he did marry, is one of the most attractive portraits in Meredith's gallery of women. From the moment she is first seen until she passes into memory, it is evident that she was possessed of that strong, beautiful, and noble womanhood to which Sandra Belloni attained after years of chastening

disappointment. She loved Nevil Beauchamp, but
her affection did not blind her to his fundamental
weakness. Even such limitations as her education
imposed upon her thought did not greatly lessen that
all-inclusive quality of mind for which grandeur is
hardly too strong a term. The silence with which
she endured the assumption of her father and of
Everard Romfrey, that women are incapable of deep
thought or of clear insight, is evidence that she possessed the very powers which those men denied to her
sex. Indeed, her attitude went far towards putting
them in the wrong; for her strength of character in
abstaining from self-defence, threw the burden of
proof upon them; and it became evident that they
were sentimentalists, blindly accepting traditional
ideas about woman's place in the world. It is a
trifle hard, perhaps, to reconcile this side of Cecilia
Halkett's character with that which permitted her to
receive Blackburn Tuckham's proposal at a time
when she must have been confident that Nevil Beauchamp was on his way to make offer of his hand. But
Meredith seldom presents his readers with ideal conditions, that is with conditions which are ideal from
the sentimental point of view. He is a realist in the
sternest sense of the term; and his problem is the
presentation of man and woman in the making, of
man and woman struggling, albeit with many re-
verses, towards that perfection of soul which Meredith himself believes is the purpose and secret of this
world's existence.

In his discussion of this problem Meredith feels
it pertinent to give time to the study of the una-

wakened as well as to the wakened, to those who are
content to remain in bondage as well as to those who
have heard the call to freedom. This, then, is the
reason for Reneé de Croisnel's existence. She is
very beautiful; she is attractive to everyone of those
impulses of passion which have caused the heart of
man to hold his intellect in subjection; she is, it
might almost be said, an embodiment of the temptation which the monks of the middle ages saw in every
woman—the temptation which sought to bind the
soul to earth and to stifle every aspiration to spiritu-
ality. The asceticism of the old churchmen would
undoubtedly have been termed a sentimentalism by
Meredith, but he could not have denied that in their
crude way, they were endeavoring to give voice to a
criticism of their age which he constantly preached
against his own. It sounded loudly in "The Ordeal
of Richard Feverel"; it was not absent, although
breathed more gently, in "Evan Harrington," and
in the two novels dealing with Sandra Belloni's
career; it rose to shrillness in "Rhoda Fleming";
and with changed qualities of tone it persisted in
those pages which dealt with the Princess Ottilia
and Reneé de Croisnel. The conclusion, however,
is not to be drawn that Meredith looked upon the
presence of passion in men and women as working
a necessary degradation of character. If that had
been his attitude, he would himself have deserved
the shafts of ridicule which he was directing against
the world as painted in the characters and the incidents of his novels. His hope was to make mankind
see that passion must be subdued to intellect before

there can be any great growth of soul; and that, as a necessary corollary, woman will remain the temptress, just so long as men act upon the tacit understanding that she exists as the coy but willing victim of his pleasure. The long continued and wide extended acceptance of this interpretation of the use of women, has produced, according to Meredith, a false balance in society, and he felt that it was his mission to point out that the resulting evil is working its own punishment. Women who accept the conditions either actively or passively, either knowingly or blindly, he thought, must be brought to see that they themselves perpetuate the degradation from which they suffer most; and men who persist in believing that women have not grown beyond what they were in the childhood of the race retard thereby not only their own advancement, but the progress of the world as well. So must we go on, said Meredith in "The Sage Enamoured and the Honest Lady,"

"Until those twain, who spring the root and are
The knowledge in division, plight a troth
Of equal hands; nor longer circulate
A pious token for their current coin
To growl at the exchange; they, mate and mate,
Fair feminine and masculine shall join
Upon an upper plain, still common mould,
Where stamped religion, and reflective pace
A statelier measure, and the hoop of gold
Rounds to horizon for the soul's embrace.
Then shall these noblest of the earth and sun
Inmix unlike to waves on savage sea.
But not till Nature's laws and man's are one,
Can marriage of the man and woman be."

Insistent as Meredith is in all of his novels upon the subject of woman's rightful place in life, the dominant tone in "Beauchamp's Career" was not woman, but politics. This, perhaps, is the reason why the novel is frequently spoken of as being unsuccessful. Outside of England, the average novel reader is too little concerned with the difference between the political parties of that country to be interested in a story which makes a discussion of them an important point; and in England itself it is very probable, as in other lands, that the rank and file of citizens are Liberals or Conservatives as much from absence of thought as from its presence. It might be expected, then, that the book would prove little popular, that even the conscientious reader should be advised to practise here and there the useful art of skipping, and that Dr. Shrapnel should be designated as "an unmitigated old bore." None the less, the thoughtful reader must find interest in the fact that "Beauchamp's Career" presented a new phase of Meredith's art, and that it gave insight into the mind of an author whose personality is not more easily discoverable in his works than was Browning's in his poems.

It is of some interest, then, to know that Meredith is an extreme Liberal in politics and is wholly out of sympathy with the existence of an aristocratic class and of an established church. He even goes so far as to speak in approval of women being granted the right of suffrage, thus taking ground in advance of many of his own party. His word on the matter might, of course, have been anticipated by any analytic reader of the novels, but his letter to *The Times* not so very long ago created some flurry. It was called out by what Meredith himself had to admit, was the result of mistaken zeal on the part of certain women who attempted to obtain by an irregularity what they could not get by due process of law. True to the methods which he followed in all his novels he approved where he could, but he did not hesitate to disapprove where necessity seemed to require. In part he wrote:

"The choicer spirits of men do now see that women have brains, and can be helpful to the hitherto entirely dominant muscular creature who allowed them some degree of influence in return for servile flatteries and the graceful undulations of the snake —admired, yet dreaded. Women must have brains to have emerged from so long a bondage. In the present instance, it is the very excellence of their case that inflames them. The mistake of the women has been to suppose that John Bull will move sensibly for a solitary kick. It makes him the more stubborn, and such a form of remonstance with him alienates the decorous among the sisterhood, otherwise not adverse to an emancipation of their sex. It cannot be repeated, if the agitating women are to have the backing of their sober sisters. Yet it is only by repetition of this manner of enlivening him that John Bull (a still unburied old gentlemen, though not much alive) can be persuaded to move at all. Therefore, we see clearly that the course taken by the suffragists was wrong in tactics. It may be argued likewise that the punishment inflicted on them has magnified the incident foolishly."

Meredith's later radicalism in politics and his earlier sympathy with the Liberal party have more than once been the cause of some carping on the part of those who cannot reconcile his holding such political ideas with his having served as an editor about 1860 upon *The Ipswich Journal* and *The Morning Post*. Both of these papers, it is true, were organs of the Tory party, but there was nothing occurring at that time in political England which could lay Meredith open to the charge of insincerity in writing leaders for the periodicals mentioned. It is said, however, that he found the work irksome, although he did sometimes take up the cudgels against members of his own party when he thought that their enthusiasm carried them too far. It was in this spirit that he wrote:

"With Mr. Cobden to interpret the laws to us, Mr. Bright to regulate their application, and Mr. Pease to control our passions, we are likely to do well. Were England subjected to the rule of the triumvirate, our difficulties with foreign nations would be short. Mr. Cobden would declare them to be in the right, Mr. Bright would proclaim us to be in the wrong, and then the final adjuration of Mr. Pease to lead us to adopt brotherly love as our emblem would come in with singular sweetness and unction."

This passage is unmistakably in Meredith's own style, as are many others now buried in old files of the papers to which they were contributed. Their author practised no economy in his flow of trenchant humor and biting satire when he thought occasion

called for a display of wit.   A further extract, although having no great bearing politically, may be
given to show how Meredith dealt with other matters of public interest.   It was currently reported, it
seems, that Lord Palmerston, the Liberal Prime
Minister, was to be called into court by an indig-
nant husband.   The situation was too ludicrous for
Meredith's gravity, and he felt compelled to give
way to the inspiration of the Comic Muse.   After a
long article on the matter he summed up his ideas in
these words:

"But rumor is a wicked old woman.   Cannot
something be done to stop her tongue?   Surely
one who is an octogenarian might be spared.   We
are a moral people, and it does not become us to
have our Premier, agile though he be, bandied
about derisively like a feathered shuttlecock on the
reckless battlefield of scandal.   For ourselves, hearing much, we have nevertheless been discreetly re-
served, but now the veil is drawn by a portion of the
Press, and not so delicately but that the world is
taught pretty plainly things concerning the Eternal
Youth in office, and the fatal consequences of his
toasts to the ladies which may make some of them
blush.   We are indeed warned that nothing less
than an injured husband has threatened and does
really intend to lay an axe to the root of our Premier's extraordinary successes in a certain awful
court.   We trust that rumor again lies; but that she
is allowed to speak at all, and that men believe her
and largely propagate her breathings, is a terrible
comment on the sublime art of toasting the ladies

as prosecuted by aged juveniles in office. It is a
retribution worthy of a Greek tragedy. We are determined to believe nothing before it is proved. It is
better to belong to the laughed-at minority who decline
to admit that the virtue has gone out of our Premier
than to confirm a shameful scandal, the flourishing
existence of which is sufficient for our moral."

From this arraignment of a gray-haired Peer
whom rumor looked upon as little better than a
reprobate, it may be well to turn aside for a moment
to Meredith's sonnet upon the death of a statesman
who went down to his grave clothed with dignity
and honor.

HAWARDEN

> When comes the lighted day for men to read
> Life's meaning with the work before their hands
> Till this good gift of breath from debt is freed,
> Earth will not hear her children's wailful bands
> Deplore the chieftain fall'n in sob and dirge;
> Nor they look where is darkness, but on high.
> The sun that dropped down our horizon's verge,
> Illumes his labor through the travelled sky,
> Now seen in sum, most glorious; and 'tis known
> By what our warrior wrought we hold him fast.
> A splendid image built of man has flown;
> His deeds inspired of God outstep a Past.
> Ours the great privilege to have had one
> Among us who celestial tasks has done.

But interest in Meredith's own political ideas and
in his characterizations of Prime Ministers must not
tempt us to stray too far from the field of his novels.
"Beauchamp's Career," it should be said in passing,
showed in its style a marked increase in those earlier

tendencies of its author on one hand to pile figure upon figure and on the other to force some simile or metaphor to curvet and caper until the reader grew dizzy.   This lack of self-restraint on Meredith's part undoubtedly contributed to prevent the book from gaining any marked popularity; and possibly his whimsical statement in an early chapter, that the reader need not look for any plot in the story, was not without similar influence.   Just what Meredith meant by such a warning is not very clear, for certainly the novel has far greater unity than had its immediate predecessor, and it is hardly less rich in variety of incident than "Evan Harrington" or even "Vittoria." Perhaps Meredith intended to imply nothing more than that he was incapable of weaving plots of such complexity as made the fame of Wilkie Collins and Charles Reade. If this is the conclusion to be drawn, he certainly had the courage of his convictions, for in his next book, "The Egoist," he showed that interest may be awakened and enthusiasm carried to the highest pitch by an extended work of fiction which is as bare as a rock of even the suspicion of a plot.   All that Meredith undertook to do in the seven hundred pages of what has come to be regarded as his greatest work was to show how a young woman broke an unwelcome engagement. Defoe's "Robinson Crusoe" may unquestionably be termed a romance without a heroine, Thackeray certainly called "Vanity Fair" a novel without a hero; but here was a work of fiction undoubtedly unique in the history of literature, —a story without a plot!

In the four years which intervened between the appearance of the final chapters of "Beauchamp's Career" in *The Fortnightly Review*, for December, 1875, and the publication in 1879 of "The Egoist" in book form without the medium of a periodical, Meredith found time to make three experiments in short-story writing, and to read a lecture before The London Institution. These four pieces of work, "The House on the Beach," the address on "The Idea of Comedy and of the Uses of the Comic Spirit," "The Case of General Ople and Lady Camper," and "The Tale of Chloe," all appeared in *The New Quarterly Magazine*, the first three in the numbers for January, April, and July, 1877, respectively, and the last in the issue for July, 1879. As the stories were not published in book form until fifteen years had passed, and the lecture not until score had gone by, Mr. J. M. Barrie, writing in *The Scot's Observer* for November 24, 1888, rather aptly termed them "The Lost Works of George Meredith." But Mr. G. S. Street was even more fortunate when in *The Yellow Book* for April, 1895, he hit upon the expression, "Mr. Meredith in Little," as a title for his review of the collected stories. Mr. Street's theme was announced in these words:

"In 'The House on the Beach,' you have Mr. Meredith, as it were, in his bones. In 'The Case of General Ople and Lady Camper' you have him alive and imperfect. In 'The Tale of Chloe' you have him consummate."

One may be permitted, perhaps, to dissent from the characterization of the second story, but we

cannot help feeling that Mr. Street was sure of his
ground and trustworthy in his conclusions.

"The House on the Beach" was certainly a piece
of work in Meredith's early manner.   Martin Tinman and his sister, Mrs. Cavely, might easily have
been mistaken for characters drawn by Dickens;
Annette Smith was of the type portrayed by Thackeray in Amelia Sedley; and Mrs. Crickledon in some
respects was George Eliot's Dolly Winthrop trans-
ported from the village of Raveloe to the Cinque
Port of Crikswich.   Various phases of sentimentality,
moreover, were attacked; and the heroine was all
but allowed to become the victim of her mistaken
devotion to a conventionality.   Still, despite this return to earlier methods and ideas, the story by no
means shows that Meredith's hand had lost its cunning, or that his power of invention had waned.
Van Diemen Smith was made too pathetic, through
being wounded in the house of his friend, to be the
subject of anything but sympathetic laughter, even
when his fears led him to picture himself in a ludicrous position.   Still greater skill was shown in
the manipulation of circumstances by which Tinman's deep and successful scheme to silence Little
Jane's craving for an increase of wages received its
reward in making her become the instrument which
laid bare his far deeper and much meaner plan to
flay once more the feelings of his friend.   Finally,
the description of the storm demands mention at
least, since, in spite of the strictest economy of
words, Meredith makes his readers feel the fury of
the wind and the destruction of the flood.

"The House on the Beach," humorous on the whole, possessed certain sombre elements and showed an interesting exhibition of nemesis; but "The Case of General Ople and Lady Camper" was a skit in Meredith's very lightest manner. Its characters moved in the world of which Meredith wrote with most ease; and Elizabeth Ople, faintly as she was drawn, was obviously related to Janet Ilchester and Cecilia Halkett, while Lady Camper was almost a forestudy of Mrs. Mountstuart Jenkinson in "The Egoist." It is not without interest also to know that the title of Meredith's tenth novel, "One of Our Conquerors," was anticipated in the first chapter of this story, and actually mentioned in the last. Mr. Street will have it that by bringing about the marriage of Lady Camper to General Ople, Meredith spoiled a brilliant and delicious farce. It is true that the suddenness with which the engagement was precipitated produces a feeling of shock in the reader's mind; but surely the mental torture endured by the General while he was being pruned of his sentimentalism and egoism rendered him not undeserving of the reward which he at last obtained. The reader's imagination, moreover, clearly perceives that the married life of the General and his wife must have been of a piece with their strange courtship, for Meredith pointed out that the man was not tuned, but only tunable, and likely, therefore, to be a permanent fund of amusement for the Lady's humor. No doubt there were other things of which the retired officer had to be broken besides his tendency to talk of residences that were "gentlemanly" and sights that were "sweetly pretty;" but it is to be hoped that a reduction to collarless imbecility was seldom necessary to bring him into proper subjection.

If the story of the General and the Lady through its inclusion of a striking phrase has any right to be considered a preliminary sketch or forestudy for "One of Our Conquerors," certainly "The Tale of Chloe" may be looked upon as a pendant to "The Adventures of Harry Richmond." It will perhaps be remembered that when the hero of the last-named novel was a small boy, his father taught him to speak with precocious superciliousness of the dairymaid who became the Duchess of Dewlap. An episode in the life of this same young woman soon after her name became enrolled in the Peerage, formed the subject matter of the third and most important of Meredith's short stories. The chief interest of the reader, however, must centre not so much about the young Duchess as about Chloe, "that most admirable woman whose heart was broken by a faithless man ere she devoted her wreck of life to arrest one weaker than herself on the descent to perdition." The story, as told, was a cameo rather than a piece of sculpture, a miniature rather than a painting; but it showed none the less the touch of a master's hand. The atmosphere was that of the age of the minuet, of powder and lace. Yet to the attractive melancholy with which authors always invest scenes of that period, Meredith added an element which took the story wholly out of the realm of comedy. Chloe, who tied a knot in a silken cord at each fresh instance of her lover's unfaithfulness, and who at last put the tangled strands to a strange and terrible use, was hardly less perfectly portrayed than the heroine of a Greek drama. The critic, therefore, did not greatly err when he called her one of the noblest figures in tragic story, and held that he who told the tale of her last unhappy days, spoke with consummate art and perfect skill.

If such words of praise seem a trifle extravagant to have been called forth by a form of literature in which Meredith never did more than perform a few experiments, they certainly cannot be looked upon by any fair-minded reader as being excessive, when applied to the long novel which appeared in the same year with "The Tale of Chloe." Nevertheless, "The Egoist" is not acceptable to every reader. If it has been made an object of idolatrous worship by Stevenson, it has been torn to shreds and tatters by William Watson. If the former spoke of it almost as if he felt himself treading upon holy ground, the latter in offering his words of censure recalled the fable of the bull in the China shop. The creator of "the dainty rogue in porcelain" might have trembled at first for the safety of his wares, but upon reassuring himself that they were above his bovine visitor's huge antics, he no doubt settled down to quiet laughter.

"No milder word than detestable," said Mr. Watson in his article, "no milder word than detestable can be applied to the preposterous style—and vile as it is, it is surpassed by the, what shall one call it? Intellectual coxcombry seems a blunt phrase but is

any courteous phrase available that will adequately
describe the airs of superiority, the affectations of
originality, the sham profundities, the counterfeit
subtleties, the pseudo-oracularisms of this book?—
Without constructive ability, without power to con-
ceive and fashion forth realizable human creatures,
wi hout aptitude for natural evolution of incident,
without the instinct for knowing what will keep company awake—Mr. Meredith can do anything better
than he can tell a story."

The citadel against which Mr. Watson hurled this
diatribe showed no sign of yielding, probably because "The Egoist" is something entirely different
from what the critic supposed it to be.   It is not a
story in the ordinary sense, it is a study in character;
its author used the methods not of the novelist, but
of the dramatist; he treated language as if it were
in a plastic rather than in a fixed state, that is, he
discarded the rules of the prose writer and availed
himself of the privileges of the poet; and finally he
did not aim so much to amuse as to instruct, for the
purpose of the book is to make the reader turn his
criticising eye inward upon himself, rather than outward upon his fellowman.

The story is vouched for by Stevenson, that a
sensitive youth went to Meredith with the complaint that he had been held up to ridicule in the
person of Sir Willoughby Patterne.   "You are
mistaken," said the great novelist in reply, "the
Egoist is not you, he is all of us."   This fact, that
Meredith's readers are almost always driven to self-
analysis is perhaps the chief cause of his being called

a pessimist and a cynic. To see our neighbors under
the lash contributes mightily to our amusement no
doubt, and goes far to awakening a spirit of thank-
fulness that we are not as others are; but our
laughter grows hollow and our satisfaction ceases,
when we feel the flick of the whip upon our own
shoulders.   Yet it is to a full realization of the value
of looking upon oneself in a humorous or even a
ludicrous light, that Meredith would bring every
man.   In that, he believes, rests the hope for
the future, whether of the person or of the race;
for if a man can look upon himself and his deeds
with healthy laughter, there is little danger of his
becoming sour or morbid; and whatever his failure,
he will be able to learn from his mistakes and to
determine with renewed strength not to bequeath
to posterity a tumbled house.

The chief men and women of "The Egoist," where
this lesson is taught with the greatest insistence, for-
bid anything like a summarizing characterization.
The book must be taken in its entirety, or be left
alone.   Sir Willoughby, Clara Middleton, Lætitia
Dale, and perhaps even Vernon Whitford, Mrs.
Jenkinson, and Crossjay Patterne mean almost
nothing when reduced to lower terms than those in
which Meredith himself presents them.   They must
be seen, now by themselves giving out such native
lustre as they possess, and now in company with one
another that the interplay of their brilliance may
call out flashes which would otherwise not even be
guessed at.   In other words, they are human beings
with all the unexpected inconsistencies which one

often sees in real life, but which one is always surprised to find in novels. It is futile to ask whether Clara Middleton possessed sufficient strength of character to break her engagement, had circumstances not assisted her; it is useless to inquire if a man would conduct himself as Sir Willoughby did in his eager desire to escape a second jilting; it is time thrown away to wonder whether Lætitia could really have brought herself to accept her quondam lover when she saw him shorn of the glamour with which she had invested him. These are questions which can have no answer, for the ways of Meredith's characters are not less inscrutable than the conduct of men and women in life. The reason, therefore, why "The Egoist" gives us pause is, not that it is unreal, but that it is too real. It is a scourging, a flagellation, a cutting to the quick. Meredith may be pleased to call it "A Comedy in Narrative," and the reader may be led thereby to expect opportunity for abundant laughter. He will not be disappointed, it is true; but if he reads between the lines, if he hears the message of the author, his amusement will be grim rather than hilarious, thoughtful rather than explosive.

Wonderful as "The Egoist" is, however, unique as most critics concede it to be, it unmistakably belongs to the genus which includes Meredith's other novels. " The Book of the Egoist," that remarkable collection of aphoristic comments upon life and conduct from which frequent quotation is made, is put to the same use in this work as was "The Pilgrim's Scrip" in "The Ordeal of Richard Feverel" and the

sayings of the Philosopher in "Sandra Belloni."
Mrs. Mountstuart Jenkinson has all the penetrative
power of Lady Camper, and by a single phrase hits
off a character as successfully as by a few strokes of
her pencil the Lady pilloried the conduct of her
middle-aged lover.   Dr. Middleton is not less obtuse
than General Ople, and in the wilful blindness of
his selfishness fully as odious.   He is as politely deferential to his daughter, as was Colonel Halkett to
his, and when there is a clash of opinions, strives to
be as patient; but he has, like the Colonel, the conventional belief that women are to be guided or even
commanded if need be, since their intellectual qualities are at best but rudimentary.   Vernon Whitford
belongs in the group of which Professor von Karsteg,
Dr. Shrapnel, and Nevil Beauchamp are likewise
members, as also at times are Austin Wentworth
and Seymour Austin.   Clara Middleton, of course,
is the third and greatest in the trio which, besides
herself, is made up of Janet Ilchester and Cecilia
Halkett; but she has qualities which remind the
reader more than once of Sandra Belloni at her best.
Indeed, Clara Middleton seems to be the perfect
flower of Meredith's earlier studies in womanhood,
as almost beyond a doubt she is the ideal to which his
later creations were never more than approximations.
     Appearing in 1879, "The Egoist" stood in point
of publication midway between George Eliot's
"Daniel Deronda," which preceded it by three
years, and Henry James's "The Portrait of a Lady,"
which followed it by two.   These data are hardly
important in themselves, but the fact that Gwendolen

Harleth, the heroine of the former novel, and Gilbert
Osmond, the heroine's husband in the latter, are
both pronounced egoists, affords some opportunity
for comment.   The presence of Mr. Middleton, a
curate, in "Daniel Deronda" and of the Rev. Dr.
Middleton in "The Egoist" is of course no more
than an accident; but Gwendolen's posing as Saint
Cecilia at the organ and taking satisfaction in the
admiration of her mother and the housekeeper,
brings up the scene in which Sir Willoughby, when
a child, mounted a chair and cried out to his ador-
ing aunts, "I am the sun of the house!"   For a
long period of years, neither the man nor the woman
had had their power or their general superiority dis-
puted, with the result that the man before whom
Isabel and Elinor Patterne bowed down in worship,
and the woman toward whom her mother was always
in an apologetic state of mind, had each developed
a strong determination to have what was pleasant
with an absolute fearlessness in making themselves
disagreeable or dangerous when they did not get it.
Added to this, they both had "that spontaneous sense
of capability, some happy persons are born with,
so that any subject they turn attention to, impresses
them with their own power of forming a correct
judgment on it."   Still, despite this interesting
parallel which might be carried even further, it
would be rash to assert any actual connection between Meredith's novel and George Eliot's.   Nothing further can be proved than that both authors,
at about the same time, felt impelled to make studies
of characters dominated by supreme selfishness.

Nor can a much stronger case be made out by any who may profess to believe that Henry James was indebted to Meredith.   The styles of the two authors have much in common, even to the frequent use of witty epigrams or sharp aphorisms.   Gilbert Osmond, too, is enough different from Sir Willoughby to be startlingly like him.   A dilletante, Osmond delighted to dabble in poetry and painting; a pseudo-scientist, Sir Willoughby spent much time in his laboratory: to their acquaintances the former always appeared to believe that he had descended from the gods, the latter seemed always to be breathing fumes from votive censers.   Sir Willoughby hoped to find in Clara an echo, a mirror; Osmond asked himself in contemplating Isabel Archer, "What could be a happier gift in a companion than a quick, fanciful mind, which saved one repetitions, and reflected one's thoughts upon a scintillating surface?"   Each flattered himself that he would have the forming of his wife's mind which was to be attached to his own "like a small garden-plot to a deer-park.   Osmond saw himself raking the soil gently and watering the flowers, weeding the beds and gathering an occasional nosegay;" Sir Willoughby, of course, would not permit himself the use of such fanciful terms, for he felt that he had risen above the plane of poets; but he pictured a scene in which he so guided, so watched over, so instructed his wife, that she became his second-self.   Luckily for Clara Middleton she escaped being sacrificed upon the altar of egoism, but Isabel Archer suffered the darker fate.   In portraying her married life, Mr. James, probably all uncon-

sciously to himself, gave a sort of sequel to "The
Egoist," or rather what would have been a sequel,
had Meredith brought his novel to a close with the
union of Sir Willoughby to "the dainty rogue in
porcelain" instead of to the lady with "a romantic
tale on her eyelashes." What Clara Middleton
would have become, had circumstances not permitted
her release from an egoist, that Isabel Archer became. Looking upon his cousin in after years
Ralph Touchett saw that she had completely
changed.

"Her light step drew a mass of drapery behind
it; her intelligent head sustained a majesty of orna-
ment. The free, keen girl had become quite another person; what he saw was the fine lady who was
supposed to represent something. 'What did Isabel represent?' Ralph asked himself; and he
could answer only by saying that she represented
Gilbert Osmond. 'Good heavens, what a function!'
he exclaimed. He was lost in wonder at the mys-
tery of things."

Much more closely related to "The Egoist" than
either "Daniel Deronda" or "The Portrait of a
Lady" was Meredith's own work called "The Tragic
Comedians." Sigismund Alvan, the hero of that
book, was a study in egoism, even more pronounced,
indeed, if less subtle than Sir Willoughby. Like the
English baronet, the Hungarian socialist took possession of a young woman's heart before her reason
had asserted itself; and though Clotilde von Rüdiger
was far inferior in every way to Clara Middleton,
Alvan melodramatically and almost hysterically re-

peated the essential acts of Sir Willoughby's comedy.
He looked upon the lady as the quarry, himself as
the hunter. He expected to find in her "a sprightly
comrade, perfectly feminine, thoroughly mastered,
young, graceful, comely and a lady of station. Once
in his good keeping her lord would answer for her.
And this," he felt, "was a manfully generous view
of the situation." At a time when circumstances
thundered that he and she must be forever separated, he recalled to her by letter the day when they had
stood together in glorious sunshine planning the work
of the New Republic. As he wrote, he seemed to see
that "his moral grandeur on that day made him live
as part of the splendor." With that in mind he began to ask himself, "Was it possible for the woman
who had seen him then, to be faithless to him?
The swift deduction from his own feelings cleansed
her of a suspicion to the contrary, and he became
light-hearted." Thus swayed by his heart rather than
by his head, he permitted himself an extravagance
of language and conduct which his reason, when it
began to stem the current of his tumultuous blood,
plainly taught him would cause him to look little less
than ridiculous, if the lady should slip from him.
The thought filled him with agony. "Anything,"
he cried, "but that! She will not refuse; I am
bound to think so in common respect for myself.
I have done tricks to make me appear a raging ape
if she—Oh! she cannot, she will not refuse!" Beside himself with fear, he looked for comfort within,
and he found it by magnanimously thinking that he
was without meanness of soul. "He had, he felt, a

broad, full heart for the woman who would come to him, forgiving her, uplifting her, richly endowing her!"

All of these feelings were Sir Willoughby's as well as Alvan's. His hasty engagement to Clara, his desire that she should reflect him and him only, his determination to mould her mind, his fear that she would escape him, his wish to be a conqueror, his agony at the thought that he might be made the subject of contemptuous laughter, his willingness to go to any extreme if he might stand unashamed before the world, all are matched by the impulses of Alvan's heart. Considering this similarity of character between the heroes, one is led to ask how it came about that "The Egoist" should be considered the greatest of Meredith's novels, and "The Tragic Comedians" the least significant. The conclusive answer is found in the very brief statement, that "The Tragic Comedians" is not to be regarded as a novel at all. By this is meant, not that it is too short, although as originally published in *The Fortnightly Review*, from October, 1880, to February, 1881, it consisted of only fifteen chapters, but that it is neither more nor less than a plain presentation of those relations between the famous German socialist, Ferdinand Lassalle, and Helene von Dönniges which resulted in the death of the former from wounds received in a duel with Yanko von Racowitza. Strangely blind to this fact, which was known at the time when the book was published, and totally forgetful that Meredith in the prologue expressly states that the pair of tragic comedians belong to history, "breathed the stouter air than fiction," and that not a single incident was invented, the critics have persisted in testing the work as a novel, and have therefore found room for little but disparagement.

But George Meredith's reputation as a novelist and poet, and his evident desire that "The Tragic Comedians" should be looked upon as a story, both demand that some reason must be sought for the existence of a work which, treating fact without invention, is yet neither biography nor history; and surrounding actual persons and events with imagination, is yet in no true sense fiction.   Now the word "fantastical" has frequently been directed against the novels of George Meredith on the score that they give no pictures of possible life.   Its reiteration at last provoked reply and the answer took the form of "The Tragic Comedians."   Meredith may well be heard in his own defence:

"The word 'fantastical' is accentuated in our tongue to so scornful an utterance that the constant good service it does would make it seem an appointed instrument for reviewers of books of imaginative matter distasteful to those expository pens.   Upon examination, claimants to the epithet will be found outside of books and of poets, in many quarters, Nature being one of the prominent, if not the foremost.   Wherever she can get to drink her fill of sunlight, she pushes forth fantastically.   As for that wandering ship of the drunken pilot, the mutinous crew and the angry captain, called Human Nature, 'fantastical' fits it no less completely than a continental baby's skull-cap the stormy infant.   Our sympathies, one may fancy, will be broader, our critical acumen shrewder, if we at once accept the thing as a part of us and worthy of study. The pair of tragic comedians of whom there will be question pass under this word as under their banner and motto. Their acts are incredible . . . yet they are real creatures, exquisitely fantastical, strangely exposed to the world by a lurid catastrophe."

With these words in mind, the reader of "The Tragic Comedians" plainly perceives that Sir Willoughby Patterne is no impossible personage, for Ferdinand Lassalle did his deeds in actual life before him; that Nevil Beauchamp's treatment of Reneé de Croisnel upon two memorable occasions, was but the appearance in fiction of the great socialist's conduct, first when dominated by his heart, and later when ruled by his head; and finally that Richard Feverel's foolish persistence in a course of action which darkened his life forever, might be matched with an event in real life.

The style of "The Tragic Comedians" on the whole is remarkably unlike that of any of Meredith's other works, although now and then, rather strangely, one seems to catch a glimpse of his early manner, as seen in "Farina." There is almost a complete absence of the aphorisms and epigrams which readers of Meredith always expect; and certainly no one can justly complain that the book is in any way obscure in expression or meaning. The sentences are brief, so frequently brief that the writing might be termed feverish. Accordingly, "The Tragic Comedians," despite its value from some points of view, might be said much more properly than "The House on the Beach" to represent Mr. Meredith in his bones. It is certainly the least significant of his works and cannot be regarded as an important contribution to literature. Nevertheless, the Prologue and the last chapter are typical of the novelist's writing. Certain paragraphs of the conclusion remind the reader of the closing words of "Vittoria," and have an added interest in that they give voice to some of Meredith's conceptions of life.

"Silent was that house of many chambers. That mass of humanity profusely mixed of good and evil, of generous ire and mutinous, of the passion for the future of mankind and vanity of person, magnanimity and sensualism, high judgment, reckless indiscipline, chivalry, savagery, solidity, fragmentariness, was dust. The two men composing it, the untamed and the candidate for citizenship, in mutual dissension pulled it down. He perished of his weakness, but it was a strong man that fell. If his end was unheroic, the blot does not overshadow his life. His end was a derision because the animal in him ran him unchained and bounding to it. A stormy blood made wreck of a splendid intelligence. . . . That last word of his history ridicules the eulogy of partisan and devotee, and to commit the excess of worshipping is to conjure up by contrast a vulgar giant; for truth will have her just proportions, and vindicate herself upon a figure over-idealized by bidding it grimace leaving appraisers to get the balance of the two extremes. He was neither fool nor madman; nor man to be adored: his last temptation caught him in the season before he had subdued his blood, and amid the multitudinously simple of this world stamped him tragic comedian: that is, a grand pretender, a self-deceiver, one of the lividly ludicrous whom we cannot laugh at, but must contemplate to distinguish where the conduct strikes the discord with life. . . . The characters of the host of men are of the simple order of the comic; not many are of a stature and a complexity calling for the junction of the two muses to name them."

With the publication of "The Tragic Comedians" in book form, late in 1880, Meredith closed the third decade of his literary career, the period of free range. From many points of view the ten years thus designated may be looked upon as the most important part of his life as author. The several works then produced evinced a sense of proportion, a consciousness of mastery, a disregard of arbitrary methods, which could not be unreservedly predicated of him in 1869 when his work as a journeyman was brought to an end. On the other hand, although it cannot be denied that he remained in full possession of all his powers through that later period which may be termed the decade of concentrated interest, the very fact that there was a limitation of range made it clear that in all probability the time of expansion was over, and that thereafter whatever energy remained in store would endeavor to put itself forth not in outspreading branch nor in upreaching stem, but rather in leaf and fruit and flower. At all events, the following decade of Meredith's literary career was not noted for the production of any such remarkable story as "The Ordeal of Richard Feverel," or of any such unusual study of character as "The Egoist;" but it was marked by the publication of "Diana of the Crossways," a novel which gained immediate popularity, and by the appearance of three other sustained works of fiction which attracted a respectful audience, if they did not earn undivided admiration. The battle had been long and hard, but few felt safe in denying that Meredith had proved himself a conqueror. Clearly his rightful place was among the leaders, in company with Dickens and Thackeray and George Eliot.

V

THE MASTER-WORKMAN

THE PERIOD OF CONCENTRATED INTEREST—"DIANA
OF THE CROSSWAYS"—"ONE OF OUR CONQUER-
ORS"—"LORD ORMONT AND HIS AMINTA"—"THE
AMAZING MARRIAGE"—THE MEREDITH SCHOOL.

AFTER the artisan has shown himself sufficiently
a master-workman to be received with noticeable respect by serious-minded men, he may not unjustly
feel it his privilege to give emphatic expression to
any thought which he deems important. Up to
the time when critics somewhat freely admit that
he is a stable living force, he is often compelled
to make use of his powers in vindication of his
right to be considered at all; but when indifference
has given way to attention, and censure to approval,
he may lay aside conscious effort to please others,
and rest assured of a considerable audience interested in what he is doing to please himself.

Now there can be but little doubt that "The
Adventures of Harry Richmond" and "The Egoist"
placed Meredith high in the ranks of English novelists, and convinced many conservative readers that
he was worthy of much more than mere passing
notice. If therefore he had ceased to write in
1880, he would not have been denied a permanent

and honored place in literature. Indeed, it may be questioned, in spite of the fact that his popularity increased with his later novels, whether the works which he wrote after the year just mentioned were in any way necessary to the stability of his renown. Nevertheless, during the decade beginning in 1885, he felt moved to produce four sustained pieces of fiction which may be said to belong to a period of concentrated interest, inasmuch as each of them dealt with complexities rising out of an unsuitable marriage. In "Diana of the Crossways" is given the story of a woman, who marrying without love, was afterward separated from her husband and made to take an anomalous and unhappy position before the world; in "One of Our Conquerors" is presented a study of the attitude taken by society towards a man and a woman living together in a union unsanctioned by Church and State but regarded, none the less, as sacred by the two chiefly concerned; and in "Lord Ormont and His Aminta" and also in "The Amazing Marriage," the reader is confronted with the unhappiness which results from a marked discrepancy between husband and wife in matters of rank, age, or inclination. With the possible exception of the second, these four stories amply repay those who read simply to be amused, but for others who look upon the novelist as having a mission beyond that of giving mere pleasure, they furnish in addition much food for thought.

It may be concluded from these facts that Meredith found in certain phases of the marriage relation some of the gravest problems furnished by modern society. That he looked upon the questions as being more than a mere source of material for the novelist, is certainly shown by the fact that long after he had ceased the formal writing of fiction, he permitted himself to speak upon them at some length. The interview, as it was reported in *The London Daily Mail*, for September 24, 1904, stirred up so much comment both in England and in America that a few weeks later, Meredith in self-defence was led to break his usual silence upon personal matters, and to say that, at least in some respects, he had been misrepresented. As, however, he did not state that he wished to withdraw from the position which he was asserted to have taken, his earlier remarks are of some interest both in themselves and on account of their connection with the fundamental ideas of his later novels. In part he was accredited by *The Daily Mail* with saying:

"It is a question in my mind whether a young girl married, say at eighteen, utterly ignorant of life, knowing little, as such a girl would of the man she is marrying, or of any other man, or of the world at all, should be condemned to live with him for the rest of her life. She falls out of sympathy with him, say, has no common taste with him, no real communication with him except a physical one. The life is nearly intolerable. Yet many married women go on with it from habit or because the world terrorizes them. Certainly, however, one day these present conditions of marriage will be changed. Marriage will be allowed for a certain period, say ten years, or, well I do not want to specify any particular time. . . . It will be a great shock, but look back and see what shocks there have been and what changes nevertheless, have taken place in this marriage business in the past! The difficulty is to make English people face such a problem."

Although this idea of the optional marriage broken or renewed at the expiration of a fixed period, had been thrown out by Colney Durance in "One of Our Conquerors," it may be doubted whether Meredith, while writing his last four novels, had really made the theory a part of his own philosophy of life. Nevertheless, he did show clearly, that to his mind, society must needs enter into a careful study of the troubles resulting from strained marriage relations. In the hope, therefore, of awakening serious thought upon the matter, he unmistakably called upon the reader to sympathize with Diana Warwick despite her erratic career, to admit the injustice of the world in its attitude toward Nataly and Nesta Radnor, to feel that the elopement of Weyburn and Lady Aminta was justifiable, and to see that a renewal of the union between the Earl of Fleetwood and his wife was impossible. From this, it must be evident to one who looks beneath the surface, that as the earlier novels were an attack upon a sentimental deference to various long unquestioned ideals, these later works were a sturdy assault upon the seemingly impregnable conventionality which looks upon the marriage bond as indissoluble.

"Diana of the Crossways," the earliest of these somewhat daring novels, made its first appearance as a story of twenty-six chapters in *The Fortnightly*

Review, where it ran from June to December, 1884. As there published, it carried the fortunes of the heroine up to the point, where the opportune arrival of Lady Dunstane at the bedside of her friend saved Diana from death. The narration then closed, rather abruptly perhaps, with a note to the effect that those who cared for more of the erratic woman would find it in the extended chronicle. The meaning of this statement was made clear early in the following year when, by the insertion of numerous paragraphs, by a renumbering of chapters, and by the addition of seventeen more carrying on Diana's story to her marriage with Redworth, the "extended chronicle" was printed as a three-volume novel. The book became immediately successful, and the demand for it was so great that three editions were exhausted before the year was out. This popularity, furthermore, awakened a widened interest in the author's earlier writings and led Meredith to sanction the publication of a collected edition of all his prose work. Nor did the liking for Diana's story prove ephemeral. After successfully weathering an unusually sharp and witty burlesque in *Punch* where, in the issue for October 18, 1890, Mr. Rudolph Lehman published a skit under the heading, "'Joanna of the Cross Ways,' by George Verimyth, author of 'Richard's Several Editions,' 'The Aphorist,' 'Shampoo's Shaving Pot,' etc., etc.," the book continued to be in steady demand; and from all present appearance, it bids fair to be widely read even by the third and fourth generations.

The story, it is true, moves with a certain swing and dash, which in part explains its perennial popularity, but the marked interest with which its first appearance was greeted, was due, no doubt, to the belief that in Diana Warwick was portrayed the famous and popular Mrs. Caroline Norton.   Both were Irish women of remarkable beauty, Diana a daughter of old Dan Merion, a wit of no little reputation; Mrs. Norton a granddaughter of Richard Brinsley Sheridan, the dramatist.   Each married after an acquaintance altogether too brief, and almost from the beginning suffered from the husband's unfounded jealousy.   Each after a time was made the subject of a ridiculous divorce suit, Augustus Warwick claiming that he had been injured by Lord Dannisburgh, the Honorable George Norton that he had suffered at the hands of Lord Melbourne.   Moreover. each of the women wrote novels which were well received by the public; and finally Mrs. Norton for a time was under the unjust suspicion of having betrayed the confidence of a cabinet minister, just as Mrs. Warwick in the story imparted Percy Dacier's secret to Marcus Tonans.   In passing, it is of interest to learn that the publication of "Diana of the Crossways" revived the almost forgotten scandal about the Honorable Mrs. Norton, and led to an investigation which wholly exonerated the lady from blame.   In consequence of this inquiry, recent editions of the book bear an introductory note written in Meredith's characteristic style:

"A lady of high distinction for wit and beauty, the daughter of an illustrious Irish house, came under

the shadow of calumny. It has latterly been ex-
amined and exposed as baseless. The story of
'Diana of the Crossways' is to be read as fiction."

The discovery that Diana Warwick had a possible
prototype in life was one of no very great difficulty, since Mrs. Norton—or rather, Lady Sterling-
Maxwell, as by a second marriage she became—
was well known and popular in England, almost
from the time of her entrance into society until the
day of her death in 1877. But twenty years after
the publication of "Diana of the Crossways," an
anonymous writer in *Scribner's Magazine*, for February, 1905, pointed out that a parallel no less interesting than that existing between Diana Warwick
and Mrs. Norton, might be drawn between the same
heroine and the French writer who called herself
George Sand. Both were noted for their wit, as might
be expected indeed since one was of Gaelic the other
of Gallic blood. Each became united early in life
to an uncongenial husband whose nature led the wife
in either case to seek happiness in separation. Both
became interested in the political matters of their
respective countries, and both turned their hands
to the writing of novels, for which they drew abundant material from their own experiences and from
those of men and women surrounding them. Both
were harassed by money cares, and were driven to
extraordinary methods to escape them. Both were
beset by lovers and found consolation in male friend-
ship; and finally each emerged from her many di-
verse perplexities into a state of peace, Diana becoming united with the patient and loyal Redworth,

and Madame Dudevant entering upon a well-earned tranquil existence at the close of her almost heroic struggles to reconcile passion and reason. One learns, also, perhaps not without some surprise, that Diana Warwick's French prototype, whom Meredith probably did not have in mind, and her English fore-runner, whom he certainly did, were almost exactly contemporary in their lives; for they were born within five years of each other, and hardly a twelve-month separated the days of their death.

With the shades of two such famous women watching over her creation, Diana Warwick might well be expected to stand by herself in the gallery of Meredith's art. Yet as a matter of fact she now and then betrays, without detriment to herself or to her maker, a touch or even a trait which shows her unmistakable relationship with other women wrought by the same hand. Her easy, or rather, her uncon-scious disregard of certain minor social conventionali-ties, and her complete fearlessness or forgetfulness of possible gossip about her conduct, both recall Sandra Belloni; while her power of penetration and her firmness of character, both make her seem at times not unlike Cecilia Halkett. All in all, how-ever, she is much more like Clara Middleton than she is like any other woman whom Meredith has drawn: that is, a rapid reading of "The Egoist" and of "Diana of the Crossways" leaves the impression that under the same conditions "the dainty rogue in porcelain" and "old Dan Merion's daughter" would each have conducted herself in no wise differ-ently from the other. Still, at no time could Diana

Warwick be mistaken for any of the several other attractive women appearing in Meredith's novels, as, for instance, Janet Ilchester and Cecilia Halkett, distantly viewed in memory might sometimes be. They, and many others with them, have the reader's admiration and respect; but Diana has more, she has his pity and his love.   Despite the trial to which her erratic conduct puts one's patience, despite her woeful lack of wisdom when one would expect it to be most abundant, despite her audacious irresponsibility, her bewildering inconsistency, her incalculable impulsiveness, one does not hesitate to be enrolled beneath Tom Redworth's banner, and to follow the lady with that leader's perfect confidence and trust.

The story in which the fortunes of this beautiful and attractive heroine were narrated, starts the reader's mind now and then upon lines of thought leading to sources from which consciously or unconsciously Meredith might have received some minor suggestions.   In the first place, although "Diana of the Crossways" is hardly a political novel in the same sense that "Beauchamp's Career" is, it certainly produces so nearly the effect of Trollope's "Parliamentary Series" as to make one feel that Lady Glencora and Mrs. Max Goesler and John Grey are just on the point of making their appearance and entering into conversation with Diana and Redworth. Perhaps, too, this illusion is strengthened somewhat by the realization on the reader's part that Diana's separation from Augustus Warwick, and his subsequent threat to take legal measures for the restoration of marital rights, are almost exactly a repetition of Laura Kennedy's experiences with her husband as related in "Phineas Redux." Again, Warwick's accusations against Lord Dannisburgh in addition to being those of the Honorable George Norton against Lord Melbourne, were likewise those which rumor, nearly fifty years ago, said were to be made against Lord Palmerston, and which Meredith, it should not be forgotten, saw fit to comment upon in his news-paper days.

Furthermore, here, as elsewhere, Meredith seemed to draw from his own earlier works. Diana's love for "antiques," to which she ascribed her liking for Lord Dannisburgh, is, as a phrase, traceable to Lady Camper's stinging comment upon the amorous General Ople's endeavor to be chivalrous, even after he had her word that she was seventy years old. Arthur Rhodes, in his devotion to Diana, is Braintop reproduced with certain improvements from "Sandra Belloni"; Lord Dannisburgh is the Duke of Bel-field from "Evan Harrington," but so much nobler in character, despite his many failings, as to be not un-worthy of a place near the elder Duke of Omnium in Trollope's "Can We Forgive Her" and "Phineas Phinn." Lady Dacier in her sanctimonious su-periority might have been studied from Mrs. Grandi-son in "The Ordeal of Richard Feverel"; and Mrs. Wathin is a gossip possibly sketched, though some-what coarsely perhaps, from the same model which furnished the delicate drawings of Lady Busshe and Lady Culmer in "The Egoist." On the whole, however, all these similarities are so remote as to be little more than fanciful; and do not in any way prevent "Diana of the Crossways" from being regarded as one of Meredith's most original and most important contributions to literature.

For a time after the publication of Diana's story, Meredith's career as a novelist seemed to be at an end.   If by chance he was mentioned at all, his critic usually spoke of him as being an unsuccessful competitor with Dickens and Thackeray rather than as a living author.   Nevertheless, Meredith was by no means keeping silence.   Occasional contributions in prose and verse were printed in *The Fortnightly Review*, *The Pall Mall Gazette*, and elsewhere; and two important volumes of poetry were published in successive years, "Ballads and Poems of Tragic Life," in 1887, and "A Reading of Earth," in 1888. The latter book was closely related in contents with "Poems and Lyrics of the Joy of Earth" which had appeared five years before; that is, two years in advance of "Diana of the Crossways"; while the earlier volume had considerable in common with the partly suppressed collection of 1862, "Modern Love and Poems of the English Roadside with Poems and Ballads."   Even a somewhat cursory reading of Meredith's books of verse beginning with the "Poems" of 1851, and passing on through the four volumes just mentioned to the three succeeding collections, "The Empty Purse," published in 1892; "Odes in Contribution to the Song of French History," in 1898, and "A Reading of Life," in 1901; will show that he was developing a philosophy and pointing out a unity between Man and Nature such as had not been preached by any earlier English poet—a philosophy and a unity, indeed, which, as early as 1883, Meredith himself summed up in a single sonnet:

EARTH'S SECRET

Not solitarily in fields we find
Earth's secret open, though one page is there;
Her plainest, such as children spell, and share
With bird and beast; raised letters for the blind.
Not where the troubled passions toss the mind,
In turbid cities, can the key be bare.
It hangs for those who hither thither fare,
Close interthreading Nature with our kind.
They, hearing History speak, of what men were,
And have become, are wise. The gain is great
In vision and solidity; it lives.
Yet at a thought of life apart from her,
Solidity and vision lose their state,
For earth, that gives the milk, the spirit gives.

Certain phases of this philosophy—of this need for man to learn from Nature whether she appear in field or wood or in the thickly populated city—may be found in every one of Meredith's novels. But it is safe to say that in "One of Our Conquerors"— the novel to which Meredith unexpectedly treated his readers in 1891—there is a stricter adherence than in any of his other prose works, to the terms which he systematically employed in the poems bearing the burden of his message. Earth and Nature, for instance, are used almost interchangeably; and either or both may be referred to as the Great Mother in the sense that from her all things spring. On the other hand, Society, together with the laws and the conventionalities which Society has dictated, is given the designation of Circumstance. Now, according to Meredith, these two forces, to one of which Man owes his origin, and by the other of which, when it acts alone, he is more often delayed than assisted in his advancement towards fullest development, are not always mutually helpful. Between them, rather, Man is carrying on an "epic encounter." Nor seldom is he in a quandary. Often he is compelled to pause and ask himself, Is Man in fact harmonious with the Great Mother when he yields to the pressure of his nature—that is, to his impulsive human nature?   To this question his reason can give but one answer, No! "Man may be rebellious against his time and his Laws, but if he is really for Nature, he is not lawless." Where, then, he may justly inquire, is to be sought the power, the wisdom which shall dictate the laws transcending those formulated by Society?   It is found resident, reason again replies, in the Intellect, that attribute of Man which distinguishes him from the brute, and which by its development has filled the Great Mother with joy.   Not yet, however, is she sure that Man is to be her crowning work. The heart, that is the beast within, would ravin hourly if it could, nor is the Intellect at all times the conqueror. The head may yet be the victim; the heart may yet gather force again to be

> "The lion of our deserts' trodden weeds;
> .   .   .   .
> Again to be the lordly paw
> Naming his appetites his needs
> Behind a decorative cloak."

In this struggle between the heart and the head for
supremacy, Circumstance, the collective term by
which Meredith names the methods agreed upon
by man as being those best suited for his life with
his fellows, is far less helpful to the head, and gives
far more assistance to the heart than should be expected. Man, however, is not himself unaware of
the conflict, and he even feels called upon now and
then to make his excuse to the Great Mother. As
Meredith puts it at the beginning of the ninteenth
chapter of "One of Our Conquerors":

"There is at times in the hearts of all men of active
life a vivid wild moment or two of dramatic dialogue
between the veteran antagonists, Nature and Circumstance, where they, whose business it should be
to be joyfully one, furiously split; and the Dame is
up with her shrillest querulousness to inquire of her
offspring for the distinct original motive of his conduct. . . . If he be not an alienated issue of the
Great Mother, he will strongly incline to her view,
that he put himself into harness with a machine
going the dead contrary way of her welfare and thereby wrote himself a donkey for his present reading.
. . . But it is asked by the disputant, If we had followed her exclusively, how far should we have
travelled from our starting point? We of the world
and its prizes and duties must do her an injury to
make her tongue musical to us, and her argument
worthy of our attention!"

Society or Circumstance, Meredith, of course,
would not look upon as being always reprehensible;
but when, by misdirection or perversion, it stands

in the way of Man's advancement, it could not to
his mind be too severely condemned. It is this
thought which spurred him to make in his many
novels repeated attacks upon the widespread and
unquestioning acceptance of traditions and established customs. In "One of Our Conquerors"
this war upon sentimentalism, as he called it, was
especially directed against the shallowness of religion as commonly received, and against the denial
to woman of her proper place in the present scheme
of things. Meredith, it is true, did not in his
work make any direct and sustained assault upon the
church; but he did take evident delight in heaping
ridicule upon the clergymen of his novels, nearly all
of whom were guilty of an elephantine belief in their
own superiority. The colorless curate of Lobourne
in "The Ordeal of Richard Feverel" and the Reverend Mr. Marter in "Sandra Belloni" are of course
hardly more than lay figures; but the Honorable
and Reverend Herbert Duffian in "Evan Harrington" and the Reverend Dr. Middleton in "The
Egoist," unlike as they are in many respects, might
very easily be regarded as representatives of that
type of minister whose choice of profession is due,
not to the winsome attractiveness of the Nazarene,
but rather to mere accident or to thoughtless following of the line of least resistance.

Not far removed from these two men although
much more ponderous in every way is the Reverend
Septimus Barmby. Appearing early in "One of Our
Conquerors," he became almost omnipresent, for even
in his absence the stentorian booming of his voice,

like "the rolling roar of curfew," seemed to be in constant reverberation. Devoted to the spirit of things that are, he could not interpret the fundamental ideas of Christianity in such a way as to make them a help in solving the most important problems of modern society. Regarding himself in his office far too seriously, he directed his eye towards old institutions and was blind to the changes taking place about him. He failed to see that education is becoming less and less the mission of the Church, and thus he remained a member of that class whom Meredith had in mind when in a recent interview he said:

"I hope that ultimately we shall take teaching out of the hands of the clergy and that we shall be able to instruct the clergy in the fact that Christianity is a spiritual religion and not one that is to be governed by material conditions. A spiritual God I most perfectly believe in. I have that belief constantly before me—I feel it within me; but a material God that interferes in material, moral affairs I have never seen; and it is, I am sorry to say, for the material God that the clergy seem to be striving."

Of far greater importance than Meredith's arraignment of the clergy and their calling, was his criticism of the place which Society has accorded to women. Of course Skepsey's belief that girls have but one mission on earth and should therefore be healthy for the sake of it, may be dismissed with a smile. Few men nowadays are willing to confess that they hold to the idea, although silence by no means necessarily proves the absence of belief.

Colney Durance undoubtedly overstated the truth
when he declared that woman, because of her education, is unfitted to speak an opinion on any matter
external to the household; but he made Nataly Radnor see plainly that society "gives an exotic fostering
to the senses of women instead of the strengthening
breath of vital air, and that, as a result, the model
women of men make pleasant slaves, not true mates."
So true is this in general, so thoroughly is woman
the slave of existing conventions, so surely is she the
artificial production of a state that exalts her while
she sacrifices daily and hourly to the artificial, that
Victor Radnor's opinions may be regarded as being
those of "the entrenched majority."   What would be
the result, he asked himself, if men could "deorient-
alize their gleeful notion of women and dis-Turk
themselves by inviting woman's voluble tongue to
sisterly occupation in the world, as in the domestic
circle?"   In reply he had the old argument, itself a
series of questions, "Is she moral? Does she mean
to be harmless?   Is she not untamable Old Nature?
Would she not, when once on an equal footing with
her lordly half, show herself that wanton old thing,
the empress of disorderliness?"   Thus rendered ap-
prehensive, Radnor allied himself with the average
man, "objecting to the occult power of women, as
we have the women now while legislating to maintain them so, and forbidding a step to a desperately
wicked female world lest the step should be to
wickeder."   Radnor's opinions of course were far
from being Meredith's own.   By his very method of
presenting them, he made it evident that he looked

upon them with contempt, and that he was freely offering himself as the voluntary champion of woman-
kind.   That he found himself at the head of no
numerous host was due perhaps to the fact that an
enthroned Society by its advocacy of existing laws
and rules and habits had produced in woman "those
timidities, at present urging her to support Estab-
lishments."

The vehicle by which Meredith conveyed to his
readers these radically destructive criticisms of long
accepted ideas, was a story not unlikely in itself to
shock the British public.   In early manhood a
certain Mr. Victor Radnor married a wealthy
woman, several years his senior.   Tiring of her, he
became interested in a Miss Nataly Dreighton, to
whose attractive qualities his wife was constantly
calling his attention.   After a struggle to remain
true to his marriage vows, he deserted Mrs. Burman Radnor in the company of her young friend,
and entered into a union which both he and Miss
Dreighton looked upon as sacred.   The novel opens
at a time when their daughter was entering upon
womanhood and is concerned with the treatment
which society meted out to her and her parents.
Thus baldly told, the story could not be objected
to on the ground that the situations were impossible
or that they were not at least occasionally ac-
quiesced in by modern society.   The immorality
of which the book was accused lay, it was admitted, not so much in the plot as in the teachings.   Two persons had violated the laws of the
Established Church, yet the reader was expected

to approve of their conduct. Their daughter, albeit innocent, was none the less illegitimate, yet Meredith was willing to lift a free-lance in her defence. This certainly was carrying things with a pretty high hand. "Why, the very foundations of society are being attacked!" cried the horrified critic. "Pray, what would Mr. Meredith have? Does he not realize that these ideas are subversive of Church and State—nay, that they are even more —say anarchical in the extreme?" Now, it is not at all unlikely that Meredith knew what he was about. A close observer of society, he detected more than one spot of weakness; and thereupon, with unflinching hand, he pointed out the source of trouble and suggested what to his mind would work a cure. He could not agree with one of his characters who freely admitted the errors of society, but felt that "the assertion of our individuality in opposition to the Government of Society—this existing Society—is a toss of the cap for the erasure of our civilization," rather he held with that other who "flung the gauntlet at externally venerable Institutions and treated Society as a discrowned monarch on trial for an offence against a more precious: viz., the individual cramped by brutish laws: the individual with the ideas of our times, righteously claiming expansion out of the clutches of a narrow old-world disciplinarian—that giant hypocrite."

If the teachings and the plot of "One of Our Conquerors" had not stood in the way of its popularity, its style alone would probably have kept it as little known as it is. Meredith has always been accused, and perhaps not unjustly, of being a maker of phrases. By this is not meant here, his power of epigrammatic utterance, a power which John Morley praised with no uncertain tone in an address on "Aphorisms," but rather his tendency to treat language as material which lends itself to any shaping. This characteristic of his style is in almost direct opposition to clearness, which has come to be looked upon as the chief desideratum of the essayist and the novelist. Meredith, however, seemed often to prefer the involved to the simple, the ornate to the plain; and in "One of Our Conquerors" the tendency certainly became an obsession. The reader is not told in so many words that Radnor kissed his wife, but that "he performed his never-omitted lover's homage," Mr. Fenellan did not drink the Old Veuve, but "crushed a delicious gulp of the wine that foamed along the channel of flavor"; Skepsey instead of feeling the size and hardness of the butcher's arm, "performed the national homage to muscle"; and in giving a cordial greeting to Lady Grace, "Victor's festival-lights were kindled, beholding her; cressets on the window-sill, lamps inside." Such writing, it cannot be denied, is both bewildering and exasperating to almost every reader; and Meredith, therefore, had no just cause of complaint if his own joy in weaving such fantastic garments for his thought was his chief reward. Certainly after the publication of "One of Our Conquerors," many of his old readers fell away or at most contented themselves with memories of what he had written before, while the

younger generation who, like Sarah Battle, occasionally found time to turn aside from whist-playing
and to unbend the mind over a book, took no special
pleasure in anything which Meredith had to say.

Radically different as "One of Our Conquerors"
was from Meredith's earlier novels in its strongly
didactic tone, its plot, and its strangely involved
style, the book struck its roots deep into all that its
author had published before it.   Egoism and sentimentalism were still made objects of attack; Colney
Durance was a maker of phrases, as were Mrs.
Mountstuart in "The Egoist," and Adrian Harley in
"The Ordeal of Richard Feverel"; the Duvidney
sisters in their worship of their cousin Victor Radnor were like the Patterne ladies in their blind adora-
tion of the egoistical Sir Willoughby, while in their
prim regard for the proprieties, they showed themselves to be what the unmarried Pole sisters must
in their old age have become.   Mrs. Marsett is un-
deniably like Mrs. Mount, although, happily, Nesta
Radnor's endeavor to save the woman from herself
was much more successful than was Richard Feverel's attempt to reclaim the woman who had been
hired to entice him away from his wife.   Again, the
several references in Chapter Five to the Rajah's
visit to London recall more than one passage in
"The Shaving of Shagpat," while the street brawl
has not a little in common with the tent scene in
"Sandra Belloni."   Even more striking than this is
a remarkable similarity between a passage in the
novel and the first poem of "Modern Love."
Although Nataly Radnor could not approve of her

husband's scheme for the great assembly at Lakelands, she would not in any way undertake to thwart or
disappoint him. Stifling her own feelings, therefore,
"She could have turned to him, to show him she
was in harmony with the holy night and loving
world but for the fear founded upon a knowledge of
the man he was; it held her frozen to the semblance
of a tombstone lady beside her lord in the aisle where
honor kindles pitchy blackness with its legions at
one movement. Verily it was the ghost of Mrs.
Burman come to the bed, between them."

Nearly thirty years before, Meredith had written
of a husband and wife between whom the spirit of
jealousy had risen; and at that time he used almost
exactly the same thought and phraseology:

> "By this he knew she wept with waking eyes:
> That at his hand's light quiver by her head,
> The strange low sobs that shook their common bed,
> Were called into her with a sharp surprise,
> And strangled mute, like little gaping snakes,
> Deadly venomous to him. She lay
> Stone-still, and the long darkness flowed away
> With muffled pauses. Then, as midnight makes
> Her giant heart of Memory and Tears
> Drink the pale drug of silence, and so beat
> Sleep's heavy measure, they from head to feet
> Were moveless, looking through their dead black years,
> By vain regret scrawled over the blank wall.
> Like sculptured effigies they might be seen
> Upon their marriage tomb, the sword between;
> Each wishing for the sword that severs all."

It is, furthermore, of some interest to discover that
a strong tendency to use the methods of Dickens re-

appeared after many years in this later novel. Skepsey, the pugilist, and Martha Pridden, the evangelist, are quite in Dickens's style, and their union is just what the elder novelist would have brought about. The Reverend Septimus Barmby and the Reverend Groseman Buttermore must have been fellow-workers with the Reverend Mr. Chadband, although, despite their heavy self-respect, they are much more delicately drawn. The statement that "Mrs. John Cormyn entered voluminous, and Mrs. Peter Yatt effervescent" shows the influence of Dickens's well-known custom of reducing character or appearance to a single trait without loss of illusion; and evidently the whole chapter describing the concert at Lakelands, and that other dealing with the agony which the Duvidney ladies were made to suffer by their lapdog's disgraceful behavior are in the manner of the master of English caricature. It would seem from this that Meredith in his later novels showed at least a slight tendency to return upon himself, to revert to methods employed in his earliest work. Certainly, when the reader is told, almost as the last word in "The Amazing Marriage," that Carinthia Jane married Owain Wythan, "because of his wooing her with dog's eyes instead of words," he must feel, recalling the references to the "old dog's eyes" in Ripton Thompson's head, that Meredith had harked back to a passage in his first novel.

Although "One of Our Conquerors" never enjoyed any great popularity, there was an attempt at the time of its publication to place it before a larger audience than had been reached by any of

Meredith's other works upon their first appearance. To this end, therefore, beginning in October, 1890, and running well on into the following year, the novel was printed simultaneously in *The Fortnightly Review* of London, *The Australasian* of Melbourne, and the Sunday issues of *The New York Sun*. Immediately upon its completion as the leading serial in each of these periodicals, it was of course published in book form. Even before that, however, it had been pretty severely dealt with by the critics, but Meredith was not to be provoked to any attempt at self-defence. Nevertheless, his next novel, "Lord Ormont and His Aminta" seemed to betray a willingness on his part to profit from the words of those who had spoken in disparagement of the earlier work, for if the style of "One of Our Conquerors" may be described as ornate, intricate, and obscure, surely that of the novel which succeeded it must be looked upon as simple in the extreme. Readers of *The Pall Mall Magazine*, where the latter story appeared between December, 1893, and July, 1894, were especially struck by this remarkable change of method, and commented somewhat forcibly upon the fact. From this, two opposite effects resulted: on one hand, those readers who felt a sort of sentimental superiority through a professed or an actual liking of Meredith's earlier style, deplored what they regarded as a falling off in his powers; on the other, many who had never been able to read Meredith at all, freely admitted their pleasure in a work unmarred by what they had been accustomed to term a tendency towards a senseless jugglery with words.

Thus, on the whole, "Lord Ormont and His Aminta" rather added to its author's fame than detracted from it, for if there really was an appreciable lessening in the number of old admirers, there was a compensating accession of new readers, many of whom soon had their eyes opened to the value of his earlier and more important works.

But whatever influence the voice of the critic may be assumed to have had upon the diction of "Lord Ormont and His Aminta," it did not cause Meredith to suspect the validity of his message, nor lead him to build his plot in accordance with commonly accepted ideas of morality. He was, perhaps, less formally didactic in this novel than in the one preceding it, but that he did not withdraw from his position of attack upon popular opinions about the marriage relation was made clear in at least two ways; he evidently approved of Aminta's determination to leave Lord Ormont when she found that she did not love him; and he had no hesitation in picturing her later life with Weyburn upon the Continent as one of unalloyed happiness. She had idealized Lord Ormont and for that sentimentalism she was subjected to a period of suffering. After a time, when she became better acquainted both with herself and her husband, she undertook to adjust her life to conventional theories and bear without complaint the yoke which she had impulsively taken upon herself. While the roseate hues were thus giving place to gray, as Meredith puts it in another connection, Aminta was thrown into close companionship with her husband's private secretary, Matthew

Weyburn, who happened to have been an acquaintance of her school-girl days. Without effort on the
part of either to avoid the other, since neither he
nor she for one moment contemplated the possibility
of a change in their relations, the two for many
months lived side by side as friends. Then, in one
of those rare moments of far-reaching vision which
Meredith, no less than Browning, insists are sometimes given to mankind, the Lady Aminta and
Matthew Weyburn saw "the difference between
men's decrees for their convenience, and God's
laws." From then on, Meredith managed matters
with even more than his usual skill, so much so, indeed, that the reader, when he lays down the book,
is somewhat shocked to realize that he has almost
unconsciously been led into an approval of what
society regards as an immoral situation.

Closely related, or even almost unified, as "One
of Our Conquerors" and "Lord Ormont and His
Aminta" are seen to be from the point of view of
the teaching which they have in common, they afford
an unusually systematic, and therefore striking contrast in details of plot-structure. Victor Radnor
married a woman much his senior, Lord Ormont one
many years his junior; Nataly Dreighton found herself excluded from society because her union with
Radnor was illegal, Lady Aminta was not given the
place which was her due, despite the fact that she
was truly the wife of the disappointed military hero;
Radnor endeavored to force Nataly to a place which
she did not desire, Lord Ormont refused to allow
his wife to take a position where she wished to stand;

Mrs. Burman was abandoned by her young husband, Lord Ormont by his young wife. Both the elder man and the elder woman lived many years, and thus prevented the marriage of those who had deserted them; but each forgave the unhappiness which had been inflicted, and in dying removed the obstacle which interfered with the legal union of the younger husband and the younger wife. At this point, however, the contrast in details was again resumed. Hastening home with the news of Mrs. Burman Radnor's death, Victor found Nataly dying, and in the agony of his grief and disappointment gave way to a mental derangement from which he never recovered. Lord Ormont, on the other hand, six months before his death accidentally encountered Matthew Weyburn in Switzerland, and, although shocked at the meeting with his wife's companion, gave him such courtly treatment as caused Aminta, when she heard of it, to say, "I thank heaven we know him to be one of the true noble men." Beyond this the reader learns little but that Aminta became a widow. Meredith leaves it to our imagination to decide whether she and Weyburn felt the need of a clergyman's blessing, or whether they regarded the approval of conscience as all-sufficient.

Closely related by similarity of teaching and by contrast of detail as "Lord Ormont and His Aminta" is with the novel which immediately preceded it, it is not less strongly, although perhaps less systematically, connected with still other works by Meredith. On the whole, the atmosphere is reminiscent of "Diana of the Crossways" and anticipatory of

"The Amazing Marriage," while in particular Aminta's ride to Steignton in some ways recalls the journey of the Duchess of Dewlap down to Bath in "The Tale of Chloe"; and the chapter entitled *A Marine Duet* carries back one's thought to Richard and Lucy meeting as Ferdinand and Miranda and to Wilfred and Sandra sitting beside Wilming Weir. Again the school life at Cuper's is strikingly suggestive of Harry Richmond's experience at Rippenger's; and certainly the interest taken by Weyburn and Eglett in English pugilism brings to mind Skepsey's main source of pleasure on one hand, and the chief incident of the Earl of Fleetwood's rather grim bridal trip on the other.

In the matter of character study, too, similar connections may be pointed out: Lady Charlotte Eglett in her indifference to Aminta's fate is like Mrs. Lovell in her unsympathetic attitude toward Dahlia Fleming; Mrs. Nargett Pagnel in her affected pronunciation and her insistence upon an assumed pedigree reminds a reader of the Countess de Saldar; and even Weyburn in his position as secretary to Lord Ormont recalls Evan Harrington in his relation to the Honorable Melville Jocelyn. All in all, therefore, despite a reduction in number of characters, and a change in matter of diction, "Lord Ormont and His Aminta" does not, as some critics would have us believe, stand apart from Meredith's other novels. A little reflection shows the threads of connection between it and them to be many and vital.

Before the story of Lord Ormont's married life

was reprinted as a book from the pages of *The Pall
Mall Magazine,* the firm of Charles Scribner's Sons
announced that arrangements had been made with
Mr. Meredith to publish, as the leading serial of
their magazine for 1895, a novel which he called "The
Amazing Marriage." The title suggested that
Meredith was still interested in problems presented
by relations existing between man and wife; and when
the story appeared, its readers found that the author
was studying the unhappy marriage from a new point
of view. It did not involve the question of the elderly
husband and the young wife as presented in "Lord
Ormont and His Aminta," or of the young husband
and the elderly wife as given in "One of Our Conquerors"; neither, as in both these novels, were matters
complicated by the introduction of a union obviously
suitable yet defiantly illegal. Instead, the conditions
assumed were not much unlike those in "Diana of
the Crossways." As there was no discrepancy in
age between Dan Merion's daughter and Augustus
Warwick, so there was none between Carinthia
Kirby and the Earl of Fleetwood; but there was such
a difference of taste in one case, and of taste and rank
in the other, as to bring about a separation of husband
and wife. Each of the husbands found himself at
last in a ridiculous position, with nobody but himself
to blame. Warwick drove Diana from him by fostering a foolish jealousy, Fleetwood deserted Carinthia
because he could not brook her birth and breed-
ing. Each of the men in time had his eyes opened
to his error, but only to find that the day for
repentance had gone by. When they would wil-

lingly have offered devoted allegiance to the women
whom they had scorned, they found themselves unable to awaken any sympathetic response.

Thus, in the main, the situations in the two novels
are parallel, and such differences as are to be sought,
must be looked for, not in details of plot, but in matters of character. The reader sees Augustus Warwick almost not at all, but thinks of him as a force
inferable only through his effect upon Diana, where-
as Lord Fleetwood, proud and erratic, cruel and
selfish, is almost never absent from the scene, and
stands out hardly less strongly than Sir Willoughby
Patterne or Nevil Beauchamp in Meredith's earlier
novels. A much more striking contrast in character study, however, is that existing between the
heroines of the two stories. Diana Warwick is always hasty and impulsive, the Countess of Fleetwood
is never other than calm and statuesque; one is at all
times nervously a-quiver, the other firmly self-con-
trolled; the former is restless, acquisitive, and passionate, the latter is patient, receptive, and restrained. This antithesis of character might be
carried out in almost endless detail; but convincing
evidence of the complete contrast between Diana
and Carinthia may be found in two citations from
the novels in which the women appear. In the
first Diana is pictured as walking in the woods
with Redworth three days before her marrage
to him.

"She was Irish; therefore intuitively decorous in
amatory challenges and interchanges. But she was
an impulsive woman, and foliage was thick around,

only a few small birds and heaven seeing; and peni-
tence and admiration sprang the impulse. It had
to be this or a burst of weeping:—she put a kiss upon
his arm. She had omitted to think that she was
dealing with a lover, a man of smothered fire, who
would be electrically alive to the act. Redworth had
his impulse. He kept it under—she felt the big
breath he drew in. . . . The impulse of each had
wedded; in expression and repression; her sensibility
told her of the stronger."

Beside this may be placed the passage in which
the Countess of Fleetwood took leave of her husband.
Towards the end of a long conversation in which he
strove to win her back to her old regard for him, she
silenced him in these words:

"'Do not beg of me, my lord. I have my brother
and my son. No more of husband for me! God
has given me a friend, too,—a man of humble heart,
my brother's friend, my dear Rebecca's husband.
He can take them from me; no one but God. See
the splendid sky we have.'—With these words she
barred the gates on him; at the same time she be-
stowed the frank look of an amiable face and brilliant
in the lively red of her exercise, in its bent-brow
curve along the forehead, out of the line of beauty,
touching, as her voice was, to make an undertone
of anguish swell an ecstasy. So he felt it, for his
mood was now the lover's."

Surely two things are made clear by these quotations: first, the marked contrast between the wom-
en; and then, perhaps of even more importance
than that, the strong moral basis which underlies

Meredith's assault upon the conventional marriage arrangements of the present day.

Aside from the fact that "The Amazing Marriage" is closely connected in one way and another with the three prose works which immediately preceded it and which with it constituted Meredith's main contribution to literature during a period of concentrated interest, it is a matter of some interest that his last piece of fiction should have elements gathered from every one of his earlier novels. To go back to Meredith's second period—the first of his novel writing—it is clear that Sir Austin Feverel's "Pilgrim's Scrip" bears very nearly the same relation to "The Ordeal of Richard Feverel" as Captain John Kirby's "Book of Maxims" to "The Amazing Marriage." Again, although Gower Woodseer in the latter work may, perhaps, be in some respects a study of Robert Louis Stevenson, he is none the less a reappearance of John Raikes from "Evan Harrington." That he is more complex and better bred, one cannot deny, but surely his worry about his shabby clothes, and his marriage with Madge Winch recall Raikes's care for his dilapidated hat, and his union with Polly Wheedle. From another point of view, that of love for nature, it is true that Woodseer has little in common with Raikes; but this only serves to bring him into relationship with another character drawn by Meredith—Vernon Whitford in "The Egoist." Further, the love which Carinthia and Chillon Kirby have for each other is much like that existing between Georgiana Ford and her half-brother Merthyr Powys, in both "Sandra Belloni" and "Vittoria"; and it may also be held, perhaps, that the elder Countess of Fleetwood by her refined cruelty more than once reminds the reader of the von Lenkenstein ladies in "Vittoria." Again, the Earl's return to Carinthia after the ill-treatment which he had dealt out to her, and his disappointment that her love was no longer his, both of course suggest the similar situation in "Rhoda Fleming."

On the other hand, it must be admitted that the connection between "The Amazing Marriage" and the first two novels of Meredith's third period is not very strongly pronounced, unless it may be thought that the elder Woodseer has something in common with Captain Jasper Welsh in "The Adventures of Harry Richmond," and that the Lady Arpington was drawn from the model which furnished Rosamund Culling in "Beauchamp's Career." But the Earl of Fleetwood, in his egoistical determination to keep his word at any cost, and in his eager desire to escape being made ridiculous, is beyond a doubt like Sir Willoughby Patterne in "The Egoist," and, therefore, also like Sigismund Alvan in "The Tragic Comedians." Finally, so far as minor characters are concerned, the Ladies Endor, Eldritch, and Cowry, as studies of gossips, are second only in importance to the inimitable Ladies Bussche and Culmer in Meredith's greatest work.

The more important lines of relationship between "The Amazing Marriage" and the earlier novels of Meredith's fourth period have already been pointed out in another connection; but it may be added in passing, that old John Kirby had the same reasons as had Lord Ormont for being dissatisfied with the treatment which his country accorded him, and that Carinthia's engagement, which was as hasty as Diana's to Warwick or as Aminta's to Ormont, was followed like theirs by a long period of unhappiness due, in keeping with Meredith's theories, to the lady's permitting her heart to act without the guidance of her reason.

This endeavor to show that Meredith's latest prose-work is to a great extent the product of forces resident in all his earlier novels, is not unlikely to give offence to many of his admirers; as also is the assumption persisted in, throughout this whole study, that a network of analogies and similarities binds his novels into what might be termed a fabric of firmest texture. Doubtless some readers of Meredith would be inclined to feel that not a few of the threads are pretty tenuous; yet all but those whose enthusiasm blurs their vision must see that, large and thickly settled as the world of Meredith's novels is, its chief inhabitants, if not all of one nation, are plainly all of one family. If it be objected that this proves too much in that it detracts from Meredith's fame rather than adds to it, the reply must be made that no one more quickly than Meredith himself would regret the existence of a renown built upon insecure foundations. "Lord, save me from my friends," has been the prayer of many a man before the present time, as it will be that of many another in time to come; and Meredith unfortunately has not been without a bitter knowledge of the need of that

petition. He is a great novelist—the greatest, let it
be conceded for the nonce, among English writers—
but he is not Shakespeare, as some admirers would
have us believe, nor perhaps, save now and then,
even Shakesperean, as others would strive to make
us admit. That he has firmly placed himself in no
mean niche in the temple of permanent literature,
only a blinded or a prejudiced observer can deny;
but to assert that he is one of that company to
which, as yet, only Homer and Dante and Shakespeare belong makes both Meredith and his undis-
criminating admirers ridiculous.

In general, of course, it is always hazardous to
prophesy the permanence of any man's fame; still,
from at least one point of view, it can be asserted
without hesitation that Meredith's name must be remembered as long as English literature shall endure.
Unlike most other writers whose real influence has
been felt only by some subsequent generation, Meredith has permeated the work of his contemporaries.
By this is meant that he has awakened such general
respect as to make him acceptable without envy to
the other novelists of at least his later years.   They
acknowledge his superiority, they look upon him as
unapproachable, they call him Master.   In evidence
of this, one may note the fact that in present dis-
cussions of novels the critic nearly always refers to
George Meredith as a standard of measurement.
Nor, indeed, is that the only use to which the
great writer and his novels are put.   It is, of course,
to be expected that Meredith's name would be
mentioned by Hall Caine in an article on "New

Watchwords in Fiction," and by Herbert Paul
in his "Apotheosis of the Novel under Queen Victoria"; but one is a bit startled at finding a quotation from "Diana of the Crossways" in an account of
"The Development of Decorative Electricity" and at
discovering a reference to its author in a discussion
of "The Humor of the Colored Supplement." And
allusions to Meredith abound elsewhere than upon
the pages of periodical publications. Thomas
Humphry Ward's "Reign of Queen Victoria" and
Justin McCarthy's "History of Our Own Times"
each of course gives a note of considerable length
upon Meredith; Robert Louis Stevenson's letters,
Oscar Wilde's essays, Algernon Charles Swinburne's
critical articles, and William Sharpe's biographies
of Rossetti and of Browning make frequent mention
of the man and his work; a rather unusual number of books have been dedicated to him by novelists,
critics, and poets; and finally, to mention only extremes, such writers as Richard Le Gallienne, the
latest of the æsthetes worth reckoning with, and
May Sinclair, the latest of the realists exhibiting
true promise, refer in their novels to the works of
George Meredith in the calm tone with which one
mentions the assured permanence of the writings
of Molière and Goethe. Thus it is plainly per-
ceivable that the literature of the present day is
embroidered—if the figure will be allowed—thickly
embroidered, indeed, with the name of Meredith,
with the titles of his novels, and even with extended
quotations from what he has written.

But a still closer inspection of recent literature

makes it clear that Meredith is woven into the very
texture of the fabric as well as embroidered upon it.
Towards the close of the nineteenth century, Mr. T.
H. S. Escott, in his "Personal Forces of the Period,"
asserted that the late James Payn "who, as publisher's reader, saw more of manuscript novels than most
people, declared that with the acceptance of Meredith as a favorite, there appeared a distinct improvement in the literary workmanship of the documents
with which he had to deal." Ten years later in
corroboration of this statement, Mrs. Craigie did
not hesitate to say that all the most worthy of living
English novelists, with the exception of Thomas
Hardy, were distinguished disciples of George Meredith. The remark was a trifle sweeping, perhaps;
yet it is indisputable that Meredith's influence has
been strongly and widely felt. Mr. Escott finds its
leavening effect in the Australian stories of Mrs.
Patchett Martin and of Mrs. Campbell Praed, in the
critical work of Mr. Edmund Gosse and of Mr.
H. D. Traill, and in both the prose and the verse of
William Ernest Henley. Others have gone so far as
to assert that nearly every recent story of adventure,
whether it be Stevenson's "Kidnapped," or Hope's
"Prisoner of Zenda," or Hewlett's "Forest Lovers,"
can be traced more or less directly to "The Adventures
of Harry Richmond"; while with as little discrimina-
tion the poems of James Thomson, the novels of
Robert Hichens, and the plays of Bernard Shaw
in their expression, their psychology, or their wit
are often assumed to be the aftermath of Meredith's first reaping. Such hypotheses break down

by their own weight; still, although at the risk of writing oneself among the makers of them, one feels tolerably safe in holding that many of the aphoristic utterances of Oscar Wilde would have remained unsaid, and more than one page in the work of George du Maurier and of Sarah Grand would never have reached the reader, had it not been for the novels of George Meredith. The school life depicted in "Peter Ibbetson" and in "The Martian," the beautiful Duchess of Towers, and the unfortunate Trilby O'Farrell are obviously the result of a close reading of Meredith's novels; and a mere mention of "The Heavenly Twins" or of "The Beth Book" should be a sufficient answer to the critic who regrets that literature does not possess any such adequate study of awakening womanhood as is found of adolescent boyhood in "The Ordeal of Richard Feverel."

Open to dispute as some of these specific claims may be, there can be but little doubt that Meredith has had a striking influence upon a considerable number of recent writers. As an example of the dominance which a great author sometimes exerts over a devoted disciple, one of the earlier works of Charles Marriott may be taken and subjected to close scrutiny. The table of contents of the novel entitled "The Column," in which Chapter XXVII is called "The Development of the Emotional Idea," and Chapter XXVIII "The Great Sweet Mother," shows a reader immediately, that he is in company with a scholar of the Meredith school. If, however, he is kindly disposed at the outset to give Mr. Mar-

riott the benefit of the doubt, he will find that his first
impressions are strengthened rather than weakened
when, as he turns to the story, he meets with such
characters as Caspar Gillies, and Johnnie Bargister,
and Daphne Hastings. If he does not see in the
cynicism of the first, an after study of Adrian Harley;
in the boyishness of the second, an attempted com-
posite portrait of Richard Feverel and Crossjay Patterne; and in the mingled simplicity and stateliness
of the last, a curious mosaic of Sandra Belloni, Clara
Middleton, Aminta Farrell, and Carinthia Kirby, he
must be wholly without a knowledge of Meredith's
best works. Nor does the discipleship end here.
Edward Hastings, who is "now and again letting
fall some concentrated paradox on the training of
the young," holds somewhat the same attitude
towards the world in general and towards his daughter in particular, as was characteristic of Sir Austin
in his relation to society and to his son Richard.
Gertrude Laffey, also, in her philanthropic enter-
prises may seem not unlike Lady Judith Felle; but
her real prototype is Mrs. Mount, for her temptation of Basil Waring is too much like one of the chapters in "The Ordeal of Richard Feverel" to leave a
reader very long in doubt of the connection. Finally,
so far as minor characters are concerned, Michael
Trigg, whom the village of Tregotha looked upon as
Daphne's watchdog, recalls Ripton Thompson in
his devotion to Lucy Feverel; and clearly Basil
Waring is Wilfred Pole transferred to a new field,
but still endowed with all his old time sentimentality, insincerity, and divided admiration.

Again in matters of situation and style, "The Column" plainly betrays the influence under which it was written. Caspar Gillies's band is no doubt Victor Radnor's orchestra borrowed from "One of Our Conquerors"; and Daphne's rending of the strings of her viola forcibly reminds one of old Belloni's breaking of the neck of his violin. Then, to go back in the plot, the betrothal in the shadow of the Grecian pillar, carries one first to the meeting at Wilming Weir and afterwards, although somewhat less surely, to Richard and Lucy in the woods near Raynham. Moreover, the conversation between Daphne and Basil about the name to be given their child, is strongly reminiscent of a similar passage in "The Amazing Marriage," as also are the changes in Daphne, when she becomes almost passionate in her motherhood, but at the same time loses the love which she once bore her boy's father.

These many scenes, furthermore, are presented in language which could only have been studied in Meredith's books. This is evident, not simply in that Mr. Marriott wrote—to choose at random—"The widening of the doors of her discretion was admirably gradual," but in that a comparison may frequently be set up between the two authors as when, for instance, one reads in "The Column," "The clamour of the sea-birds dropped to a gobbling murmur so absurdly suggestive of dinner conversation that the girl laughed aloud" and is immediately led to remember that Meredith wrote in "The Egoist" many years ago, "The downpour pressed down on the land with a great roar of eager gobbling, much like that

of the swine's trough fresh filled." It may also be
pointed out in passing that Mr. Marriott twice em-
ploys a device used by Meredith in the forty-third
chapter of "Rhoda Fleming" to make the reader
cognizant of the fact, that beneath a conversation
of no great depth, a real conflict of souls is going
on. Both Richard Le Gallienne and Paul Elmer
More have quoted the passage from Meredith for
entirely different reasons, although they unite in
praising it for its high realism; but Mr. Marriott's
unquestioning adoption of his master's method shows
him to be a disciple indeed.

Without seeking to inquire whether Mr. H. G.
Wells does actually show the influence of Meredith
in the opening chapters of "Love and Mr. Lewis-
ham," or whether the sources of "The Beloved Vaga-
bond," by W. G. Locke, may really be sought
in "The Adventures of Harry Richmond"; without
undertaking to do more than notice the statement of
Mr. W. R. Nicoll that both George Gissing and
Thomas Hardy openly admitted that but for the encouragement which they received from Mr. Meredith as publisher's reader, they would never have
devoted themselves to writing, one may feel safe in
assuming that the thoroughness with which Meredith and his work are embedded in present-day
literature, will prevent his being ignored by any
future student, however distant the point of view,
or however cursory the glance. Such immortality
is, in the literary world, but little different from
that in the spiritual world, as suggested by George
Eliot in the poem, "O, may I join the Choir

Invisible!" The woman's teaching is, that having lived, we continue to exist until the end of time, by virtue of the influence which we exert over those whom we meet, and which they extend to those who follow them. Unsatisfactory as such immortality seems to the many, it is none the less based upon an assured scientific fact, and is, therefore, indisputably certain. Admitting then, for the moment, all that the most adverse critics have said against Meredith, that his style is insufferably bad, that his method could not be conceivably worse, that his characters are wholly impossible, and that his mission is foolishly vain, no one, whether admirer or not, can deny that he is assured of a position neither insignificant nor inconspicuous.

But to not a few of his readers, Meredith seems deserving of much more than that kind of immortality which rests upon the mention of his name by other authors and upon the formative influence obviously exerted by his writings. The knowledge of what must be is greatened in the minds of many by faith in what will be: and when that faith is put to trial, they are far from feeling that it is without a substantial basis in reason. Still, if such have learned anything from their reading of the man whom they delight to honor, they hesitate to name his absolute place. Whatever the impulse of the heart, they know that it should be tempered by the working of the brain; and they therefore do not undertake to assert more than that Meredith must be regarded as no unworthy companion of the greatest English novelists. If the sneer of the critic accuses them of having but faint confidence in their belief, they are not betrayed into fruitless wrangling or loud defence. Serenely unmoved, they let Meredith speak for himself. Surely no just man can find fault with the intermingling of honest pride and sincere humility behind that sonnet, to which Meredith, writing in his middle age, gave the name of "Internal Harmony."

> "Assured of worthiness we do not dread
> Competitors; we rather give them hail
> And greeting in the lists where we may fail:
> Must, if we bear an aim beyond the head!
> My betters are my masters: purely fed
> By their sustainment I likewise shall scale
> Some rocky steps between the mount and vale;
> Meanwhile the mark I have and I will wed.
> So that I draw the breath of finer air,
> Station is naught, nor footways laurel-strewn,
> Nor rivals tightly belted for the race.
> Good speed to them! My place is here or there;
> My pride is that among them I have place:
> And thus I keep this instrument in tune."

Truly such calm self-analysis explains the remarkable patience with which Meredith awaits the decision of the wise years. If in the words of Lowell,

> "Some innate weakness there must be
> In him who condescends to victory
> Such as the present gives and cannot wait
>   Safe in himself as in a fate,"

Meredith through the absence of such weakness, shows himself endowed with noble strength and

manly power.   A prophet, it has been said, is not
without honor save in his own country; and with
equal truth, it might have been added, save in his
own time.   It is the privilege of Meredith's friends,
therefore, to keep silence; for looking back from the
present through the long period of his activity, and
realizing once more the calm confidence which enabled him to go on with his work in the face of
indifference, opposition and contempt, we well
may say:

> "He knew to bide his time
> And can his fame abide."

A LIST
OF THE CHARACTERS IN
GEORGE MEREDITH'S NOVELS
WITH AN ENUMERATION OF
THE CHAPTERS IN WHICH
THEY APPEAR

French, German, Spanish, and Italian names beginning
with particles of relationship are entered under the letter
with which the chief member of the compound begins, thus:

D'AUFFRAY, AGNES, follows ATTENBURY, LADY

DE COL, MARQUIS, follows COGGLESBY, TOM

VON CREFELDT, BARONESS, follows CREEDMORE, LORD

A LIST OF CHARACTERS

A

ABARAK—Shaving of Shagpat: XII, XVI-XX, XXIII, XXIV.

ABNER—Rhoda Fleming: XLII.

ABNER, ARTHUR—Lord Ormont and His Aminta: II-IV, XI, XVI, XXVI.

ABNETT, JOSHUA—Lord Ormont and His Aminta: XXI.

ABRANE, CAPTAIN—Amazing Marriage: VII-XII, XV-XVII, XX, XXIII, XXVI, XXVIII, XXXIV, XXXV, XXXVIII-XLI, XLV.

ABRANE, RUFUS — Amazing Marriage: II, III.

ABT, HEINRICH—Farina: I.

ADDERWOOD, LORD — Lord Ormont and His Aminta: III, VI, VIII, XI-XIII, XV, XXI, XXIII, XXV, XXIX.

ADDICOTE, GILBERT — Lord Ormont and His Aminta: XIII.

ADELINE—Adventures of Harry Richmond: VII.

AENNCHEN — Adventures of Harry Richmond: XV, XXIV, XXV, XXVII, XXXI, XXXIII, XXXV, XLVIII.

AENNCHEN — Vittoria: XIII, XXVII, XXXIX, XLII, XLIV.

AEPFELMANN, HANS—Farina: I.

AKLIS—Shaving of Shagpat: XIV.

AKLIS, SONS OF—Shaving of Shagpat: V, VI, XIV, XVII, XX, XXIV.

AKLIS, BRIDES OF—Shaving of Shagpat: XIII, XIV, XX.

ALFRED, LORD—Beauchamp's Career: XLII.

ALMERYLE—Shaving of Shagpat: II.

ALONZO—see CAMWELL, AUGUSTUS.

ALPHONSE—Adventures of Harry Richmond: IV, XXIII-XXV, XXXVIII, XXXIX, XLIV, LIII.

ALTKNOPFCHEN, DAME—Farina: II.

ALTON, LORD—Adventures of Harry Richmond: XXXIX, XL, L.

ALVAN, SIGISMUND — Tragic Comedians: Introduction, I-XIX.

AMALIA, DUCHESS—Vittoria: XI-XIV, XIX, XX, XXVII, XXVIII, XXX, XXXVI, XXXVII, XXXIX, XL, XLII, XLIV, XLV.

AMELIA—Egoist: XIV.

AMMIANI, COUNT CARLO—Vittoria: I-VIII, X, XII-XXV, XXVII-XLVI.

AMMIANI, CARLO MERTHYR—Vittoria: Epilogue.

AMMIANI, COUNTESS MARCELLINA—Vittoria: XVI, XVIII, XIX, XXI, XXIII, XXIV, XXVII, XXX, XXXI, XXXIII-XXXIX, XLI-XLIII.

AMMIANI, GENERAL PAOLO—Vittoria: XIV-XVI, XXX, XXXI, XLIII.

ANDREAS—Vittoria: XXVII.

D'ANDREUZE, COUNTESS JULIA—Amazing Marriage: II.

ANDREWS, ELIZABETH—see BERRY, ELIZABETH.

ANNA, AUNT—Rhoda Fleming: XVII-XX, XXIII, XLIV.

ANTON—Amazing Marriage: V-VII.

D'ARCI—Vittoria: XXXI.

AREEP—Shaving of Shagpat: XXII.

ARLINGTON—One of Our Conquerors: IX, XXV, XXXVI, XXXIX.

ARMETT, MISS—Adventures of Harry Richmond: xxxix.

ARMSTRONG, ROBERT — see ECCLES, ROBERT.

ARNOLDO—Vittoria: xxi.

ARONLEY, LORD—see ROMFREY, EVERARD, and ROMFREY, CRAVEN.

ARPINGTON, LADY—Amazing Marriage: ii, xii, xx-xxviii, xxxvi, xxxvii, xl, xli, xlv-xlvii.

ASHWORTH — Adventures of Harry Richmond: vi.

D'ASOLA, VIOLETTA — see D'ISORELLA, COUNTESS.

ASPER, CONSTANCE—Diana of the Crossways: xv-xvii, xix, xxi-xxiii, xxvi, xxvii, xxix, xxxv-xxxvii, xxxix.

ASRAC, EBN—Shaving of Shagpat: ii.

ASSUNTA—Vittoria: xxviii.

ASWARAK, VIZIER—Shaving of Shagpat: ii.

ATTENBURY, LADY—Ordeal of Richard Feverel: iv.

D'AUFFRAY, AGNES — Beauchamp's Career: xxiii-xxv, xl, xlii, xliii.

D'AUFFRAY, M.—Beauchamp's Career: xxiii, xxiv,

AUSTIN, SEYMOUR — Beauchamp's Career: xvi-xxii, xxvi, xxviii, xxxii, xxxvii, xxxix, xlv-xlviii, liv.

AVERST, EDITH—One of Our Conquerors: xxvi, xxxv.

AVERST, SIR JOHN—One of Our Conquerors: xxvi.

AVONLEY, LORD—see ROMFREY, CRAVEN.

AZAWOOL—Shaving of Shagpat: xxi-xxiii.

AZROOKA—Shaving of Shagpat: xxii.

B

BAERENS, GOTTFRIED—Case of General Ople and Lady Camper: i, vi, viii.

BAERENS, MRS.—Case of General Ople and Lady Camper: i, vi, viii.

BAGARAG, SHIBLI—Shaving of Shagpat: i, iii, v-xxi, xxiii, xxiv.

BAGENHOPE — Adventures of Harry Richmond: liii.

BAIRAM, DR. BENJAMIN—Ordeal of Richard Feverel: xviii, xxv, xlv.

BAKER—Adventures of Harry Richmond: iii.

BAKEWELL, MRS.—Ordeal of Richard Feverel: vi, xi, xxv, xxvi.

BAKEWELL, TOM—Ordeal of Richard Feverel: iii-xiii, xx-xxvi, xxviii-xxxi, xxxiv, xxxvii-xxxix, xliii, xliv.

BALDERINI, AGOSTINO—Vittoria: i-viii, x, xii, xv, xvi, xviii-xxi, xxxi, xxxv, xxxix, xlii-xlvi.

BANDELMEYER, GREGORIUS —Adventures of Harry Richmond: xxxii.

BANDINELLI, GIULIO — Vittoria: i-v, xxxvi, xl-xliv.

BANNERBRIDGE, CHARLES ADOLPHUS — Adventures of Harry Richmond: ii-iv, xix, xl, li, lii.

BANNERBRIDGE, MISS—Adventures of Harry Richmond: ii, ix, xliv.

BANNISTER, MRS.—One of Our Conquerors: xxiii.

BANTAM, THE—see JINKSON, GILES.

BARBARA, LADY — Beauchamp's Career: xlii.

BARCLAY—Egoist: xix, xxv, xxvii, xxix.

BARCLAY, COLONEL—Rhoda Fleming: xxi, xxii.

BARCOP, MRS.—Case of General Ople and Lady Camper: ii, iv, vi, vii.

BÄRENLIEB—Farina: xiii.

BARLEY, SUSAN—see DEWLAP, DUCHESS OF.

BARMBY, REVEREND SEPTIMUS—One of Our Conquerors: iv, viii, ix, xi, xiv-xviii, xxi, xxii, xxiv, xxv, xxvii-xxxiii, xxxvi-xxxix, xli, xlii.

BARNES—Diana of the Cross-ways: XLIII.

BARNES, MR.—Evan Harrington: I, II, VII.

BARNSHED — Adventures of Harry Richmond: VI.

BARRETT, LADY—Sandra Belloni: X, LV.

BARRETT, SIR JUSTINIAN—Sandra Belloni: X, LV.

BARRETT, PERCIVAL—Sandra Belloni: LV.

BARRETT, PURCELL—Sandra Belloni: VII-X, XIV-XVII, XIX, XXI-XXIII, XXIX, XXXI, XXXIII, XXXIV, XXXVII-XL, XLIII, LV-LVII.

BARRINGTON, LADY—Evan Harrington: I.

BARRINGTON, MRS. — Evan Harrington: XXII.

BARTHOLOMEW, PETER—Sandra Belloni: XI.

BARTLETT—Adventures of Harry Richmond: XLIII.

BARTLETT—Diana of the Cross-ways: XII, XL.

BARTLETT—Egoist: XVII.

BASKELETT, CAPTAIN CECIL —Beauchamp's Career: II, XI, XIV, XIX-XXII, XXVI, XXVIII-XXXII, XXXIV, XXXVI, XXXIX, XL-XLV, XLVIII, LII, LV.

BASKELETT, SIR JOHN AND LADY—Beauchamp's Career: XXXIII.

BATTISTA—Vittoria: X.

BAYNES — Sandra Belloni: XXXIV, XXXVII.

BAYRUFFLE, HONORABLE MRS.—Sandra Belloni: XXXIV, XXXVII, LVI.

BEAMISH, BEAU — Tale of Chloe: I-VIII, X.

BEAN, DR.—Rhoda Fleming: XIX.

BEATRICE—Lord Ormont and His Aminta: III.

BEAUCHAMP, ELIZABETH MARY—Beauchamp's Career: II, III, XVI, XXVI, XXVIII, XXXII, XXXVII, XXXIX.

BEAUCHAMP, LADY EMILY—Beauchamp's Career: II.

BEAUCHAMP, NEVIL—Beauchamp's Career: I-LVI.

BEAUCHAMP,COLONEL RICHARD—Beauchamp's Career: II, XXVI, XLIX.

BEAUCHAMP, ROSAMOND—see CULLING, ROSAMOND.

BEAUMARIS, LORD—Adventures of Harry Richmond: XXXIX.

BEAZLEY, MR.—Ordeal of Richard Feverel: XVI, XXVI.

BEL, AUNT—see CURRENT, ISABELLE.

BELFIELD, DUKE OF—Evan Harrington: XIV, XVI, XVIII, XIX, XXI, XXII, XXIV, XXIX-XXXIII, XXXVII, XXXIX, XLI.

BELLONI, EMILIA ALESSANDRA, also known as VITTORIA CAMPA—Sandra Belloni: I-XV, XVII-LIX. Vittoria: II-XLIV, Epilogue.

BELLONI, GUISEPPE—Sandra Belloni: V, VI, XXV, XXVI, XXX, XXXII, XXXIV, XXXIX, XL, XLVIII, L, LII, LIV.

BELLONI, MRS.—Sandra Belloni: VI, XXXIX, XLVII-L, LII, LIX. Vittoria: V, VIII, XI, XIII, XIV, XX, XXVII, XXXV.

BELMARAÑA, COUNT — Evan Harrington: III, IX.

BELTHAM, DOROTHY — Adventures of Harry Richmond: I, III, IV, VII-XI, XIV, XVIII-XX, XXII, XXXVI-XXXVIII, XL, XLIII, XLIV, XLVII, XLVIII, L-LVI.

BELTHAM, SQUIRE HARRY LEPEL—Adventures of Harry Richmond: I-IV, VI-IX, XI, XII, XIV, XVIII-XX, XXII, XXV, XXVII, XXX, XXXVI-XLI, XLIII, XLIV, XLVI-LIII, LVI.

BELTHAM, MRS.—Adventures of Harry Richmond: IX, XXIII, XLI.

BELTUS, LADY—Lord Ormont and His Aminta: XXIII.

BENCH, WALTER—Lord Ormont and His Aminta: XII.

BENJAMIN—One of Our Conquerors: IV.

BENLEW, ROBERT I—Lord Ormont and His Aminta: XXII.

BENLEW, ROBERT II—Lord Ormont and His Aminta: XXII, XXVI, XXX.

BENLEW, ELIZABETH EG-
LETT—Lord Ormont and His
Aminta: XXII.

BENLOMIK—Vittoria: X.

BENNETT, BURLEY — Evan
Harrington: XXII.

BENSON—Ordeal of Richard
Feverel: IV, V, VII, X, XIII, XX-
XXIV, XXXI, XXXIII, XXXIV,
XLIV.

BEPPO—Sandra Belloni: LIX.
Vittoria: III-VI, XI-XV, XXVI-
XXVIII, XXXI, XXXII, XXXV,
XXXVII-XXXIX, XLII, XLIV-XLVI.

BERNARDUS, FATHER—Vit-
toria: XXVII, XXVIII.

BERRY, ELIZABETH — Ordeal
of Richard Feverel: I, XXVI,
XXVIII-XXXII, XXXIV, XXXVII-
XLI, XLIII-XLV.

BERRY, MARTIN—Ordeal of
Richard Feverel: XXI, XXII,
XXV, XXVI, XXVIII, XXX, XXXVII,
XXXIX-XLI, XLIII, XLIV.

BERTHA OF BÖHMEN—Far-
ina: VI.

BHANAVAR THE BEAUTIFUL
—Shaving of Shagpat: I, II, X.

BIGGOT, TOM — Beauchamp's
Career: IV.

BIGNET, MADAME BLANCHE
—Adventures of Harry Richmond: XXXII.

BILLET, SIMON—Rhoda Flem-
ing: XX.

BILLING—Rhoda Fleming: XVIII,
XXIV.

BILLING, MRS.—Rhoda Flem-
ing: XXIV.

BILTON, STEPHEN — Rhoda
Fleming: XVII-XXI.

BLACHINGTON, ADOLPHUS—
One of Our Conquerors: XVII.

BLACHINGTON, LADY ROD-
WELL—One of Our Conquer-
ors: XVII, XX-XXII, XXIV, XXVII,
XXXVI.

BLACHINGTON, SIR ROD-
WELL—One of Our Conquer-
ors: XIV, XX-XXII, XXIV, XXVII,
XXXVI.

BLAIZE, GILES — Ordeal of
Richard Feverel: II-XI, XV, XXII,
XXIII, XXVI, XXVIII-XXX, XXXIV,
XLI, XLIII, XLV.

BLAIZE, TOM—Ordeal of Richard Feverel: I, IX, XX, XXII-
XXVI, XXVIII, XXXIV.

BLANCOVE, ALGERNON—
Rhoda Fleming: I, V-IX, XII,
XIV-XVIII, XX-XXXIV, XXXVII,
XXXVIII, XLII-XLV, XLVII, XLVIII.

BLANCOVE, EDWARD—Rhoda
Fleming: I, V-XII, XVI, XVIII, XX-
XXIX, XXXI-XXXVIII, XLI, XLIII-
XLVIII.

BLANCOVE, SQUIRE—Rhoda
Fleming: I, VI, VIII, XV, XVIII,
XXVI, XXXII, XXXVIII, XLI.

BLANCOVE, SIR WILLIAM—
Rhoda Fleming: VI, VIII, XI, XII,
XVI, XXI, XXII, XXV, XXVI,
XXXI-XXXIV, XXXVI, XXXVII,
XLII, XLVIII.

BLANDISH, LADY EMMELINE
—Ordeal of Richard Feverel: I,
IV, XI-XVI, XX, XXII-XXV, XXVIII,
XXX, XXXIII-XXXVIII, XL, XLI,
XLIV, XLV.

BLASS-GESELL—Farina: XI, XII.

BLATHENOY, JACOB—One of
Our Conquerors: IX, XIII, XX-
XXII, XXIV, XXV, XXX, XXXI.

BLATHENOY, MRS.—One of
Our Conquerors: XVII, XX-XXII,
XXIV, XXV, XXIX-XXXII.

BOB—Evan Harrington: XIII.

BOBINIKENE, M.—One of Our
Conquerors: XIX, XLI.

BODDY—Adventures of Harry
Richmond: XLVIII, LIV.

BOLLOP—Ordeal of Richard Feverel: III.

BOLTON, LADY BETTY—see
EDBURY, MARQUISE OF.

BOLTON, MRS.—see SWEET-
WINTER, MABEL.

BONNER, JULIANA — Evan
Harrington: XIV-XIX, XXI, XXIII-
XXV, XXVII, XXIX-XXXII, XXXV-
XLIII, XLV.

BONNER, MR.—Evan Harring-
ton: XXVII, XXXI.

BONNER, MRS.—Evan Har-
rington: IX, XIV-XVII, XIX, XXV,
XXVII, XXIX, XXXII-XXXIV,
XXXVII-XL, XLIII.

BOOLP—Shaving of Shagpat: II.

BOON, JONATHAN—Lord Or-
mont and His Aminta: XIX.

BOOTLBAC—Shaving of Shag-
pat: XXI-XXIV.

BOROLICK, ALGY — Beau-
champ's Career: XX, XXI

BOULBY, DICK—Rhoda Flem-
ing: XVIII.

BOULBY, HARRY — Rhoda Fleming: XVIII, XIX, XLVI.

BOULBY, MRS.—Rhoda Fleming: XVIII-XXI, XXIII, XLIV, XLVI.

BOUTHOIN, DR.—One of Our Conquerors: XIX, XXI, XXIV, XXVIII, XXXVI.

BOYLE & LUCKWORT, CHEMISTS—One of Our Conquerors: XIII, XVIII.

BOYNE, MR.—Rhoda Fleming: III, VI.

BRADDOCK, THORPE & SIMNEL, SOLICITORS—Diana of the Crossways: XIII, XIV, XVII, XXIII, XXIX, XXXVII.

BRAILSTONE, LORD—Amazing Marriage: III, XV-XVII, XXIII, XXIV, XXVIII, XXXIV, XXXIX, XLI, XLIII-XLVII.

BRAINTOP — Sandra Belloni: XXIV-XXVI, XXIX, XXXI-XXXV, XXXVII, XXXVIII, LIII, LIV, LIX.

BRANCIANI, COUNT—Sandra Belloni: L-LII; Vittoria: XXVI.

BRANCIANI, COUNTESS—Sandra Belloni: L-LII.

BRANKSBURNE, MARY—Ordeal of Richard Feverel: XXXII.

BRAWNLEY, MR.—Ordeal of Richard Feverel: VI.

BRAYDER, HONORABLE PETER—Ordeal of Richard Feverel: XXXIV-XXXVI, XXXIX, XLIII.

BREEKS, MRS.—Sandra Belloni: VIII, XI.

BRIDES OF AKLIS—see AKLIS, BRIDES OF.

BRIDGENORTH—Diana of the Crossways: XXVI.

BRIDGES, MRS.—Diana of the Crossways: XII.

BRISBY—Adventures of Harry Richmond: XLII.

BRISBY—Diana of the Crossways: VIII, XI.

BRISK, REVEREND — Beauchamp's Career: XVII.

BROADMEAD, FARMER — Evan Harrington: XI-XJII, XVII.

BRONCINI, COUNT—Vittoria: IX, XXVI.

BROWNSON, JOHNNY—Beauchamp's Career: XIX.

BROWNY—see FARREL, AMINTA.

BRUNHILD—Farina: II.

BULSTED, GREGORY—Adventures of Harry Richmond: IX, X, XIX, XXXVI-XXXVIII.

BULSTED, CAPTAIN WILLIAM—Adventures of Harry Richmond: IX, X, XV, XVIII-XX, XXXVII-XLI, XLIII, XLVI, XLIX, LIII, LV, LVI.

BULSTED, MRS. WILLIAM—see RIPPENGER, JULIA.

BURDOCK, WILL—Sandra Belloni: XI.

BURGIN, MR.—Adventures of Harry Richmond: XXIII, XXXVII, LIII.

BURLEY — Evan Harrington: XVIII, XXI.

BURNLEY, LORD ALFRED—Beauchamp's Career: XXVI, XLII.

BURT, MR.—Rhoda Fleming: III, VI.

BURT, MARY—Rhoda Fleming: I.

BUSBY, LORD—Diana of the Crossways: XXX.

BUSBY, ROBERT—Diana of the Crossways: XXX.

BUSRAC, EBN — Shaving of Shagpat: IV.

BUSSHE, LADY—Egoist: II-V, XVII, XXV, XXIX, XXXIV-XXXVII, XLI, XLIII-L.

BUSSHE, LORD JOHN—Egoist: XVII.

BUTTERMORE, REVEREND GROSEMAN—One of Our Conquerors: VII, XIII, XIV, XXIX, XXXI, XXXVI, XXXIX, XL.

BUXLEY, EDWARD—Sandra Belloni: I, II, XV-XVII, XXVII, XXIX, XXXI, XLII.

BUXTON, DR.—Lord Ormont and His Aminta: XIV.

BYSTOP—Adventures of Harry Richmond: VI.

C

CADDIS, MR.—One of Our Conquerors: xx, xxi, xxxvi.

CADWALLADER — Amazing Marriage: xxxiv.

CALLET, MADAME ARMANDINE—One of Our Conquerors: iii, viii, ix, xiii, xiv, xxi, xxii, xxxvi, xxxix.

CALLIANI, GIULIO—Lord Ormont and His Aminta: xii, xxx.

CAMERON, MRS.—Sandra Belloni: l.

CAMILLA—Vittoria: xvii, xix-xxi, xxii, xxv, xxxi, xxxii, xl.

CAMPA, VITTORIA—see BELLONI, EMILIA; ALESSANDRA.

CAMPER, LADY ANGELA—Case of General Ople and Lady Camper: i-viii.

CAMPER, SIR SCROPE—Case of General Ople and Lady Camper: i, ii.

CAMWELL, AUGUSTUS—Tale of Chloe: ii, iv, v-viii, x.

CANTOR, LADY—One of Our Conquerors: xxvi.

CAPES, MR.—Egoist: xxxv.

CAPES, SIR JOHN — Rhoda Fleming: xvi, xxi, xxii, xxiv.

CAPPERSTON, SIR WALTER —Diana of the Crossways: xiv.

CARDI, PIETRO—Vittoria: xv, xxix.

CAREY, LORD AND LADY— Rhoda Fleming: xxii.

CARIGNY—Adventures of Harry Richmond: xxxii, xliv.

CARLING, MR.—One of Our Conquerors: iv, vi, vii, xii, xiii, xix, xxi, xxii, xxx, xxxi, xxxvi, xxxix, xli.

CARLING, MRS.—One of Our Conquerors: vii.

CARLO ALBERTO — see CHARLES ALBERT.

CARMINE, LADY—One of Our Conquerors: xx, xxi.

CARNISCHI—Vittoria: xxxi.

CARPENDIKE, MR. — Beauchamp's Career: xix, xx.

CARR, LORD ALONZO—Adventures of Harry Richmond: xlvii.

CARRINGTON, LOUISA—Evan Harrington: xiv, xix-xxi, xxiv, xxvii, xxx-xxxii, xxxvi, xxxvii, xli.

CARSTAIRS—Lord Ormont and His Aminta: xxiii, xxix.

CARTHEW, MRS. — Amazing Marriage: xiii, xiv, xx.

CASELDY, SIR MARTIN—Tale of Chloe: ii-x.

CATHAIRN, LADY—Diana of the Crossways: xx.

CATKIN—One of Our Conquerors: iv, xiv, xv, xviii, xx, xxii, xxv, xxxiii, xxxvi, xl.

CATMAN—Adventures of Harry Richmond: v, vi.

CAUSITT, DR. PETER—Lord Ormont and His Aminta: xvi.

CAVELY, MARTHA—House on the Beach: i-xii.

CAWTHORNE, DR.—Amazing Marriage: ii, iii.

CHARLES—Evan Harrington: v.

CHARLES ALBERT, KING OF SARDINIA—Vittoria: i, ii, iv, v, viii, xxx-xxxii, xxxiv-xxxviii, xli-xlv.

CHARNER, DANIEL—Amazing Marriage: xlv.

CHASSEDIANE, JENNIE—Adventures of Harry Richmond: xxxii, xxxviii, xxxix, xli-xliv.

CHAUNTER — Adventures of Harry Richmond: vi.

CHECCO—Vittoria: x, xvi.

CHERSON, MRS. FERDINAND —Diana of the Crossways: xxvii.

CHESSINGTON—Egoist: xxxiv.

CHIALLO, CAPTAIN—Lord Ormont and His Aminta: xii, xxv.

CHICKLEY, MRS.—Sandra Belloni: xxv.

CHIEF, THE—Vittoria: i-vi, viii, x-xii, xv-xviii, xxiv, xxvii, xxx, xxxv-xxxvii, xl, xliii, xliv.

CHILLINGWORTH, LADY CHARLOTTE — Sandra Belloni: x, xiv, xv, xviii, xix, xxiii, xxvi, xxviii, xxx-xxxvii, xl, xlvi, l, lii-liv, lvi-lviii.

CHIPPS, MR.—Sandra Belloni: XXI, XXII.

CHIUSE, VINCENTINO—Lord Ormont and His Aminta: XII.

CHLOE—see MARTINSWARD CATHERINE.

CHRIMHILD—Farina: II.

CHUMP, MARTHA—Sandra Belloni: IV, V, VII, XIV-XVII, XIX, XXI-XXIII, XXVII, XXIX, XXXI-XXXVII, XLII, LIII-LVI, LIX.

CHUMP, MR.—Sandra Belloni: XV, XVI, XIX, XXIV, XXXII, XXXIII, XLII, LIV.

CLANCONAN, LORD—One of Our Conquerors: XXVII, XXIX-XXXI, XXXV.

CLÉMENCE, MADAME—Amazing Marriage: XI.

CLIFFORD, DR. — Ordeal of Richard Feverel: XII, XX, XXIII-XXV.

CLUNGEON, JIMMY—Tale of Chloe: V.

COGGLESBY, ANDREW—Evan Harrington: III-V, VII-IX, XVIII-XXXI, XXXIII, XXXVII-XLI, XLIV, XLVI, XLVII.

COGGLESBY, MRS. HARRIET —Evan Harrington: III, V, VII-IX, XIII, XIV, XIX, XX, XXV; XXVII, XXXVIII, XL, XLI, XLIV, XLVI, XLVII.

COGGLESBY, TOM—Evan Harrington: V, VIII, XI, XII, XVII, XVIII, XXV-XXXII, XXXVI, XXXVII, XXXIX, XLI, XLIV, XLVI, XLVII.

DE COL, DUCHESSE DA ROSTA—Evan Harrington: XXI.

DE COL, MARQUISE—Evan Harrington: IX.

COLEWORT—One of Our Conquerors: XLI.

COLLESTON, MARQUIS OF— Lord Ormont and His Aminta: XVI.

COLLETT—Lord Ormont and His Aminta: I, XVIII, XXIV, XXVI, XXVIII, XXX.

COLLETT, SELINA—Lord Ormont and His Aminta: I, VI, X, XIV, XVIII, XXI, XXIII-XXVI, XXVIII, XXX.

COLLETT, MRS.—Lord Ormont and His Aminta: XXVII, XXVIII, XXX.

COLUMELLI — Amazing Marriage: XXVIII, XXXIX, XLVII.

COMBLEMAN, ADMIRAL— Evan Harrington: I, III, IX, XIII.

CONLEY, FARMER—Evan Harrington: XXX.

CONLEY, MISSES—Evan Harrington: XXX, XXXI.

CONNING, MARIA—Evan Harrington: XIII, XIV, XIX, XXI, XXIX, XXXIII, XXXVII.

CONSTANTINE, PRINCE— Tragic Comedians: I.

CONRAD, KAISER — Farina: XIV.

COOP, JANE — Lord Ormont and His Aminta: XII.

COOP, MARTHA MARY—Lord Ormont and His Aminta: XII.

COOP, ROBERT—Lord Ormont and His Aminta: XII.

COPLEYS, THE—Sandra Belloni: III, XIX, XXI, XXVII.

COPPING, SQUIRE AND MRS. —Evan Harrington: XXII.

COPPING, TOM—Evan Harrington: XIII, XX.

CORBY, SIR MEESON—Amazing Marriage: VII-IX, XI, XII, XX, XXIII, XXIV, XXXV, XXXIX, XLI, XLV, XLVII.

CORFE, COLONEL—One of Our Conquerors: XX, XXI, XXXVI.

CORMYN, DR. JOHN AND MRS. —One of Our Conquerors: IV, VIII, IX, XI, XVIII, XX, XXII, XXIV, XXV, XXXVI-XXXVIII, XL, XLI.

CORNEY, DR.—Egoist: X, XV, XIX, XXVI, XXVII, XXXII, XLII, XLIV,-XLVII, L.

CORTE, UGO—Vittoria: I-V, VII, XII, XVIII, XXX, XXXI, XXXIV, XXXVI, XL-XLIV, XLVI.

COUGHAM—Beauchamp's Career: XVI, VIII-XX.

COURTNEY, MISS—Diana of the Crossways: XXVIII.

COWRY, LADY—Amazing Marriage: XII, XXIII, XXVIII, XLV.

COXWELL,—Evan Harrington: VII, XXVI.

CRANE, LORD AND LADY— Diana of the Crossways: XIV.

CREEDMORE, LORD—Diana of the Crossways: XV, XIX.

VON CREFELDT, BARONESS LUCIE — Tragic Comedians: II, V, VII-XV, XVII, XIX.

CRESSETT, COUNTESS FANNY—Amazing Marriage: I-V, XII, XIII, XV, XXIII, XXV, XXVI, XXIX, XXXV, XXXIX, XLIV.

CRESSETT, JR.—Amazing Marriage: IX, XI, XII, XXXV, XXXIX, XLI, XLIII, XLVI, XLVII.

CRESSETT, EARL OF—Amazing Marriage: I-III.

VON CRESTOW, COUNT AND COUNTESS—Tragic Comedians: II, V.

CRICKLEDON—House on the Beach: II-V, VII, XI.

CRICKLEDON, MRS.—House on the Beach: III-VIII, XI.

DE CROISNEL, COMTE CRESNES—Beauchamp's Career: V-IX, XI, XXIII-XXV, XXXIV, XXXVII, XLI.

DE CROISNEL, RENÉE—Beauchamp's Career: V-XI, XIII, XIX-XXVI, XXX, XXXII, XXXIV, XXXVII, XXXIX-XLVI, XLVIII, LI, LII, LV.

DE CROISNEL, CAPTAIN ROLAND—Beauchamp's Career: V-X, XXIII-XXVI, XXXIV, XXXVII, XXXIX-XLIII, XLV, LV.

CROOKLYN, PROFESSOR — Egoist: XXVII, XXIX, XXX-XXXVIII, XLI,

CROOM, JACOB—Egoist: XXVI.

CROYSTON, LADY — Beauchamp's Career: LV.

CROYSTON, LORD — Beauchamp's Career: XXXII, XXXVII, LV.

CRUCHI, JACOPO—Vittoria: XXV, XXVI, XXVIII, XLVI.

CRUCHI, ROSETTA—Vittoria: XXV.

CRUMMINS, NED—House on the Beach: II.

CUFF, COLONEL EVANS—Beauchamp's Career: XI.

CULBRETT, STUKELY—Beauchamp's Career: I-III, XI, XIV, XVII, XX, XXI, XXVI, XXXIII, XXXV-XXXVIII, XLIII, XLIV, XLIX, LV.

CULLING, MR.—Beauchamp's Career: I, II, IX, X, XIV.

CULLING, ROSAMUND—Beauchamp's Career: I-V, VIII, IX, XI-XIV, XVII, XXII, XXV, XXVI, XXVIII, XXX, XXXIII-XXXVII, XXXIX-XLV, XLVIII-LIII, LV, LVI.

DE CULME, LADY—Lord Ormont and His Aminta: XI-XIII.

CULMER, LADY—Egoist: II, V, X, XXIX, XXXIV, XXXVI, XXXVII, XLIII-XLVI.

CUMNOCK, CAPTAIN—Lord Ormont and His Aminta: XVIII-XXI.

CUPER, MR.—Lord Ormont and His Aminta: I, II, IV, V, IX, XI-XIII, XXIV, XXVI.

CURATE OF LOBOURNE—Ordeal of Richard Feverel: IV, XIII, XV.

CURRENT, ISABELLE—Evan Harrington: XVI, XVIII, XXII, XXIV, XXIX, XXX, XXXIII, XXXVII.

CURRIE, FRED — Ordeal of Richard Feverel: XXXIV.

CURTIS, DICK—Rhoda Fleming: XVIII, XXIII.

D

DACIER, LADY—Diana of the Crossways: XVII, XIX, XXVII.

DACIER, LORD—Diana of the Crossways: XIX, XX.

DACIER, PERCY—Diana of the Crossways: XIV-XLI, XLIII.

DALE, LÆTITIA—Egoist: II-IV, VI-XI, XIII-XX, XXII-XXV, XXVII, XXIX-XXXIV, XXXVI-L.

DALE, MR.—Egoist: II-IV, X, XIII-XVI. XXXIII, XXXIX, XL, XLII-XLVI, XLVIII, XLIX.

DANCE, ARTHUR—Diana of the Crossways: XI.

DANDY—Evan Harrington: VII, IX, XXVI.

DANMORE, LADY—Lord Ormont and His Aminta: XXIX.

DANNISBURGH, LORD—Diana of the Crossways: I, VI, VII, XIV, XVI-XXI, XXVI, XXVII, XXXV, XLI.

DANNY, MR.—One of Our Conquerors: XXI.

DANVERS—Diana of the Cross-
ways: IX, XI-XIII, XXII, XXIV-
XXVII, XXIX, XXX, XXXII, XXXVI,
XXXVIII-XL, XLII, XLIII.

DARLETON, LUCY—Egoist:
XXI-XXV, XXVII, XLVII.

DARLEY, ABSWORTHY AND
MISSES — Ordeal of Richard
Feverel: XVIII.

DARLINGTON, GENERAL—
Egoist: XXIV, XXV.

DARTFORD, LORD—Sandra
Belloni: X.

DE DARTIGUES, COMTE—
Evan Harrington: V.

DAUPHIN, THE—Adventures of
Harry Richmond: XLII.

DAVENPORT, MOLLIE—Or-
deal of Richard Feverel: XX,
XXII, XXIII, XXV.

DAVIS—Adventures of Harry
Richmond: VI.

DAVIS—Adventures of Harry
Richmond: IX.

DAVIS, MOTHER — Amazing
Marriage: XXV.

DAVIS — Beauchamp's Career:
XIX, XX.

DE CRAYE, LIEUTENANT
HORACE—Egoist: X, XI, XIII,
XVII-XXVI, XXVIII-XLIV, XLVI-
XLVIII, L.

DEHORS, ARMAND—Egoist: X.

DELZENBURG, COUNT—see
ERNEST.

DELZENBURG, COUNTESS OF
—see OTTILIA, PRINCESS.

DENEWDNEY, LADY—Advent-
ures of Harry Richmond: XXI,
XXII.

DENHAM, HARRY — Beau-
champ's Career: XXVIII, L, LIV,
LVI.

DENHAM, JENNY — Beau-
champ's Career: XI, XII, XIX,
XXVII, XXIX, XXX, XXXII,
XXXIII, XXXV, XXXIX, XLII, XLV,
XLVIII-LVI.

DERING, CUTHBERT—Diana
of the Crossways: XXIV, XXXVIII,
XLII.

DERRY, JACK—Diana of the
Crossways: III.

DESBAROLLES, M.—Advent-
ures of Harry Richmond:
XXXII.

DESBOROUGH, COLONEL—
Ordeal of Richard Feverel: XX,
XXIII.

DESBOROUGH, LUCY—Ordeal
of Richard Feverel: VIII, IX, XI,
XIV, XV, XIX-XXIII, XXV-XXXII,
XXXIV, XXXV, XXXVII-XLV.

DESBOROUGH, MRS.—Ordeal
of Richard Feverel: XXX.

DESPRES, M.—Ordeal of Richard Feverel: XLV.

DESTRIER, LORD — Advent-
ures of Harry Richmond: XX,
XXIII, XXXIX, XL-XLV, XLVII,
XLIX, LV, LVI.

DETTERMAIN,—Adventures of
Harry Richmond: XXIV, XXV,
XXVII, XXXIX, XLI, XLIV, XLVII.

DEVEREUX, LOUISE WAR-
DOUR—Beauchamp's Career:
XIX-XXII, XXXIII, XXXVII-XXXIX,
XLII, XLV, XLVIII, XLIX, LI, LII,
LVI.

DEVEREUX, WARDOUR—
Beauchamp's Career: XX, XXI,
XXXIII, XXXVIII.

DE WITT, CAPTAIN JORIAN—
Adventures of Harry Rich-
mond: XXI-XXIII, XXXII, XXXIX,
XLI-XLIV, XLVII, L-LIII.

DE WITT, BRAMHAM—Advent-
ures of Harry Richmond: XLI,
XLII, XLVII.

DEWLAP, DUCHESS OF—Tale
of Chloe: I-VIII, X.

DEWLAP, DUKE OF—Tale of
Chloe: I-III, X.

DEWSBURY, ANASTASIA —
Adventures of Harry Rich-
mond: XXIII, XXXIX, LII, LIII.

DEWSBURY, ELIZABETH—
Adventures of Harry Rich-
mond: XXXIX.

DIANA OF THE CROSSWAYS—
see WARWICK, DIANA AN-
TONIO.

DICK—Adventures of Harry
Richmond: IV.

DICKETT—Beauchamp's Career:
XXX.

DISHER, AUGUSTUS—Advent-
ures of Harry Richmond: XLVII.

DISHER, DOLLY—Adventures
of Harry Richmond: XLVII.

DISHER, MR.—Adventures of
Harry Richmond: XLVII.

VON DITTMARSCH, CAPTAIN —Adventures of Harry Richmond: XLVII, XLVIII.

VON DITTMARSCH, MRS.—see SIBLEY, LUCY.

DOB—Shaving of Shagpat: XXI-XXIV.

DOLCHESTER, LADY—Adventures of Harry Richmond: XLI.

DOLLIKINS—Beauchamp's Career: XX, XXI.

DOLOROSO, DON—Evan Harrington: IV.

DORIA, MISS—Ordeal of Richard Feverel: XXXV.

DOUBLE, JOSEPH—Adventures of Harry Richmond: XI-XIV.

DOUBLEDAY—Evan Harrington: VII.

DOVILI, ANGELO — Vittoria: XV.

DREIGHTON, COLONEL SELWIN—One of Our Conquerors: XI.

DREW—Adventures of Harry Richmond: V, VI, XIII.

DREW, JOHN THOMAS—Beauchamp's Career: XI.

DUBBIN—Evan Harrington: XIV, XXX.

DUBBLESON—One of Our Conquerors: XLI.

DUCIE, VIVIAN—Beauchamp's Career: XIX, XXIV-XXVI.

DUFFIAN, HONORABLE AND REVEREND HERBERT— Evan Harrington: XL, XLIV, XLVI, XLVII.

DUFFIELD, LORD—Amazing Marriage: III.

DULAC, LORD AND LADY— Diana of the Crossways: XXV.

DUMP, CHARLES — Amazing Marriage: II, III.

DUMP, MARY—Amazing Marriage: III.

DUNSTANE, CAPTAIN LUKEN —Diana of the Crossways: II-VIII, XII-XIV, XVIII, XIX, XXI, XXVI, XXVII, XXXVI, XXXVII, XXXIX-XLIII.

DUNSTANE, LADY EMMA—Diana of the Crossways: II-XXI, XXIII-XXVII, XXIX-XXXI, XXXVI-XLIII.

DUPERTUY, MADAME — Adventures of Harry Richmond: XXXII.

DURANCE, COLNEY—One of Our Conquerors: I, III-XXV, XXVII-XXIX, XXXI, XXXV-XLII.

DURANDARTE—One of Our Conquerors: XX, XXI, XXXVI, XLI.

DURHAM, CONSTANTIA—Egoist: I-III, VI, VII, IX, X, XII, XVI, XXI, XXII, XXIV, XXIX, XXXV-XXXVII, XXXIX, XLII, XLV.

DURHAM, SIR JOHN—Egoist: III.

DURIETTE, M.—Diana of the Crossways: XV.

DUVIDNEY, MISSES DOROTHEA AND VIRGINIA—One of Our Conquerors: VIII, XVIII, XIX, XXII-XXVI, XXVIII-XXX, XXXIII, XXXIV, XXXVI, XXXVII, XL.

DYKES, MAJOR—Adventures of Harry Richmond: XIX.

E

ECCLES, JONATHAN—Rhoda Fleming: XIV, XVII-XXIV.

ECCLES, ROBERT — Rhoda Fleming: I, II, IV, V, VII, IX, X, XIII, XV, XVII-XXV, XXX, XXXII, XXXIII, XXXV-XXXIX. XLI-XLVIII.

ECKERTHY, TOM—Adventures of Harry Richmond: VII-IX, XXIII, XL, XLIII.

EDBURY, LADY MARIA—Adventures of Harry Richmond: XXXIX, XLI, XLII, XLIV, XLV, XLIX, LIII.

EDBURY, MARCHIONESS OF —see SERENA, MARCHIONESS OF EDBURY.

EDBURY, MARQUIS THE ELDER—Adventures of Harry Richmond: XLIV, LIV.

EDBURY, MARQUIS THE YOUNGER—see DESTRIER, LORD.

EDELSHEIM, MAJOR—Adventures of Harry Richmond: XXXII.

EDWARDS, HOWELL—Amazing Marriage: XXVIII-XXXIII.

EGLETT, LADY CHARLOTTE —Lord Ormont and His Aminta: II-XI, XIII-XVII, XX-XXVI, XXVIII-XXX.

EGLETT, MR.—Lord Ormont and His Aminta: II, III, XIII, XXII, XXIII, XXV, XXVI.

EIGHTEENTHCENTURY,THE —see GRANTLEY, GREAT-AUNT.

ELBURNE, COUNTESS—Evan Harrington: XXV, XL, XLIII.

ELDRITCH, LADY—Amazing Marriage: XII, XXIII, XXVIII, XLV.

ELECTOR AND ELECTRESS OF BAVARIA—Farina: VI.

ELLING, LADY—Rhoda Fleming: XVI, XXIV, XXVII.

ELLING, LORD—Rhoda Fleming: VI, XI, XVI, XXI, XXII, XXIV.

ELSEA, LADY — Beauchamp's Career: XXXIX, XLIV.

ELTHAM, LORD—Sandra Belloni: LVII, LVIII.

EL RASOON—Shaving of Shagpat: XXII.

EL ZOOP—Shaving of Shagpat: XXII.

EMERLY, MADAME — Tragic Comedians: VIII.

EMILIO—Vittoria: XXXVII, XLIV.

EMPSON—Lord Ormont and His Aminta: XIII.

ENCHANTRESS, T H E — see MOUNT, BELLA.

ENDERMAN, FRANZ—Farina: I.

ENDOR, LADY—Amazing Marriage: XII, XXIII, XXVIII, XLV.

ENRICO—Vittoria: XLIV.

VON EPPENWELZEN, MARSHAL ALBRECHT WOHLGE-MUTH—Adventures of Harry Richmond: XV-XVIII, XXIV, XXVII.

ERNEST, PRINCE OF EPPEN-WELZEN-S A R K E L D—Adventures of Harry Richmond: XIV-XVII, XIX, XXV-XXVIII, XXXI-XXXVI, XXXVIII, XL, XLI, XLIII-XLV, XLVIII-LIII, LVI.

ESQUART, LADY—Diana of the Crossways: XIV-XVI, XVIII, XXII, XXV, XXVII, XXVIII.

ESQUART, LORD—Diana of the Crossways: XIV-XVI, XVIII, XXV, XXVII.

ETHERELL, CHARLES—Adventures of Harry Richmond: XLIV, XLVII.

EUGÈNE—Vittoria: XI, XV.

EVELEEN—Adventures of Harry Richmond: VII, XLVI.

EVREMONDE, EVELYN—Evan Harrington: XVIII-XXII, XXIV, XXV, XXVII, XXX-XXXIV.

EVREMONDE, CAPTAIN LAWSON—Evan Harrington: XXX, XXXI, XXXIV.

EZNÔL, ABOO—Shaving of Shagpat: XXIV.

F

FAKENHAM, ADMIRAL BALDWIN—Amazing Marriage: II, III, VI, VII, XI-XIII, XV, XIX-XXII.

FAKENHAM, CURTIS—Amazing Marriage: II, III.

FAKENHAM, GEOFFRY—Amazing Marriage: II.

FAKENHAM, HENRIETTA—Amazing Marriage: III, V-VII, IX-XIII, XV, XVII, XIX. XX, XXII-XXVIII, XXX, XXXV, XXXVI, XXXIX, XLIII-XLVII.

FAKENHAM, COUNTESS LIVIA—Amazing Marriage: III, V, VII-XIII, XVII, XIX-XXVIII, XXXV, XXXIX-XLI, XLIII, XLV-XLVII.

FALARIQUE, M.—One of Our Conquerors: XIX, XXIV, XXVIII, XLI.

FALMOUTH — Adventures of Harry Richmond: XLII, XLIII.

FANNING, GENERAL—One of Our Conquerors: IX.

FANNING, MRS.—One of Our Conquerors: XVII, XX, XXI, XXIV, XXXVI.

FARINA—Farina: I-XVII.

FARINA, FRAU—Farina: VI, VII.

FARNLEY, MR.—Evan Harrington: XXXI.

FARRELL, AMINTA—Lord Ormont and His Aminta: I-XXX.

FARRELL, CAPTAIN ALGER-NON—Lord Ormont and His Aminta: VI.

FARUGINO—Vittoria: XV.

FEATHERDENE — Ordeal of Richard Feverel: IV.

FECKELWITZ, JACOB BAUM-WALDER—Vittoria: XIII, XXV-XXVIII, XXXIX, XLII, XLV.

FEIL—Shaving of Shagpat: XXII, XXIII.

FELLE, LADY JUDITH—Ordeal of Richard Feverel: XXXIV, XXXIX, XLI, XLII.

FELLE, LORD—Ordeal of Richard Feverel: XXXIV, XLII.

FELLINGHAM, GENERAL—House on the Beach: VIII, IX, XI.

FELLINGHAM, HERBERT—House on the Beach: II-XII.

FELLINGHAM, MARY—House on the Beach: IX-XII.

FELTRE, LORD—Amazing Marriage: XXI, XXII, XXVI-XXVIII, XXXIII, XXXVII-XLIV, XLVI, XLVII.

FENBIRD & JAY, CHEMISTS—One of Our Conquerors: XIII.

FENCASTER, MARCHIONESS GRACEY—Lord Ormont and His Aminta: XII.

FENELLAN, CAPTAIN DART-REY—One of Our Conquerors: IV-VI, X, XV, XVI, XVIII, XIX, XXI, XXIV, XXV, XXVII, XXIX-XLII.

FENELLAN, GENERAL—One of Our Conquerors: XIX.

FENELLAN, MRS. HENNEN—One of Our Conquerors: III, XIX, XXV.

FENELLAN, SIMEON—One of Our Conquerors: I-IX, XI-XIV, XVI, XVII, XIX, XXI, XXII, XXIV, XXV, XXXI, XXXIII, XXXV-XXXVII, XXXIX-XLII.

FENN, LAURA—Ordeal of Richard Feverel: XXXVIII.

FENN, MR.—Diana of the Crossways: XXI.

FENNELL, MASON—Amazing Marriage: XXXIV.

FERBRASS, MR.—Beauchamp's Career: XVIII, XX.

FERNAWAY, JONATHAN—Egoist: XXVI.

FESHNAVAT, VIZIER—Shaving of Shagpat: I, III, V, VI, VIII-XI, XIV, XVI, XVIII-XXIV.

FETTLE, SIMON—Amazing Marriage: II.

FEVEREL, CAPTAIN ALGER-NON—Ordeal of Richard Feverel: I, IV, VIII, X-XII, XV, XXIII, XXV, XXVI, XXVIII, XXXII, XXXIV, XXXVII.

FEVEREL, SIR AUSTIN ABS-WORTHY BERNE—Ordeal of Richard Feverel: I, II, IV-XVIII, XX-XXVI, XXVIII-XLI, XLIII-XLV.

FEVEREL, LIEUTENANT CUTHBERT—Ordeal of Richard Feverel: I.

FEVEREL, HIPPIAS—Ordeal of Richard Feverel: I, IV, X, XII, XX, XXIII, XXV, XXVI, XXVIII, XXIX, XXXII-XXXIV, XXXVII, XLI, XLIV.

FEVEREL, LADY—Ordeal of Richard Feverel: I, XII, XXIV, XXXVII, XXXVIII, XL, XLI.

FEVEREL, LUCY—see DES-BOROUGH, LUCY.

FEVEREL, SIR PYLCHER—Ordeal of Richard Feverel: XVII.

FEVEREL, RICHARD DORIA—Ordeal of Richard Feverel: I-XLV.

FEVEREL, RICHARD II—Ordeal of Richard Feverel: XLI-XLV.

FEVEREL, VIVIAN—Ordeal of Richard Feverel: I.

FINCHLEY, ISABELLA — Lord Ormont and His Aminta: III, VI-VIII, X-XV, XVII, XIX, XXIII, XXV, XXX.

FINCHLEY, LAWRENCE—Lord Ormont and His Aminta: III, VIII, XV, XXX.

FISKE, ANNE—Evan Harrington: II, VII, IX, XXVI.

FISKE, BARTHOLOMEW—Evan Harrington: VII.

FITZGERALD, JUDGE—Diana of the Crossways: XXX.

FLATSCHMANN, COLONEL — Vittoria: X.

FLEETWOOD, COUNTESS—see KIRBY, CARINTHIA JANE.

FLEETWOOD, DOWAGER COUNTESS—see FAKENHAM, COUNTESS LIVIA.

FLEETWOOD, EARL OF—see RUSSETT, EDWARD.

FLEISCHER, ADOLPH—Lord Ormont and His Aminta: xii, xxx.

FLEMING, DAHLIA — Rhoda Fleming: i-xxv, xxvii-xxxix, xli-xlviii.

FLEMING, RHODA — Rhoda Fleming: i-xv, xix, xxiii, xxv, xxvii, xxix-xxxiii, xxxv-xlviii.

FLEMING, SUSAN — Rhoda Fleming: i-iii, v, vii, ix, xi, xxv, xlii.

FLEMING, WILLIAM JOHN—Rhoda Fleming: i-iv, vii, ix-xv, xix, xxv, xxx, xxxii, xxxiii, xxxv, xlvii.

FLIPPER—Amazing Marriage: xv.

FLITCH, MR. and MRS.—Egoist: xi, xvii-xix, xxii, xxiv, xxviii-xxx, xxxiv-xxxvi, xlix.

FLOYER, MARIANA—One of Our Conquerors: xxxvii.

FÖHRENDORF, COUNTESS OF —see AMALIA, DUCHESS.

FORD, GEORGIANA—Sandra Belloni: xxvii, xxviii, xxxi, xxxii, xxxiv, xxxvi, xxxvii, xli, xliii, xlvi-l, liii, liv, lvi, lix. Vittoria: xix, xxxii, xxxv, xxxviii.

FOREY, ANGELICA and MATILDA—Ordeal of Richard Feverel: xxxii.

FOREY, BRANDON and CLARENCE—Ordeal of Richard Feverel: xxxii.

FOREY, CLARE DORIA—Ordeal of Richard Feverel: i, iv, v, x-xiv, xx, xxviii, xxix, xxxii, xxxiv, xxv, xl, xliv, xlv.

FOREY, HELEN DORIA—Ordeal of Richard Feverel: i, iv, xii-xv, xxiv, xxix, xxxii, xxxiv-xxxviii, xl, xliv, xlv.

FOREY, MR.—Ordeal of Richard Feverel: xxxii.

DE FORMOSA, DUKE and DUCHESSE DE FORTANDIGUA—Evan Harrington: iii.

FORTH, DRUMMOND—Evan Harrington: xii-xiv, xxv, xxvii, xxx-xxxiv, xliii.

FOSTER—Diana of the Crossways: xii.

FOULKE, SQUIRE—Evan Harrington: i.

FRANCIS—Amazing Marriage: viii, ix.

FRANCO — see REMAUD, FRANK.

FRANCOIS—Beauchamp's Career: viii.

FRANKENBAUCH—Farina: x.

FREBUTER, GENERAL GEORGE—Evan Harrington: v.

FRED—Evan Harrington: xxvi, xxx.

FREDERICKS, COLONEL—Sandra Belloni: xxxvi.

FREDERICKA, PRINCESS — Adventures of Harry Richmond: xvi.

FREDI—see RADNOR, NESTA VITTORIA.

FRIM, NICHOLAS—Evan Harrington: xxiii, xxv, xxxviii.

FRITZ—Farina: x

G

GAINSFORD—Sandra Belloni: xv, xvi, liv, lv.

GAMBIER, CAPTAIN AUGUSTUS FREDERICK — Sandra Belloni: vi, x-xii, xviii, xix, xxi, xxvii, xxviii, xxxi, xxxiii, xxxiv, xxxvii, xlii, xlvi, xlvii, liii, lvii. Vittoria: vi, x, xvii-xix, xxvii, xxviii, xxxii, xxxv.

GAMMON, MASTER — Rhoda Fleming: ii, vii, xiii-xv, xxv, xxxiii, xxxix, xli-xliv, xlvii.

GANNETT, DR.—Beauchamp's Career: xlviii-liii.

GANNIUS, DELPHICA—One of Our Conquerors: xix, xxiv, xxvi, xxviii, xxxvii, xli.

GANNIUS, DR.—One of Our Conquerors: xix, xxiv, xxviii, xxxvi.

GARBLE, DAME—Rhoda Fleming: xviii.

GARDNER, LADY SUSAN—Beauchamp's Career: xxvi.

GARNER, MARY—Ordeal of Richard Feverel: XX.

GARRAVEEN—Shaving of Shagpat: V, VII, XI, XII, XIV, XV, XVII, XVIII.

GELLER, ERNEST—Farina: I.

GIACINTA—Vittoria: XI, XX, XXII, XXIII, XXVI, XXXI, XXXV, XXXIX, XLV.

GIESSLINGER, KÄTCHEN—Vittoria: XXIII.

GIRLING, JOHN—Sandra Belloni: XI.

GLADDING, MR.—One of Our Conquerors: IX.

GLOSSOP, DR.—Amazing Marriage: XIII, XXXIV, XL, XLV, XLVII.

GOODWIN, CLARA—Adventures of Harry Richmond: IV, XIV, XV, XVIII-XX, XXXVIII, XLVII, XLVIII, L.

GOODWIN, COLONEL — Adventures of Harry Richmond: IV, XIV, XVIII-XX, XXXVIII, XLVII, XLVIII, L.

GOORELKA—Shaving of Shagpat: IX-XII, XVIII, XXIII.

GOREN, MR.—Evan Harrington: II, IV, V, VII, IX, XVI, XVII, XXVI, XXXVIII-XL.

GOSHAWK, THE — see GUY, THE GOSHAWK.

GOSLING, ADELINE—Rhoda Fleming: XVI, XIX, XX, XXV.

GOSLING, MR. and MRS.—Case of General Ople and Lady Camper: II, VI, VII.

GOSLING, MRS.—Rhoda Fleming: XXI, XXV.

GOSSIP, DEBORAH—Ordeal of Richard Feverel: XVIII.

GOSSTRE, LADY—Sandra Belloni: IV, V, VII, IX, X, XIV, XV, XXVIII, XXXI, XXXII, XXXVII, XLII, XLVII, LIII, LIV, LVI.

GOWEN, DAVID—Lord Ormont and His Aminta: XII.

GRAÄTLI, COUNT — Vittoria: XIII, XXVIII.

GRAÄTLI, DUCHESS OF—see AMALIA, DUCHESS.

GRAINE, GORDEN—Evan Harrington: XVI.

GRAINE, JENNIE—Evan Harrington: XVI-XVIII, XX, XXX-XXXII.

DE GRANDCHAMP, COLONEL CÖIN — Beauchamp's Career: XXV.

GRANDISON, CAROLINE—Ordeal of Richard Feverel: XX, XXII, XXIII, XXVI, XXVIII, XXXII.

GRANTLEY, GREAT-AUNT — Ordeal of Richard Feverel: I, IX, XX, XXIII, XXV, XXVII.

GRAVES, PRISCILLA—One of Our Conquerors: IV, VIII-XI, XIV, XV, XVIII, XX-XXII, XXIV, XXV, XXXI, XXXIII, XXXVI, XXXVIII, XLI, XLII.

GREGORY, FATHER—Farina: VII-X, XIV-XVII.

GRENAT, EMILE—Lord Ormont and His Aminta: I, IV, V, XII, XVIII, XXIV, XXX.

GRIFFITH, DR.—Amazing Marriage: XXXIII.

GRIST, MESSRS., SOLICITORS —Evan Harrington: XVII, XXXII, XXXVI, XLIV.

VON GROSCHEN, FRAU—Farina: II.

VON GROSCHEN, GOTTLIEB —Farina: I-VIII, X, XIV, XVII.

VON GROSCHEN, LISBETH—Farina: II, IV, VI-VIII, XIV-XVI.

VON GROSCHEN, MARGARITA—Farina: I-VIII, X, XII-XVII.

GROSSBY, MR.—Evan Harrington: I, VII.

GUIDASCARPI, ANGELO—Vittoria: XVIII, XIX, XXI, XXIII-XXXI, XXXIII-XXXVII, XXXIX, XLI-XLIII, XLVI.

GUIDASCARPI, CLELIA—Vittoria: XXIV, XXXIII.

GUIDASCARPI, RENALDO — Vittoria: XVIII, XIX, XXIV, XXVII, XXIX-XXXIV, XLI, XLIII.

GULREVAZ—Shaving of Shagpat: X, XIV-XVII, XX, XXIV.

GUNNETT, AMABEL FRYAR —Diana of the Crossways: XXVII, XXXVI, XXXVII, XXXIX, XLI, XLII.

GUNNETT, FRAYAR—Diana of the Crossways: XLI.

GUY, THE GOSHAWK—Farina: III-IV, VIII, X-XVII

H

HABRAL — Evan Harrington:
XXII.

HACKBUT, ANTHONY—Rhoda
Fleming: II-VIII, X, XII, XIV,
XXV, XXXI, XXXIII, XL, XLII-
XLVIII.

HACKLEBRIDGE, GENERAL
—Evan Harrington: IX.

HACKMAN—Adventures of Harry Richmond: VI, VII.

HALKETT, CECILIA — Beau-
champ's Career: XI, XIV-XXIV,
XXVI, XXVIII-XXX, XXXII.
XXXVII, XXXIX, XLII, XLIV-LVI.

HALKETT, COLONEL — Beau-
champ's Career: I, III, IV, XII,
XIV-XVIII, XX, XXII, XXVI,
XXVIII-XXX, XXXII-XXXIX, XLIII,
LVI.

HALL, CAPTAIN ROBERT—
Beauchamp's Career: III, IV,
XII, XXXI.

HALLEY, LADY GRACE—One
of Our Conquerors: IV, VIII, IX,
XI, XIV-XVI, XVIII, XXVI, XXVII,
XXXI, XXXV, XXXVI.

HALLEY, LORD—One of Our
Conquerors: VIII, XVIII, XXV.

HAMBLE, MR.—Rhoda Fleming:
III, VI.

HAMPTON-EVEY, REVEREND
STEPHEN—Lord Ormont and
His Aminta: III, XIII, XVII, XXVI.

HAPPENWYLL, GENERAL —
Adventures of Harry Richmond:
XXXIV.

HAPPIT—Adventures of Harry
Richmond: VI.

HARDIST, CAPTAIN — Beau-
champ's Career: XI, XV.

HARLEY, ADRIAN—Ordeal of
Richard Feverel: I, IV-VII, X-
XIII, XX-XXVI, XXIX-XXXVI,
XXXVIII, XL, XLI, XLIV.

HARLEY, MRS. JUSTICE—Or-
deal of Richard Feverel: I.

HARRINGTON, SIR ABRA-
HAM—Evan Harrington: III,
IX, XIII, XVII, XIX, XX, XXVII,
XXXI, XXXVII.

HARRINGTON, ADMIRAL—
Evan Harrington: XXII.

HARRINGTON, EVAN—Evan
Harrington: I-XLVII.

HARRINGTON, HENRIETTA
MARIA DAWLEY—Evan Har-
rington: II, IV, V, VII, IX. XIV,
XVI, XXII, XXVI, XXVII, XXIX-
XXXIII, XXXVII, XXXVIII, XLIV,
XLVI, XLVII.

HARRINGTON, MELCHISE-
DEC—Evan Harrington: I, II,
IV-VII, XIV, XIX-XXVI, XXVIII-
XXXIII, XXXVI-XXXVIII, XLIII,
XLIV, XLVI.

HART, REVEREND SIMON—
Adventures of Harry Richmond:
IX.

HARTISTON, SIR ABRAHAM
—Diana of the Crossways: XXX.

HARTSWOOD, COLONEL—Di-
ana of the Crossways: XLI.

HARVEY, WILLIAM — Evan
Harrington: XV-XVIII, XX, XXX,
XXXII.

HATCHFORD, MARQUIS OF—
Adventures of Harry Richmond:
XLVII.

HAWKSHAW, MRS.—Evan Har-
rington: XXVI.

HEDDON, COLONEL—Advent-
ures of Harry Richmond: LIV,
LVI.

HEDDON, LIPSCOMBE — Or-
deal of Richard Feverel: XVIII.

HEDDON, LORD—Ordeal of
Richard Feverel: XVIII.

HEDDON, LUCY—Adventures
of Harry Richmond: LIV, LVI.

HEDGES, ANDREW—Diana of
the Crossways: VIII.

HEINRICH, KAISER—Farina:
I-III, VIII, X, XI, XV, XVI.

VON HELLER—Farina: III.

D'HENRIEL, COMTE HENRI
—Beauchamp's Career: XXIII-
XXV, XXXIX, XL.

HEPBURN, ALEXANDER —
Diana of the Crossways: XXVIII,
XXXIX.

HERBSTBLUM, MARTHE—Fa-
rina: II.

HERIOT, WALTER—Advent-
ures of Harry Richmond: V-IX,
XX, XXIII, XXXVI-XXXIX, XLIII-
XLV, XLIX, LVI, LVI.

HERMANN, PRINCE—Advent-
ures of Harry Richmond: XXXIV,
XLIV, LI-LIII, LVI.

HICKSON, MR.—Adventures of Harry Richmond: XXI, XXII.

HIGGINSON, LADY MARIA—Adventures of Harry Richmond: XXXVI, XXXVIII, XLI.

HILDA OF BAYERN—Farina: VI.

HILL, BEAUCHAMP—Adventures of Harry Richmond: XLII, XLIII.

HIPPERDON, NORMANTON—Adventures of Harry Richmond: XLIII, XLIV.

HIPPONY, JACK—Adventures of Harry Richmond: XLVII.

HODGES, NAT—Evan Harrington: XIII, XX.

VOM HOF, BARON—Adventures of Harry Richmond: XLIV.

VOM HOF, ECKART—Adventures of Harry Richmond: XXXII, XL, L, LI, LIII.

HOLLINGER, COUNT—Tragic Comedians: XIII, XIV, XVIII.

HOLLIS, JOHN—Beauchamp's Career: V.

HOLMES — Rhoda Fleming: XXXIV.

HOPPNER,—Egoist: IX, XVII, XXIX.

I

ILCHESTER, CHARLES—Adventures of Harry Richmond: VIII, IX, XIX, LIII.

ILCHESTER, JANET—Adventures of Harry Richmond: VIII, X, XII, XVIII-XX, XXIII, XXX, XXXVI-XLV, XLVII-LVI.

ILCHESTER, LADY MARGARET — Adventures of Harry Richmond: VIII, IX, XIX, XLI, LIII, LIV.

ILCHESTER, SIR RODERICK—Adventures of Harry Richmond: VIII, XLI, LIII, LIV.

INCHLING, MR.—One of Our Conquerors: I, XVII, XVIII, XXI, XXVII.

INCHLING, MRS.—One of Our Conquerors: XVIII, XXVII.

INES, CHRISTOPHER—Amazing Marriage: XIV-XIX, XXI, XXIII, XXV, XXIX, XXX, XXXII, XXXIII, XXXV, XXXVI, XL, XLI, XLVI.

INES, MR.—Amazing Marriage: XVIII.

ISENTRUDE—Farina: VI.

D'ISORELLA, COUNTESS—Vittoria: XVI, XXX, XXXI, XXXIV, XXXVI-XLV.

J

JACK—see RAIKES, JOHN FEVERSHAM.

JACKO—Evan Harrington: II, VII, IX.

JACOBS, MR.—Adventures of Harry Richmond: XXXIX.

DE JACQUIERES, MADAME—Diana of the Crossways: XXX.

JANE—Evan Harrington: IX.

JANE—House on the Beach: VI, XI, XII.

JANE, AUNT—Rhoda Fleming: XVII, XXIII.

JARNIMAN—One of Our Conquerors: III, IV, VII, X, XVI, XIX, XXI, XXII, XXX, XXXI, XXXVI, XL-XLII.

JARNIMAN, MRS.—One of Our Conquerors: XV.

JAYE, LADY JULIANA—Ordeal of Richard Feverel: IV.

JENKINSON, MRS. MOUNT-STUART—Egoist: II-VI, IX, X, XVII, XVIII, XXIV, XXVII-XXXIX, XLI, XLIII-XLVII, XLIX, L.

JENNA, LIEUTENANT—Vittoria: IX, X, XXIX, XXX, XXXIX, XL, XLVI.

JENNINGS, MR.—Adventures of Harry Richmond: XXXIX, XLII, XLIII.

JEREMY—Adventures of Harry Richmond: LIII.

JERIDOMANI, SIGNOR—One of Our Conquerors: XXVIII.

JIM—Sandra Belloni: II, VIII, IX, XI.

JINKSON, GILES—Ordeal of Richard Feverel: VIII-XI, XX, XXIII.

JOCELYN, ALEC—Evan Harrington: IV, XIV, XVI, XXXVII.

JOCELYN, LADY EMILY—Evan Harrington: III, IX, XIV, XVI-XXXV, XXXVII, XL, XLI, XLIII-XLVI.

JOCELYN, SIR FRANKS—Evan Harrington: III, IX, XIV, XVI, XIX, XXI, XXII, XXV, XXVII-XXIX, XXXI, XXXIII, XXXVII, XLIII, XLV, XLVI.

JOCELYN, HONORABLE HAMILTON EVERARD — Evan Harrington: XIII, XIV, XVI, XXI, XXII, XXIX.

JOCELYN, HARRY—Evan Harrington: XII, XIV-XVI, XVIII-XXV, XXVII-XXXIII, XXXVII, XL, XLIII, XLV, XLVII.

JOCELYN, HONORABLE MELVILLE—Evan Harrington: III, IV, VII, VIII, XIII-XVII, XIX-XXII, XXIV, XXV, XXVII-XXX, XXXVII.

JOCELYN, MRS.—Evan Harrington: IV, XIV, XV, XVII, XXII, XXIV, XXVII, XXIX, XXXII, XXXVII, XLIV.

JOCELYN, ROSE—Evan Harrington: III, IV, VI, VII, IX, X, XIII-XXII, XXIV, XXV, XXVII-XL, XLIII-XLVII.

JOCELYN, COLONEL SEYMOUR—Evan Harrington: XIV, XX-XXII, XXVII, XXXI, XXXVII.

JOCHANY, COUNT—Diana of the Crossways: XIV.

JOE—Rhoda Fleming: XLII.

JOHN—Ordeal of Richard Feverel: XXXVIII.

JONATHAN—Evan Harrington: VIII.

JONES, MRS. MARY—Amazing Marriage: XVIII, XIX, XXII.

JOPSON, MR.—Adventures of Harry Richmond: XXXIX.

JOSEF: Amazing Marriage: V.

JOYCE—Evan Harrington: VII.

JULINKS, MISS—One of Our Conquerors: XXI.

VON DER JUNGFERWEIDE, HEINRICH—Farina: I.

JUPP — Adventures of Harry Richmond: III.

JUTTA, PFALZGRÄFIN — Farina: VI.

K

KADRAB—Shaving of Shagpat: XI.

KADZA—Shaving of Shagpat: I, XI, XXI-XXIV.

KALTBLUT, FRAU—Farina: II.

KANE, LADY—Adventures of Harry Richmond: XLI, XLII, LVI.

KARAVEJIS—Shaving of Shagpat: XVII-XXI, XXIII.

KARAZ—Shaving of Shagpat: V-VIII, X-XII, XIV, XVI-XXI, XXIII, XXIV.

DI KARSKI, IRMA — Vittoria: XIII-XV, XVII, XIX-XXI, XXXVI, XL, XLII, XLV.

VON KARSTEG PROFESSOR JULIUS—Adventures of Harry Richmond: XXVII-XXXI, XXXIV, XLIV.

KASIRWAN, SHAH—Shaving of Shagpat: XIV.

KATH—Adventures of Harry Richmond: XXXV.

KEMPSON, MRS. — Amazing Marriage: I.

KENDALL,—Beauchamp's Career: XLIV.

KESENSKY, GRAF — Adventures of Harry Richmond: XLII, XLIII, LV, LVI.

KHIPIL—Shaving of Shagpat: III, IV, XXII.

KILLICK, SAMUEL — Beauchamp's Career: XIX, XX, LIV, LV.

KILNE—Evan Harrington: I, II, VII, XXVI.

KILTORNE, LADY CHARLOTTE—One of Our Conquerors: XIX.

KING OF OOLB—Shaving of Shagpat: VIII-XI, XXI-XXIV.

KING OF THE CITY OF SHAGPAT—Shaving of Shagpat: I, XX-XXIV.

KIOMI—Adventures of Harry Richmond: VII-IX, XVIII, XX, XXIII, XXXVI, XL, XLV-XLVII, LV, LVI.

KIRBY, CARINTHIA JANE—Amazing Marriage: I, III-IX, XI-XIX, XXI-XXXI, XXXIII-XXXV, XXXVII-XLVII.

KIRBY-LEVELLIER, CHILTON SWITZER JOHN—Amazing Marriage: I, III-VIII, X-XIII, XV, XIX-XXI, XXIV-XXX, XXXII, XXXV-XXXVII, XXXIX-XLVII.

KIRBY, CAPTAIN JOHN PETER AVASON—Amazing Marriage: I-V, XI-XIII, XV, XVII, XVIII, XXII, XXIII, XXV-XXVII, XXIX-XXXIV, XXXVI, XL, XLII, XLIV-XLVII.

KIRBY, RALPH THORKILL—Amazing Marriage: I.

KIRBY, STANSON — Amazing Marriage: I.

KIT—see INES, CHRISTOPHER.

KOLLIN, COUNT—Tragic Comedians: II-IV.

KOOROOKH—Shaving of Shagpat: XVI, XVIII-XX, XXIII, XXIV.

KORNIKOFF, COUNTESS—Adventures of Harry Richmond: LIII.

KRAUT—Farina: II, VI.

KRESNUK, KING OF GÂF—Shaving of Shagpat: XXII-XXIV.

KROOJIS—Shaving of Shagpat: V.

KROOZ EL KRAZAWIK—Shaving of Shagpat: XXI-XXIII.

L

LAMMAKIN—Beauchamp's Career: XI.

LANDLADY OF THE AURORA—Evan Harrington: VIII.

LARKINS—Adventures of Harry Richmond: VI.

LARRIAN, GENERAL—Diana of the Crossways: II-IV, VI, XI, XIII, XIV, XVIII, XXVIII, XXXV, XLIII.

LATTERS, HARRY — Rhoda Fleming: XXXI, XXXVIII.

LAUNAY, COLONEL—Diana of the Crossways: XLI.

LAXLEY, FERDINAND—Evan Harrington: XII, XIII, XV-XX, XXII-XXV, XXVII, XXIX-XXXVIII, XL, XLII, XLIII, XLV-XLVII.

LAXLEY, LORD—Evan Harrington: XIX.

LEBERN, COUNT — Amazing Marriage: V.

LEBRUNO—Vittoria: XIX-XXI.

LECZEL, GENERAL — Tragic Comedians: XVI, XVII.

LEDDINGS—Amazing Marriage: XXXII, XXXVII, XL.

LEEMAN—Lord Ormont and His Aminta: XIII.

VON LENKENSTEIN, COMMENDATORE GRAF ADELBERT—Vittoria: XI, XXVIII, XXX, XXXIII, XL, XLV.

VON LENKENSTEIN, COUNTESS ANNA—Vittoria: XIV, XVIII-XX, XXVI-XXX, XXXIII, XXXIV, XXXVI-XL, XLII, XLIV, XLV.

VON LENKENSTEIN, BIANCA—Vittoria: XI, XVIII, XXVII, XXVIII, XXX, XXXVI, XLV.

VON LENKENSTEIN, COUNT KARL—Vittoria: XXXII-XXXIV, XXXVI, XXXVIII-XL, XLV, XLVI.

VON LENKENSTEIN, COUNTESS LENA—Vittoria: IX, XIV, XVIII-XX, XXVII-XXX, XXXIV, XXXVI, XXXVIII-XL, XLV.

VON LENKENSTEIN, COUNT PAUL—Vittoria: IX, XVIII, XIX, XXVI, XXVII, XXXIII, XXXIV, XXXVII, XXXIX, XLV.

LEO—Lord Ormont and His Aminta: III, XIII.

LEONARDO—Vittoria: XX, XXI.

LESPEL, GRANCEY — Beauchamp's Career: XI, XV, XVII-XXII, XXVIII, XXXI, XXXII, XXXIX, XLV. LV.

LESPEL, MRS. GRANCEY—Beauchamp's Career: XX, XXI, XXVI, XLV, LV.

LEVELLIER, LORD—Amazing Marriage: I-III, V, XIII, XIV, XVII, XVIII, XXII, XXIV, XXVII, XXXIV, XXXV, XLII, XLIII, XLV, XLVI.

LEWISON, LADY MARY—Egoist: XXIII.

LIESCHEN—Adventures of Harry Richmond: XV, XXXIII, XXXV.

LIESCHEN—Farina: VI.

LIKA, COUNT—Adventures of Harry Richmond: XLIII.

LINNINGTON, FRED — Evan Harrington: XIII.

LISA—Vittoria: XXVII.

LIVELYSTON, LORD — Evan Harrington: IV, XIV.

LIVRET, M.—Beauchamp's Career: XXIII, XXV.

LLEWELLYN — Amazing Marriage: XXXIV.

LOCKRACE, EARL OF—Beauchamp's Career: XXXII, XXXVII.

LOEPEL, COUNT—Adventures of Harry Richmond: XXXII.

LOFTUS, ADMIRAL—Adventures of Harry Richmond: XXXIX, XLI, XLII, XLVIII, L.

LORENZO—Vittoria: IX, XLVI.

LORING, DOROTHY — Evan Harrington: XIII, XVI, XVII, XIX, XX, XXX, XXXVII, XLII.

LORING, SIR JOHN—Evan Harrington: XVI, XVIII, XIX, XXI, XXIX-XXXI, XXXIII, XXXVII.

LOTSDALE, CRANMER—One of Our Conquerors: XXI.

LOVELL, HARRY — Rhoda Fleming: VI, XXII.

LOVELL, MARGARETT—Rhoda Fleming: I, VI, VIII, IX, XVI-XXIV, XXVII-XXXII, XXXIV, XXXVI, XLIV-XLVIII.

LOWTON, SIR GEORGE—Evan Harrington: XIII.

LUCIANI BIANCA—One of Our Conquerors: XX, XXI.

LULOO—Shaving of Shagpat: XXI.

LUMLEY, CAPTAIN — Sandra Belloni: XXXVI.

LUMLEY, MR.—Adventures of Harry Richmond: XXI.

LUPIN, MRS.—Sandra Belloni: III, XV, XVI, XXVII, XXIX, XXXII, XXXIII.

LUTON, EARL OF—Adventures of Harry Richmond: XLVII.

LYDIARD, LOUISE — Beauchamp's Career: XXXIII, XXXVII, XLV.

LYDIARD, MR.—Beauchamp's Career: XII, XIX-XXI, XXVII, XXVIII, XXXIII, XXXV, XXXVII, XXXIX, XLII, XLV, XLVI, XLVIII, L-LVI.

M

MACKRELL, JOHN ROSE—Amazing Marriage: XXIII, XXIV, XXVI, XXVIII, XXXIV, XXXIX, XLV-XLVII.

MACPHERSON, DR. WILLIAM —Diana of the Crossways: XXVI, XXVII.

MAHONY, CAPTAIN CAREW —Diana of the Crossways: XIII, XXVIII.

MÄHRLEN, PROFESSOR—Adventures of Harry Richmond: XXXIII.

MALET, CAPTAIN—Adventures of Harry Richmond: XIV.

MALKIN, MR.—Diana of the Crossways: III.

MALLARD, AMBROSE—Amazing Marriage: III, XV, XVI XVIII, XXIII, XXVIII, XXXIV, XXXV, XXXIX, XLI, XLII, XLIV.

MALLOW, MRS.—Sandra Belloni: VII, XIV.

MANTON—One of Our Conquerors: XXIII, XXXIV.

MANX, QUINTIN—Diana of the Crossways: XV, XVII, XXI, XXVII, XXXIII, XXXV.

MAPLES, MRS.—Lord Ormont and His Aminta: XIII.

MARGARET—Ordeal of Richard Feverel: XXVIII.

MARIA—Vittoria: XXIV.

MARIANDAL—Amazing Marriage: III, V.

MARINI, GIULIA—Sandra Belloni: XXXVII-XL, LII, LIX.

MARINI, LUIGI—Sandra Belloni: XXXIV, XXXVII, XXXVIII, XL, XLVI-XLVIII, LIX.

MARION—Sandra Belloni: XXX.

MARK—Evan Harrington: XI, XII.

MARKHAM, NED—Ordeal of Richard Feverel: VII.

MARKLAND, MRS.—Diana of the Crossways: XXXV.

MARQUIS, THE — see HARRINGTON, MELCHISEDEC.

MARSCHATSKA—Vittoria: IV.

MARSETT, CAPTAIN EDWARD—One of Our Conquerors: XXVIII, XXIX, XXXII, XXXIV, XXXVIII, XXXIX.

MARSETT, JUDITH — One of Our Conquerors: XXVIII, XL.

MARSHALLED, KING—Shaving of Shagpat: II.

MARTER, REVEREND MR.—Sandra Belloni: XXIII, XXXIV.

MARTHA—Amazing Marriage: XXIX, XXXII, XXXIII, XXXV.

MARTHA—Lord Ormont and His Aminta: XIV.

MARTIN, ELIZABETH—Amazing Marriage: I.

MARTIN, WILLIAM—Amazing Marriage: I.

MARTINEZ, CAPTAIN—Adventures of Harry Richmond: LVI.

MARTINSWARD, CATHERINE —Tale of Chloe: II-X.

MARY — Beauchamp's Career: XLVII.

MARY—Egoist: XL.

MARY—Evan Harrington: XXVI.

MARY—One of Our Conquerors: XXVIII, XXXII, XXXIV, XXXVI.

MASNER, JOSEPH—Lord Ormont and His Aminta: I, XI, XXVIII.

MASTALONE, FILIPPO—Vittoria: II.

MATEY—see WEYBURN, MATTHEW.

MATTEO—Vittoria: XIV.

MAY, AMY—Lord Ormont and His Aminta: VI, XI, XII, XV, XVI, XVIII, XIX, XXI, XXIII, XXV, XXVI.

MAY, CAPTAIN—Lord Ormont and His Aminta: VI, XI, XII, XVI, XIX, XXIII, XXV, XXVI.

MEDOLE, COUNT—Vittoria: II, VIII, X, XII, XV, XVI, XVIII, XX, XXX, XXXI, XXXV, XXXVIII, XL.

MEDOLE, COUNTESS — Vittoria: XL.

MEEK, EZRA and JONATHAN —Amazing Marriage: XLII.

MEL—see (1) HARRINGTON, MELCHISEDEC and (2) JOCELYN, HONORABLE MELVILLE.

MELVILLE, MRS.—see JOCELYN, MRS.

MENAI, COUNTESS OF—Beauchamp's Career: XXXI.

MERCADESCO—Vittoria: XXIX.

MERION, DAN — Diana of the Crossways: I-III, V, VII, VIII, XVII, XIX, XXIII, XXVIII, XXXVII, XXXVIII.

MERION, DIANA—see WARWICK, DIANA ANTONIO.

M'GILLIPER—Beauchamp's Career: XIX.

MICHELL — Beauchamp's Career: IV, XI.

MICHIELA—Vittoria: XIV, XIX-XXI, XXIII, XXV, XXXII.

MIDDLETON, CLARA—Egoist: IV-L.

MIDDLETON, MRS. — Egoist: XX.

MIDDLETON, REVEREND DR. —Egoist: IV-XI, XIII, XV, XVII-XXVII, XXIX-XXXVII, XXXIX, XLI-L.

MILLINGTON, COLONEL—Beauchamp's Career: XXI.

MINA—Vittoria: XXVI.

MOLYNEAUX, PETER—Beauchamp's Career: XIX, XX.

MONTAGUE — Adventures of Harry Richmond: VI.

MONTAGUE—One of Our Conquerors: XXIII.

MONTAGUE, MRS.—Egoist: VII, XIX, XXIV, XXV.

MONTESINI—Vittoria: XXIX.

MONTINI—Vittoria: XIX-XXII, XXXVIII.

MONTVERT, MR. and MRS.—Diana of the Crossways: XIV.

MOODY, WILLIAM — Rhoda Fleming: XVIII, XIX, XXIV.

MORSFIELD, ADOLPHUS—Lord Ormont and His Aminta: III, VI, VIII, X-XIII, XV-XXVI, XXIX.

MORTIMER, MR.—Rhoda Fleming: XL.

MORTIMER, MRS.—Ordeal of Richard Feverel: XXXVI.

MORTON, MR.—Ordeal of Richard Feverel: II, IV, XX, XXXIV.

MORTON, RALPH BARTHROP —Ordeal of Richard Feverel: XII, XIV, XV, XXVIII, XXIX, XXXIV, XXXV, XLV.

MOUNT, BELLA—Ordeal of Richard Feverel: XXXV-XXXVIII, XLIII.

MOUNTFALCON, LORD—Ordeal of Richard Feverel: XXXIV-XXXVI, XXXIX, XLIII, XLV.

MOUNTNEY, MAB—One of Our Conquerors: XIII.

MOUNTSTUART, MRS. — see JENKINSON, MRS. MOUNTSTUART.

MUNCASTLE, MR.—Lord Ormont and His Aminta: I.

MUSTAPHA, BABA—Shaving of Shagpat: I, III, VIII, IX, XII, XIV, XX-XXIV.

MYTHARETE, PISISTRATUS —One of Our Conquerors: XIX, XXVIII, XLI.

N

NAGEN, GENERAL—Vittoria: XXXIX, XLIV-XLVI.
NASE, PFALZGRÄF—Farina: XVI.
NASHTA—Shaving of Shagpat: II.
NATKINS—Ordeal of Richard Feverel: IV.

NEWSON, MR.—Adventures of Harry Richmond: XXIV, XXV, XXVII, XXXIX, XLI, XLII, XLIV, XLVII.

NOORNA BIN NOORKA—Shaving of Shagpat: I, III, V-XXIV.

NYMNEY—Amazing Marriage: I.

O

OAKES—Lord Ormont and His Aminta: XXVIII.
OGGLER—Beauchamp's Career: XIX.
OPLE, ELIZABETH—Case of General Ople and Lady Camper: I-VIII.
OPLE, GENERAL WILSON— Case of General Ople and Lady Camper: I-VIII.
D'ORBEC, BARONNE—Beauchamp's Career: XXIII, XXV.
D'ORBEC, M.—Beauchamp's Career: XXIII, XXV.
ORMOND, CAROLINE—Beauchamp's Career: XXVI.
ORMONT, MAJOR GENERAL THOMAS ROWSLEY—Lord Ormont and His Aminta: I-XIII, XV-XXVI, XXVIII-XXX.

ORSO, COUNT—Vittoria: XIX-XXI.

OSRIC—Adventures of Harry Richmond: VII, VIII.

OTTILIA, PRINCESS WILHELMINA FREDERIKA HEDWIG—Adventures of Harry Richmond: XV-XIX, XXIV-XXXIX, XLI-XLIV, XLVII-LVI.

OTTILIA—Farina: II.

OTTO, PRINCE—Adventures of Harry Richmond: XXVI, XXVII, XXX-XXXIV, XXXIX.

OXFORD, CAPTAIN HARRY— Egoist: III, X, XXI, XXIII, XLII.

P

PAGNELL, ALFRED NARGETT—Lord Ormont and His Aminta: VI.
PAGNELL, MRS. NARGETT— Lord Ormont and His Aminta: I, III, V-VIII, X, XII, XIII, XV-XXI, XXVI.

PALMET, LORD ERNEST— Beauchamp's Career: XIX-XXI, XXVI, XXVIII-XXXI, XXXVI, XXXVII, XLIV, XLV, LV.

PAPWORTH, SIR MILES—Ordeal of Richard Feverel: II, IV-VI, XI.

PARSLEY, MR.—Evan Harrington: XIII-XV, XIX, XXV, XXVII, XXXIII, XLVII.

PARSONS, JAMES PANNERS—Lord Ormont and His Aminta: XII.

PARYLI, PRINCESS THÉRÈSE —Diana of the Crossways: XIV.

PAT—Evan Harrington: XXV.

PATTERNE, CROSSJAY—Egoist: IV, VI-XV, XVII-XIX, XXI-XXXIII, XXXVI-XLIII, XLVI-L.

PATTERNE, LIEUTENANT CROSSJAY—Egoist: I, IV, VIII, IX, XI, XXXII, XLII.

PATTERNE, LADIES ELEANOR and ISABEL—Egoist: I, II, IV, VI-X, XIV, XV, XXII, XXIV, XXV, XXIX-XXXI, XXXVI XXXVIII, XXXIX, XLI, XLIV-XLVI, XLIX.

PATTERNE, LADY—Egoist: I-VI, XIII.

PATTERNE, MRS.—Egoist: VIII, XLII.

PATTERNE, SIMON—Egoist: I.

PATTERNE, SIR WILLOUGHBY—Egoist: I-XI, XIII-L.

PAWLE, BARON—Diana of the Crossways: XXX.

PAYNE—Sandra Belloni: XXXII.

PAYNHAM, MARY—Diana of the Crossways: XVIII, XIX, XXI, XXIII, XXV, XXVII-XXX, XXXIX, XLI-XLIII.

PAYNTER—Adventures of Harry Richmond: VI.

DE PEL, COUNTESS—Evan Harrington: III.

PEMPTON, MR.—One of Our Conquerors: IV, VIII, IX, XI, XIV, XVIII, XX-XXII, XXV, XXXIII, XXXVI, XL-XLII.

PENNERGATE, MR.—One of Our Conquerors: XVIII.

PENNON, LADY—Diana of the Crossways; I, XIV, XVII, XVIII, XXI, XXIII, XXV, XXVIII-XXX, XXXIX.

PENNYCUICK, MR. — Rhoda Fleming: XL.

PENRHYS, ANNA—Adventures of Harry Richmond: XX-XXII, XXVII, XXXIX, XLI-XLIV.

PEPPEL, COMMANDER—Beauchamp's Career: XVII, XLVII.

PERICLES, ANTONIO AGIOLOPOULOS—Sandra Belloni: I-V, XVII, XXI, XXIII, XXIV, XXVII, XXX-XXXII, XXXIV, XXXVII, XXXIX, XL, XLII, LII, LIV-LVI, LVIII, LIX. Vittoria: V-VIII, XIII, XIV, XVII-XXI, XXIII, XXXI, XXXVIII, XL-XLII, XLIV.

PERIDON, MR.—One of Our Conquerors: IV, VIII, XI, XIV, XV, XVIII, XX, XXII, XXV, XXXIII, XXXVI, XL-XLII.

PERKINS — Evan Harrington: XLIV.

PERKINS, MR.—Evan Harrington: VII, XLIV, XLV.

PERKINS, MRS.—Evan Harrington: XXXI.

PERRIN—One of Our Conquerors: XXIII, XXXIV, XXXV.

PETERBOROUGH, REVEREND AMBROSE—Adventures of Harry Richmond: XXIII-XXVII, XXX, XXXIII, XXXIV, XXXVI-XXXVIII, XLI, LI.

PETTIFER, SIR WILSON—Egoist: XXXV.

PETTIGREW, MRS.—Diana of the Crossways: II, III, XIV, XVIII, XLII.

VON PFENNIG—Farina: III.

PHELPS, LUMMY — Amazing Marriage: XV.

PHILIBERTE, DAME—Beauchamp's Career: XXIII, XXIV.

PHILIPPA—Lord Ormont and His Aminta: III.

PHILLIMORE, DICK—Adventures of Harry Richmond: XLVIII.

PHIPPUN—House on the Beach: II-IV.

PIAVENI, AMALIA—Vittoria: XI-XIII, XXVIII, XL-XLII.

PIAVENI, GIACOMO—Vittoria: V, IX, XVIII, XXVIII, XXX, XXXVI.

PIAVENI, GIACOMO II—Vittoria: XI-XIII, XXVIII, XL-XLII.

PIAVENI, LAURA—Vittoria; V, VIII, X, XII-XIV, XVI, XVIII-XXI, XXIII, XXVII, XXVIII, XXXI-XXXIII, XXXV-XLVI.

PIERSON, COLONEL JOHN—Sandra Belloni: XVI, XXIII, XLIII, LII, LIX. Vittoria: VI, VIII-X, XIV, XVII, XIX-XXII, XXVIII, XXX, XXXII, XXXIX, XL.

PIERSON, LIEUTENANT—see POLE, WILFRID.

PILLIE, DR.—Evan Harrington: XI, XII.

PINNET—Lord Ormont and His Aminta: XXVIII.

PITSCREW, LORD SIMON—Amazing Marriage: II, III, XXII, XXXIV, XXXIX.

PLUMSTON, TOMMY—Tale of Chloe: V.

PLUNGER — Beauchamp's Career: XI.

POLE, ADELA—Sandra Belloni: I-V, VII-X, XIV-XVII, XIX, XXI, XXIII, XXIV, XXVII, XXIX-XXXI-XXXVII, XLII, LII-LVII, LIX. Vittoria: VI-IX, XVII-XIX, XXVIII, XXXVII-XL.

POLE, ARABELLA—Sandra Belloni: I-V, VII-X, XIV-XVII, XIX, XXI, XXVII, XXIX, XXXI-XXXVI, XLII, LII, LVI, LIX.

POLE, CORNELIA—Sandra Belloni: I-V, VII-X, XIV-XIX, XXI, XXII, XXVI, XXVII, XXIX, XXX-XXXVI, XXXVIII, XL, XLII, LII-LVII, LIX.

POLE, SAMUEL BOLTON—Sandra Belloni: I-V, VII-IX, XIV-XVII, XIX, XXIII-XXXV, XXXVII, XXXIX, XL, XLII, LIV, LVI, LIX.

POLE, WILFRID: Sandra Belloni: I-VIII, X-XXI, XXIII, XXIV, XXVI-LIV, LVI-LIX. Vittoria: V-X, XIV, XVII-XXII, XXVII-XXX, XXXII-XXXIV, XXXVII, XXXIX-XL, XLV, XLVI.

POLLINGTON — Egoist: XXV, XXIX.

POLLINGTON, MR. and MRS.—Case of General Ople and Lady Camper: II, VI, VII.

POLLY—see WISHAW, MARY FENCE.

POLTERMORE, COLONEL—Tale of Chloe: VII, VIII, X.

POONEY, SIR ALFRED—House on the Beach: VII.

POSTERLEY, REVEREND ABRAM—One of Our Conquerors: XXIII, XXIV, XXIX, XXX, XXXIII.

POSTILLION—Evan Harrington: VI, VII.

POTTIL, SIR HUMPHREY and LADY—One of Our Conquerors: XXII, XXIV.

POTTS, CHUMLEY—Amazing Marriage: III, X-XII, XV-XVIII, XXIII, XXVI, XXVIII, XXXIV, XXXVII, XXXIX-XLII, XLIV, XLV.

POTTS, COLONEL JACK—Amazing Marriage: II.

POWYS, MERTHYR — Sandra Belloni: V, X, XV, XVIII, XXVII-XXIX, XXXI, XXXII, XXXIV, XXXVII, XXXVIII, XLI, XLIII, XLV-L, LII, LIV, LVI, LVIII, LIX. Vittoria: XIII, XIX, XXVII, XXVIII, XXXII, XXXV, XXXVI, XXXVIII-XLVI.

PRANCER — Beauchamp's Career: XI.

PRIDDEN, MARTHA—One of Our Conquerors: XXXI, XXXIII, XXXIV, XXXVII, XXXIX, XLI, XLII.

PRINCE PALATINE OF BOHEMIA—Farina: VI.

PRYME, SIR TWICKENHAM—Sandra Belloni: X, XV-XVII, XIX, XXVII, XXXI, XXXIII, XXXIV, XXXVI, XXXVII, XLII, LV, LVII, LIX.

PULLEN—Diana of the Crossways: XL.

PURLBY, COLONEL—Diana of the Crossways: XIV.

DE PYRMONT, GEORGES—Vittoria: XIII, XIV, XIX, XX, XXII.

Q

QUATLEY, LADY—One of Our Conquerors: XXVII, XLI.

QUATLEY, SIR ABRAHAM—One of Our Conquerors: XXI, XXIII, XXVI, XXVII, XXXVI, XXXVII.

QUEEN OF PORTUGAL—Evan Harrington: XXXI.

QUEENEY, JOSHUA—Amazing Marriage: XXXIV, XXXVII, XL, XLI.

QUILLETT, MRS. COWPER—Amazing Marriage: XIII, XVII.

R

RABESQURAT — Shaving of Shagpat: III, V, X, XII-XIV, XVII, XXI, XXIII, XXIV,

RABY, DUCHESS OF—Diana of the Crossways: XIV.

RADNOR, MRS. BURMAN — One of Our Conquerors: III-VIII, XI-XIV, XVI, XVIII-XXII, XXIV, XXV, XXVII, XXX, XXXVI, XXXVII, XXXIX, XLII.

RADNOR, GENERAL—One of Our Conquerors: XXII, XXIII.

RADNOR, NATALIA DREIGH-TON—One of Our Conquerors: II-VI, VIII-XIX, XXI-XXXI, XXXIII-XLII.

RADNOR, NESTA VICTORIA— One of Our Conquerors: II, III, V. VI, VIII-XLII.

RADNOR, VICTOR MONTGOM-ERY—One of Our Conquerors: I-XXVII, XXIX, XXXI, XXXIII, XXXV-XXXVII, XXXIX-XLII.

RADOCKY, PRINCE LOUIS— Vittoria: XL, XLV.

RAIKES, JOHN FEVERSHAM —Evan Harrington: X-XIV, XVI-XIX, XXV-XXXIV, XXXVI-XLI, XLV-XLVII.

RAINER, CHARLES—Diana of the Crossways: XVII, XXI, XXIII.

RAMBONI, COUNT—Vittoria: XLV.

RAMPAN, CAPTAIN—Diana of the Crossways: IV.

RANDELLER, SIR JOHN— Lord Ormont and His Aminta: III, VI, XII, XXIX.

RANDOM, MISS—Ordeal of Richard Feverel: XXXVI.

DE RASADIO, CHEVALIER MIGUEL—Evan Harrington: XXIV.

RASATI, COUNT—Vittoria: XV.

RASOON, EL—see EL RASOON.

RASTAGLIONI, COUNTESS— Beauchamp's Career: XIX.

RAVALOKE—Shaving of Shagpat: XI, XXIV.

RAVEJOURA—Shaving of Shagpat: XVIII, XX.

RAY, LADY—House on the Beach: IV.

REDDISH, LADY EVELINA— One of Our Conquerors: XXXV.

REDNER, MR.—Evan Harrington: IV.

VON REDWITZ, CHANCEL-LOR—Adventures of Harry Richmond: XXXIV.

VON REDWITZ, II—Adventures of Harry Richmond: LV, LVI.

REDWORTH, THOMAS—Diana of the Crossways: II-XVIII, XXI, XXIII-XXIX, XXXV-XLIII.

REGNAULT — Adventures of Harry Richmond: XXXII.

REM, CLEMENTINA—One of Our Conquerors: XXIII.

REM, SIR NICHOLAS—One of Our Conquerors: XXIII.

REM, REVEREND STUART— One of Our Conquerors: XXIII, XXIV, XXIX, XXX, XXXIII, XXXIV.

REMAUD, FRANK—Evan Harrington: XXVI, XXX, XL.

DE REMILLA, MARQUIS— Evan Harrington: XXI.

REWKES, DR.—Lord Ormont and His Aminta: XXVI, XXIX, XXX.

RHODES, ARTHUR—Diana of the Crossways: XVIII, XIX, XXI, XXIII,XXV, XXVII, XXVIII, XXX, XXXI, XXXV-XXXVII, XXXIX, XL, XLIII.

RIBSTONE, MRS.—House on the Beach: VI, VIII.

RIBSTONE, PHILIP — see SMITH, VAN DIEMEN (II).

RICCI, ROCCO—Vittoria: VIII, XII-XV, XIX-XXI, XXIII, XXVIII, XXXVII, XXXVIII.

RICHARDS, MR.—Adventures of Harry Richmond: XLIV.

RICHARDS, MR.—see FEVER-EL, RICHARD DORIA.

RICHMOND, AUGUSTUS FITZ-GEORGE ROY—Adventures of Harry Richmond: I-IX, XIV-XVII, XXIX, XXXII-LVI.

RICHMOND, HARRY LEPEL— Adventures of Harry Richmond: I-LVI.

RICHMOND, MARIAN — Adventures of Harry Richmond: I-III, IX, XXXVIII, LII.

RIFFORD, LADY ISABELLA— Diana of the Crossways: XXX.

RIPLEY, SIR PERKINS—Evan Harrington: XIII.

VON RIPPAU, MARGRAVINE — Adventures of Harry Richmond: XV-XIX, XXIV-XXVII, XXIX, XXX, XXXIII, XXXIV, XLII, XLVIII, LIII, LVI.

RIPPENGALE—Adventures of Harry Richmond: III.

RIPPENGER, JULIA—Adventures of Harry Richmond: IV-VI, IX, X, XVIII-XX, XXIII, XXXVI-XXXVIII, XL, XLI, XLV, XLVI, XLIX, LIII, LV, LVI.

RIPPENGER, MR.—Adventures of Harry Richmond: IV-IX, XII, XIII, XVIII.

RISBONDA, DOÑA—Evan Harrington: V.

RIVERS, MELTHUEN—Amazing Marriage: VII.

RIZZO, BARTOLOMMEO—Vittoria: II, V, VII-X, XII, XV, XVI, XVIII, XIX, XXI, XXV, XXIX, XXX, XXXIII, XXXIV, XXXVI-XLVI.

RIZZO, ROSELINA—Vittoria: VII, XV, XXIX, XXX, XXXII-XXXVI, XL-XLIII.

ROBERT—Sandra Belloni: XLVII.

DE LA ROCHE-AIGLE, MADAME LA COMTESSE—Diana of the Crossways: XXX.

ROCKDEN, LADY—Diana of the Crossways: XIV.

ROFE, SIMON—Diana of the Crossways: XX.

ROLLES, REGINALD—Case of General Ople and Lady Camper: I-VIII.

ROMARA, LUCIANO—Vittoria: XV-XVIII, XXI, XXII, XXIX-XXXI, XXXVI-XLI.

ROMARIS, PRINCE MARKO —Tragic Comedians: I, II, V, VI, XI, XII, XVII-XIX.

ROMFREY, CRAVEN—Beauchamp's Career: II. IV, XXXVII, XXXVIII.

ROMFREY, EARL I—Beauchamp's Career: II, IV, XXXVIII, XXXIX, XLI.

ROMFREY, EARL II—see ROMFREY, HONORABLE EVERARD.

ROMFREY, HONORABLE EVERARD—Beauchamp's Career: I-V, X-XIV, XVI-XVIII, XX-XXII, XXV, XXVIII-XXXIX, XLI-XLV, XLVIII-LIV, LVI.

ROMUALDO—Vittoria: XXI.

ROOMDROOM — Shaving of Shagpat: VIII, IX.

ROSELEY, ADMIRAL — Evan Harrington: I, II.

ROSELEY, LADY—Evan Harrington: I-III, XIII, XIV, XIX-XXII.

ROSTRAL, MADAME — Evan Harrington: II.

ROTHHALS, HENKER—Farina: III, VII, X-XIII.

DE ROUAILLOUT, MARQUIS RAOUL—Beauchamp's Career: VII, VIII, X, XI, XXIII-XXVI, XXX, XXXIX, XL, XLII, XLIII, XLV, LV.

DE ROUAILOUT, MARQUISE —see DE CROISNEL, RENÉE.

ROULCHOOK, EBN—Shaving of Shagpat: II.

RUARK—Shaving of Shagpat: II.

RUBREY, FRED—Adventures of Harry Richmond: XLI.

VON RÜDIGER, CLOTILDE —Tragic Comedians: Introduction: I-XIX.

VON RÜDIGER, GENERAL and FRAU—Tragic Comedians: I, IV-VI, VIII, IX, XI-XV, XVII, XVIII.

VON RÜDIGER, LOTTE—Tragic Comedians: VIII, XII.

RUDOLFO—Vittoria: XXI.

RUFO, LEONE—Vittoria: XV, XXIX, XXXIII, XXXIV, XXXVII.

RUFUS, SERJEANT—Diana of the Crossways: XXX.

RUKROOTH—Shaving of Shagpat: II.

RUNDLES, MISS—Amazing Marriage: XVII, XXXVII, XL.

RUNDLES, MR.—Amazing Marriage: XV, XVII, XIX.

RUNNINGBROOK, TRACY—Sandra Belloni: IV, V, VIII, X, XXIII, XXV, XXXI, XXXII, XXXIV, XXXVIII, XLII-XLIV, XLVI, XLVII, LVI-LVIII.

RUSSETT, EDWARD—Amazing Marriage: II, III, VI-XXI, XXIII, XLVI.

RUSSETT, JOHN EDWARD—Amazing Marriage: XXXV, XXXVII, XL, XLII, XLVI.

S

SADDLEBANK, ANDREW — Adventures of Harry Richmond: v-viii, xi, lv.

DE ST. OMBRE, M.—Amazing Marriage: x, xxiii, xxiv, xxviii, xxxv, xxxix.

DE SALDAR, CONDE SEÑOR SILVA DIAZ—Evan Harrington: iii-v, xiv, xix-xxi, xxvii, xxx, xl, xliv, xlvii.

DE SALDAR, COUNTESS LOU-ISA—Evan Harrington: iii-ix, xiii-xxvii, xxix-xliv, xlvi, xlvii.

SALLÂP—Shaving of Shagpat: xxii, xxiii.

SALLY—Evan Harrington: i, vii.

SALLY—Evan Harrington: xxvi.

SALTER, JOHN—Adventures of Harry Richmond: v-vii.

SALVOLO—Vittoria: xix, xx.

SAMPLEMAN, LADY—Adventures of Harry Richmond: xx, xxii, xxvii, xxxix, xliii, xliv, lv.

SAMUEL—Adventures of Harry Richmond: xl.

SAMUELS — Rhoda Fleming: xxxi.

SANDOE, DIAPER—see SOMERS, DENZIL.

SANDRA—see BELLONI, EMILIA ALESSANDRA.

SANFREDINI, SIGNORA GIULIA—One of Our Conquerors: iii, xxiv, xxxvi, xxxix, xli.

SANO, MARCO—Vittoria: i-v, xxx, xxxvi, xli-xliv, xlvi.

SARACCO, LUIGI—Vittoria: v, vii, viii, x, xiii-xv, xxvii, xxxii, xxxiii, xxxv, xxxvii, xxxviii, xl, xlii, xlv.

SARPO—Vittoria: xxvii, xl, xli.

SATHANAS—Farina: iv, v, viii-x, xiv, xv, xvii.

SCHILL, DIETRICH—Farina: i, xiv-xvi.

SCHLESIEN, DR.—One of Our Conquerors: iii, viii, ix, xi, xviii-xxi.

SCHMIDT, BERTHOLD—Farina: i, v, vi, xiv, xv.

SCHMIDT, CUNIGONDE—Farina: vi, xv.

SCHÖNECK, GENERAL—Vittoria: ix, xxx, xxxii, xxxiii, xxxix, xl.

SCHWARTZ — Adventures of Harry Richmond: xxiv-xxxi, xxxiii, xxxiv, xlviii, l.

SCHWEIZERBARTH—Diana of the Crossways: xv.

SCHYLL-WEILINGEN, PRINCESS OF — see AMALIA, DUCHESS.

SCOTT, JOHN—House on the Beach: xii.

SCROOM, JERRY—One of Our Conquerors: xvi.

SEDGETT, JOHN—Rhoda Fleming: xvii, xviii.

SEDGETT, MRS.—Rhoda Fleming: xviii, xxxi, xlvi.

SEDGETT, NICODEMUS — Rhoda Fleming: xviii-xxiv, xxvii, xxix-xxxi, xxxiii, xxxv, xxxvii-xxxix, xli, xlii, xliv-xlvi.

SEDLEY, MR.—Vittoria: vi, x, xix, xxviii.

SEDLEY, MRS.—see POLE, ADELA.

SEDLEY, VISCOUNTESS—Adventures of Harry Richmond: xxxix, xli.

SEGRAVE, COLONEL HIBBERT—Adventures of Harry Richmond: xlvii, l.

DE SEILLES, LOUISE—One of Our Conquerors: viii, xi, xiv, xv, xvii, xviii, xx, xxii, xxiv, xxviii, xxx, xxxiii, xxxv, xxxix-xlii.

SEMHIANS, REVEREND MANCATE—One of Our Conquerors: xix, xxiv, xxviii, xxxvi, xli.

SEQUIN, MR.—Rhoda Fleming: xl.

SERABIGLIONE, COUNT—Vittoria: xi, xviii, xx, xxviii, xxxvi, xxxix, xlv.

SERENA, MARCHIONESS OF EDBURY—Adventures of Harry Richmond: xxvii, xxxix, liv.

SEWIS, BENJAMIN—Adventures of Harry Richmond: i, vii-ix, xxxvii, xxxviii, xlii.

SHAFRAC—Shaving of Shagpat: XXI.

SHAGPAT—Shaving of Shagpat: I, III, V, VIII, IX, XI-XIV, XVI-XXIV.

SHAHPESH—Shaving of Shagpat: III, IV, XXI.

SHAHPUSHÂN — Shaving of Shagpat: XXII-XXIV.

SHALDERS, MR.—Lord Ormont and His Aminta: I, II, V.

SHALE, LORD-LIEUTENANT —Adventures of Harry Richmond: XLI.

SHALE, MR. and MRS. MATTHEW—Lord Ormont and His Aminta: XXVI.

SHALE, SUSAN:—Lord Ormont and His Aminta: XXVI.

SHAMSHUREEN SHAH—Shaving of Shagpat: I, XXIV.

SHAPLOW, BENJAMIN—One of Our Conquerors: X, XVI.

SHELLEN, T.—Lord Ormont and His Aminta: XII.

SHENKYN—Amazing Marriage: XXXIV.

SHEPHERD BOY—Ordeal of Richard Feverel: XIX.

SHEPSTER, RALPH—Tale of Chloe: IV.

SHERWIN, CLARA — Beauchamp's Career: XII, XXIX, XXX.

SHERWIN, GENERAL—Beauchamp's Career: XII, XXIX.

SHIMPOR—Shaving of Shagpat: I, V, XXII, XXIV.

SHOOLPI—Shaving of Shagpat: I, V, XXIV.

SHORNE, JULIA—Evan Harrington: XIV, XVII, XVIII, XXIV, XXV, XXVII, XXIX-XXXII, XXXVII, XL, XLII, XLIII, XLV.

SHORNE, MR.—Evan Harrington: XIII, XXIX.

SHOTTS AND COMPANY, BANKERS—One of Our Conquerors: XVIII.

SHRAPNEL, DR.—Beauchamp's Career: XI-XIV, XVI, XVII, XIX-XXII, XXVI-XXXIX, XLII-XLV, XLVIII-LVI.

SHULLUM—Shaving of Shagpat: I, V, XXIV.

SIBLEY, LUCY—Adventures of Harry Richmond: XVI, XXIV, XXVI, XXVII, XXXI, XLVI, XLVIII.

SIEGFRIED—Farina: II, VI, IX, XIII.

SILLABIN—Adventures of Harry Richmond: XXXVIII, LIII.

SIMON—Sandra Belloni: XXV.

SINGLEBY, LADY—Diana of the Crossways: XIV, XVIII, XXVII, XXVIII, XXXIX, XLI.

SKEPSEY, DANIEL—One of Our Conquerors: III, IV, IX-XI, XV-XIX, XXI, XXII, XXIV, XXV, XXVII, XXVIII, XXX, XXXI, XXXIII, XXXIV, XXXVI, XXXVII, XXXIX, XLI, XLII.

SKEPSEY, MARTHA—One of Our Conquerors: X, XV, XXIV, XXV, XXVII.

SKERNE—Evan Harrington: IV.

SLATER, SIR WEETON—Adventures of Harry Richmond: XXXIX, XLII, XLVII.

SMITH, ANNETTE—House on the Beach: II-XII.

SMITH, SULLIVAN—Diana of the Crossways: II, III, XI, XIV, XVII, XVIII, XXI, XXVIII-XXX, XXXVII XXXIX, XLIII.

SMITH, VAN DIEMEN (I)—House on the Beach: III, VI.

SMITH, VAN DIEMEN (II)—House on the Beach: II-XI.

SMITHERS, PETER—Evan Harrington: IX.

SOCKLEY, MRS.—Evan Harrington: XXVI, XLI.

SOMERS, DENZIL—Ordeal of Richard Feverel: I, IV, VI, XII, XXV, XXVIII, XXXIV, XXXVII, XXXVIII.

SOOLKA—Shaving of Shagpat: II.

SOUTHWEARE, PERCY—One of Our Conquerors: XXXII, XXXIV, XXXV.

SOWERBY, COUNTESS—One of Our Conquerors: XLII.

SOWERBY, HONORABLE DUDLEY—One of Our Conquerors: IV, VIII, IX, XI, XII, XIV-XXII, XXIV-XLII.

SPEED THE PLOUGH—see BAKEWELL, TOM.

SPELLMAN, JOHANN—Vittoria: XXV, XXVI.

SPLENDERS, LADY — Evan Harrington: IX.

STAINES, LADY—Lord Ormont and His Aminta: XIII, XV, XXIII.

STANTON — Beauchamp's Career: XLIX, LII.

STOKES, GEORGE—Evan Harrington: X, XI.

STOKES, LADY RACHEL—Adventures of Harry Richmond: XXXIX.

STÖRCHEL, DR.—Tragic Comedians: XIII-XV, XVII, XVIII.

STRÄUSCHER, HERR—One of Our Conquerors: XXIV.

STRIKE, CAROLINE — Evan Harrington: III, V, VII, XIV, XVIII, XIX, XXI-XXVI, XXX, XXXII, XXXIII, XXXVI-XLIV, XLVI, XLVII.

STRIKE, MAJOR MAXWELL—Evan Harrington: III, V, VIII, XIV, XVIII, XIX, XXI, XXX, XXXVII, XXXIX, XL, XLI.

STRIKE, MAXWELL II—Evan Harrington: V, XLIV.

DE STRODE, COUNTESS—Adventures of Harry Richmond: XLI.

SUCKLING, LORD — Rhoda Fleming: XVI, XXI, XXII, XXVI, XXVII, XXIX, XXXI, XXXVIII.

SUDLEY, COLONEL—One of Our Conquerors: XXX, XXXII, XXXIII.

SUMFIT, MRS.—Rhoda Fleming: II-IV, VII, IX, XIII, XXIV, XXXIII, XXXIX, XLI-XLIII, XLV-XLVII.

SUMNERS, THE—Sandra Belloni: II, XVII, XIX, XXVII, XXXI, XXXII, XLII.

SUSAN—Rhoda Fleming: XIX.

SWANAGE, LADY—One of Our Conquerors: XX, XXI.

SWEETWINTER, BOB — Adventures of Harry Richmond: III, XXXVII, LV.

SWEETWINTER, MABEL—Adventures of Harry Richmond: III, XXIII, XXXVII, XXXVIII, XLII, LV, LVI.

SWEETWINTER, MARK—Adventures of Harry Richmond: III, XXIII, XXXVI, XXXVII, LV.

SYBILLE, MADAME—Diana of the Crossways: XXVII, XXIX, XXXVI.

SZEZEDY, COUNTESS — Adventures of Harry Richmond: XXXIX.

T

TAPLOW—One of Our Conquerors: III, XX.

TARANI—Sandra Belloni: XLVIII.

TARTINI—Vittoria: XXX.

TCHEIK—Shaving of Shagpat: XXI.

TELLIO—Diana of the Crossways: XXVII.

TEMPLE, GUS—Adventures of Harry Richmond: V, VI, IX-XX, XXIII, XXIV, XXVII, XXVIII, XXX, XXXII, XXXVI-XXXIX, XL-XLIV, XLVII-LI, LIII, LVI.

TEMPLE, MR.—Adventures of Harry Richmond: XLII, XLIV.

TENBY, MR.—Adventures of Harry Richmond: XLII.

THEMISON, DR.—One of Our Conquerors: XIII, XIV, XVI, XVIII, XIX, XXI, XXII, XXX, XXXVI, XXXIX, XL-XLII.

THIER, SCHWARTZ—Farina: III, VII, X-XIV.

THOMSON, DR. LANYAN—Diana of the Crossways: XXVI, XXVII.

THOMPSON, LETITIA—Ordeal of Richard Feverel: XI, XXVIII, XXXII.

THOMPSON, MR.—Ordeal of Richard Feverel: VII, XI, XVI-XVIII, XXII, XXVI, XXXIII.

THOMPSON, MRS.—Ordeal of Richard Feverel: XI.

THOMPSON, RIPTON—Ordeal of Richard Feverel: I-VII, X-XII, XVI, XXV, XXVI, XXVIII-XXXI, XXXIII, XXXV-XXXVIII, XLI-XLV.

THRESHER, JOHN—Adventures of Harry Richmond: III, IV, VII, XI, XXIV, XXXVII, XLIII.

THRESHER, MARTHA — Adventures of Harry Richmond: III, XXIII, XXXVII.

THRIBBLE—Adventures of Harry Richmond: III.

THWAITES, CORPORAL — Rhoda Fleming: XXXII.

TILES, BOB—Ordeal of Richard Feverel: III-V, XI.

TIMPAN, MADAME — Sandra Belloni: XV.

TINLEY, ALBERT—Sandra Belloni: XXXI, XXXVI, XLII, LV, LVI.

TINLEY, LAURA—Sandra Belloni: I, III-V, X, XIX, XXI, XXII, XXVI, XXXVI, XLII, LV, LVI, LVIII.

TINLEY, MADELINE—Sandra Belloni: XLII.

TINLEY, RALPH—Sandra Belloni: XXXII.

TINLEY, ROSE—Sandra Belloni: XLII.

TINMAN, MARTIN—House on the Beach: I-XI.

TODDS, BEN—Amazing Marriage: XV, XVI.

TODHUNTER, JOHN PEMBERTON—Ordeal of Richard Feverel: XXXV, XL.

TODHUNTER, MRS.—Ordeal of Richard Feverel: XXXV.

TOLLINGBY — Adventures of Harry Richmond: XLIII, XLIX, LVI.

TOMBER, SIR UPTON—Amazing Marriage: II.

TOMKINS—Beauchamp's Career: XI.

TOMLINSON—Beauchamp's Career: XIX, XX.

TONANS, MARCUS—Diana of the Crossways: XVII, XVIII, XXI, XXVII, XXIX, XXXII-XXXVI, XXXVIII.

TOPF, DAME—Farina: II.

TRAMP—Adventures of Harry Richmond: VI-VIII.

VON TRESTEN, COLONEL —Tragic Comedians: IX, X, XII, XIII, XV-XVIII.

TREWINT—Adventures of Harry Richmond: XXXVII.

TREWK, NED—Sandra Belloni: XI.

TRIPEHALLOW—Beauchamp's Career: XIX, XX.

TUCKHAM, BLACKBURN — Beauchamp's Career: III, XVI, XVII, XXVI, XXVIII, XXXII, XXXVII, XXXIX, XLII, XLV-XLVIII, LI, LIII, LV, LVI.

TUCKHAM, MRS.—see HALKETT, CECELIA.

TUDOR, OWEN—Amazing Marriage: XXXIV.

TURBOT, TIMOTHY — Beauchamp's Career: XIV, XVI, XIX, XX, XXII, XXVII.

TURCKEMS, BARONESS—Adventures of Harry Richmond: XXVI, XXVII, XXX, XXXIV-XXXVI, XLVIII, L.

U

UBERLY—Adventures of Harry Richmond: X, XII, XIX, XXIII, XL, XLVIII, L.

UKLEET—Shaving of Shagpat: II.

UPLOFT, GEORGE—Evan Harrington: I, XIX-XXII, XXIV, XXV, XXVII, XXIX-XXXI, XXXIII, XXXVII, XLIII.

UPLOFT, SQUIRE—Evan Harrington: I, XIII.

URMSING, BEAVES—One of Our Conquerors: IX, XXI, XXII, XXXVI, XL, XLI.

URSEL—Adventures of Harry Richmond: XXXV.

URUISH—Shaving of Shagpat: XXIV.

V

VAUGHAN, MR.—Amazing Marriage: XXXIV.

VEEJRAVOOSH — Shaving of Shagpat: XVII-XXI, XXIII.

DE VILLA FLOR, COUNT— Evan Harrington: IX.

VINCENT, MISS—Lord Ormont and His Aminta: I, II, V, VII, XI, XII, XXX.

VISTOCQ, BARON — Rhoda Fleming: XXVII.

VITTORIA—see BELLONI, EMILIA ALESSANDRA.

VOLPO, COLONEL—Vittoria: XXXIX.

W

WADASTER, LORD—Diana of the Crossways: xxx.

WADDY, MARY—Adventures of Harry Richmond: ii-iv, xviii, xx, xxiii, xxxviii, xxxix, xlii, xliv, xlix-liv.

WAINSBY — Rhoda Fleming: xviii.

WALBURG, COUNT — Tragic Comedians: viii-x.

WARDAN, DR.—One of Our Conquerors: xxi.

WARDEN, MR. and MRS.—Case of General Ople and Lady Camper: ii.

WARING, MAJOR PERCY—Rhoda Fleming: xx, xxii-xxiv, xxvi, xxvii, xxx-xxxii, xxxviii, xxxix, xliv, xlvi, xlviii.

WARWICK, AUGUSTUS—Diana of the Crossways: i, ii, iv-ix, xiii-xv, xvii, xviii, xxi, xxiii-xxv, xxvii, xxix, xxx, xxxvi, xl, xliii.

WARWICK, DIANA ANTONIA —Diana of the Crossways: i-xlii.

WATER-LADY, THE—Farina: xii, xiii.

WATHIN, CRAMBORNE—Diana of the Crossways: xiv, xvii, xxi, xxiii.

WATHIN, MRS.—Diana of the Crossways: xiv, xvii, xxi, xxiii, xxv, xxvii, xxix, xxxv-xxxvii, xlii.

WATKYN—Amazing Marriage: xxxiv.

WAYTIS, MR.—Amazing Marriage: xxv.

WEISSPRIESS, CAPTAIN JOHANN NEPOMUK FREIHERR VON SCHEPPENHAUSEN—Vittoria: ix, x, xiv, xv, xix, xx, xxii, xxiii, xxvi-xxix, xxxiii, xxxiv, xxxviii-xl, xlv, xlvi.

WEDDERBURN, SERJEANT—Adventures of Harry Richmond: xxxix, xli, xlii.

WEDGER, TOMMY—Amazing Marriage: ii.

WELBECK—Evan Harrington: vii.

WELSH, CAPTAIN JASPER—Adventures of Harry Richmond: xii-xv, xvii-xix, xxix, xlii, liv-lvi.

WELSH, ROBERT—Adventures of Harry Richmond: xiii, xiv.

WELSHPOOL, LORD—Beauchamp's Career: xxxviii.

WELSHPOOL, COUNTESS — Beauchamp's Career: xxxiii.

WENTWORTH, AUSTIN—Ordeal of Richard Feverel: i, ii, iv, vi-xii, xx, xxv, xxvi, xxxiii, xxxiv, xli, xlii, xlv.

WENTWORTH, MRS.—Ordeal of Richard Feverel: i.

WERNER, BARON—Farina: ii-iv, vi, vii, x-xv.

WESTLAKE, MR.—Diana of the Crossways: xvii, xxiii, xxvii, xxviii, xxx, xxxv.

WEYBURN, COLONEL SIDNEY—Lord Ormont and His Aminta: iii, iv, xiv, xxiii.

WEYBURN, MATTHEW—Lord Ormont and His Aminta: i-v, vii-ix, xi-xxi, xxiii-xxx.

WEYBURN, MRS.—Lord Ormont and His Aminta: xiii-xv, xviii, xx, xxviii.

WHEEDLE, MR. and MRS.—Evan Harrington: xlv.

WHEEDLE, POLLY—Evan Harrington: xiii, xiv, xvii, xviii, xxv, xxvii, xxxii, xxxv-xxxviii, xlv, xlvii.

WHEEDLE, SUSAN—Evan Harrington: x, xi, xiii, xviii, xxv, xxx, xxxii, xxxiii, xxxvii, xl, xlv.

WHITFORD, GRACE—Egoist: xliv.

WHITFORD, MRS. -— Egoist: xxxviii.

WHITFORD, VERNON—Egoist: ii-xxx, xxxii-xxxix, xli-l.

WHITMONBY—Diana of the Crossways: xvii, xviii, xx, xxi, xxiii, xxv, xxvii-xxx, xxxiii, xxxv.

WICKLOW, MARY ANN—Rhoda Fleming: v, x, xxv.

WICKLOW, MRS.—Rhoda Fleming: v, x, xxv.

WILDER, MR. and MRS.—Case of General Ople and Lady Camper: II.

WILDJOHN, COLONEL—Egoist: XXXV.

WILHELM — Vittoria: XXVI, XXVII.

WILKINSON, PERCY—Diana of the Crossways: I.

WILLIAM—Adventures of Harry Richmond: VII.

WILLIAM—Diana of the Crossways: XXVI.

WILLIAMS, MONTEREZ—Adventures of Harry Richmond: XIX, XXXIX, XLVII.

WILMERS, DORSET—Diana of the Crossways: I.

WILMERS, HENRY—Diana of the Crossways: I, XVII, XVIII, XXIII, XXV, XXVII, XXVIII, XXX.

WILMORE, LIEUTENANT JACK—Beauchamp's Career: III, XV, XIX, XLII, XLVIII.

WILSON—Sandra Belloni: II, VI, XI.

WILSON, MRS.—Sandra Belloni: II, XI.

WILTS, LADY—Adventures of Harry Richmond: XXI, XXII, XXVII.

WILTS, MOUNTFORD—Diana of the Crossways: XXVIII.

WILTSHIRE, JOHN—Amazing Marriage: II.

WINCH, MADGE—Amazing Marriage: III, XV-XIX, XXII, XXV-XXXIII, XXXV-XLVI.

WINCH, SARAH—Amazing Marriage: XVIII, XIX, XXI, XXII, XXV, XXVIII, XXX, XXXI, XXXV, XXXVI, XXXVIII, XLVI.

WINCH, TOBIAS — Amazing Marriage: XVIII.

WINGHAM—Beauchamp's Career: XIX.

WINKRIED—Farina: II.

WINSTANLEY, MRS. GRAFTON—Diana of the Crossways: XXVII.

WINTER, VERA—Beauchamp's Career: XXVI.

WIPPERN, LORD — Rhoda Fleming: XXII.

WISHAW, MARY FENCE— Evan Harrington: VII, IX.

WITLINGTON, EARL OF— Adventures of Harry Richmond: XXXIX, XLII.

VON WOLFENSTEIN, COUNT FRETZEL — Adventures of Harry Richmond: XVI, XVIII, XXX.

WOLLASLEY, MRS.—Diana of the Crossways: XVIII.

WOODSEER, GOWER—Amazing Marriage: VI-XI, XVI-XXVIII, XXX-XLVI.

WOODSEER, MR. — Amazing Marriage: XVIII, XIX, XXI, XXII, XXV, XXXVII, XLI, XLIV.

WORCESTER, ELIZABETH — Tale of Chloe: VII.

WORRELL, MAJOR—One of Our Conquerors: XXVIII, XXIX, XXXII, XXXIII, XXXV, XXXVII-XXXIX.

WORRELL, MRS.—One of Our Conquerors: XXVIII.

WRECKHAM, MR. and MRS.— Adventures of Harry Richmond: XXXIX.

WROXETER, LORD—Diana of the Crossways: IV, XLI, XLII.

WÜRMSER—Vittoria: XXVI.

WYTHAN, OWAIN—Amazing Marriage: XVI, XXVII, XXIX-XXX, XXXIII, XXXIV, XXXVI, XXXVII, XL-XLIII, XLV-XLVII.

WYTHAN, REBECCA—Amazing Marriage: XXVII, XXIX-XXXI, XXXIII, XXXIV, XXXVI, XL, XLII, XLIII, XLVI, XLVII.

Y

YATT, DR. PETER—One of Our Conquerors: II, IV, VIII, X, XVIII, XX, XXII, XXXIII.

YATT, MRS.—One of Our Conquerors: XXII, XXXIII, XXXVI.

Z

ZÂK—Shaving of Shagpat: xxii.

ZARAGAL—Shaving of Shagpat: xxiv.

ZEEL—Shaving of Shagpat: xxi-xxiii.

ZETTLISCH, LIEUTENANT—Vittoria: xxii.

ZOFEL, COLONEL — Vittoria: xxviii, xxix.

ZOOP, EL—see EL ZOOP.

ZOORA—Shaving of Shagpat: ii.

ZOTTI—Vittoria: viii, xv, xvi, xxxv.

ZRMACK—Shaving of Shagpat: xxiv.

ZURVAN—Shaving of Shagpat: ii.

VON ZWANZIGER—Farina: iii.

ZWITTERWITZ—Vittoria: xxvi.

The Novels of George Meredith: A Study

George Meredith